Crash Course in Contemporary Reference

Recent Titles in Libraries Unlimited
Crash Course Series

Crash Course in Contemporary Reference

Francisca Goldsmith

Crash Course

LIBRARIES UNLIMITED™
An Imprint of ABC-CLIO, LLC
Santa Barbara, California • Denver, Colorado

Library of Congress Cataloging-in-Publication Data

Names: Goldsmith, Francisca, author.
Title: Crash course in contemporary reference / Francisca Goldsmith.
Description: Santa Barbara, CA : Libraries Unlimited, [2017] | Series: Crash
    course | Includes bibliographical references and index.
Identifiers: LCCN 2016030068 (print) | LCCN 2016036892 (ebook) |
    ISBN 9781440844812 (acid-free paper) | ISBN 9781440844829 (ebook)
Subjects: LCSH: Reference services (Libraries) | Reference services
    (Libraries)—United States.
Classification: LCC Z711 .G64 2017 (print) | LCC Z711 (ebook) |
    DDC 025.5/2—dc23
LC record available at https://lccn.loc.gov/2016030068

ISBN: 978-1-4408-4481-2
EISBN: 978-1-4408-4482-9

21 20 19 18 17   1   2   3   4   5

This book is also available as an eBook.

Libraries Unlimited
An Imprint of ABC-CLIO, LLC

ABC-CLIO, LLC
130 Cremona Drive, P.O. Box 1911
Santa Barbara, California 93116-1911
www.abc-clio.com

This book is printed on acid-free paper ∞

Manufactured in the United States of America

CONTENTS

INTRODUCTION

The methods and means by which professional reference work is undertaken during the second decade of the 21st century differ in many ways from the practices and resources created and refined during the last century. Yet there are overarching principles of librarianship, information management, and communication, each of which rests soundly on developments, practices, and rubrics created generations ago. This practical textbook aims to analyze the needs and expectations contemporary reference services should address and provide guidance to staff working in this area of library and information science.

The book is arranged in a dozen chapters that provide a developmental approach to exploring the issues and resources that compose the contemporary reference service milieu. We begin by examining the components of service provision, in the first three chapters and then move into exploring the current world of information sources. Next, we take a deeper view of strategies and tactics to move those resources through service practice for the benefit of our community. In the final two chapters, we discuss the contemporary models of organizing reference services work and staff development needs to conduct reference services into the near future.

My life as a reference librarian has been varied in place, time, library type and community descriptors, and roles. It has straddled eras, allowing me to work on a then cutting edge after hours local telephone reference service as well as in the consortium-based context of a virtual reference service open to the world. I've served in academic and public reference departments, and have been teaching library staff of all educational backgrounds and in all types of libraries in the practice of reference service provision. One of the enormous benefits of teaching reference methods and resources across years and through many different curricular means is the need to keep constantly abreast of innovations while also remaining aware of how those innovations are or aren't taking hold in the realm of practice. I count myself lucky to have worked with excellent reference librarians and others whose lack of skill and/or interest alerted me to the need to do soul searching of my own practices and devotion to professional development.

Thanking all the wonderful and insightful reference service teachers I have had, formally and informally as peers, along the way would create a prodigious list and many of the ones to whom I owe the most are also not interested in public acclaim. However, I will call out three very formal instructors who certainly launched my career in reference work and marked me for life as someone who is devoted to the profession.

The first is a now-deceased high school English teacher with the fortuitously punning name of Miss Judge. Helen Judge set me my first complex research assignment, back in 10th grade, and that led to a wellspring of discovery: old serials' backfiles—bound and in microfilm—as well as indexes, abstracts, and, best of all, these librarians working in the reference room whose actual job it was to help me think about resources and authority!

During my last semester as an undergraduate, the dean of the graduate school and also the professor of Renaissance history, Sister Margaret Rose Welch, suggested (at the time I thought casually, but she was probably just surreptitiously guiding me) I explore *The College Blue Book*'s listings for graduate library school programs. As a two-year-old (seriously), I had entertained notions of growing up to become a librarian, but I honestly thought I had given that up in favor of, perhaps, teaching or civil engineering or archaeology. Reading the curriculum descriptions, I was hooked.

In library school itself, I was very fortunate to study several courses related to reference with Dr. Michael Ochs. Thorough, analytical, and able to provide experiential learning that went way beyond lists of imposed questions to take to the graduate library to research, he showed me that reference services are a kind of interpretative service. One has to understand how to work between a need for information and resources that will typically not express the information neatly and quickly.

Of course, I have to thank the now 1,000 professional and paraprofessional reference service providers whose work and learning I have facilitated in formal reference studies coursework. And thank you for taking the time to move ahead into this Crash Course.

CHAPTER 1

An Overview of Professional Library Reference Service

Reference work in the library context includes an array of activities. Each one and all of them together guide community members as they search for authoritative information and referral to next steps they can take to resolve any knowledge concern. In this chapter, we will take a bird's-eye look at the hallmarks of library reference service and how library staff members undertake providing this service element to the community.

WHAT MAKES REFERENCE WORK A PROFESSIONAL JOB?

Let's start by discussing what a library reference staff member needs in the contemporary library. To do that, we need to start with noting what "professional" means in this context!

Professions are those occupations that require *defined skills and knowledge sets*, a *code of ethics*[1] employed by all in that work without deference to local prejudices or custom, and the need to pursue *ongoing training* in accord with changes in best practices as are required by new technologies or laws.

1

Think about how this definition applies to those who work in places other than a library: various forms of medical care deliverers, those working in the field of education, safety and emergency workers, and so forth. Professional staff at all levels assist the surgeon in the operating room, with skills and tasks that are essential to surgery. It's not just about the surgeon; nursing and aide positions are also professional and essential to delivering contemporary surgery. Professional work in schools includes the dedication and duties of teachers' aides, various staff assigned to monitor and pursue the needs of attendance maintenance, food services, and more.

"Professional" means working without bias. How would you respond to the firefighter who refused to save your son from a burning house because her prejudices against males outranked any ethical precept that required her to be gender-neutral in making life-saving decisions on the job? Would you trust the paralegal who has not received any continuing education, or even examined any new case law, since he began working in law in 1988?

"Professional" means conducting work so that the best job possible in any situation can be achieved. In the context of reference, it means finding accurate, relevant information for community members in locating answers to information problems.

Occupations are classified in a variety of ways, depending upon who is doing the classifying and to what purpose. For the purpose of what we are considering in this book, someone who works in any library *must*:

- Perform tasks related to the institutional mission of the library
- Have acquired a level of education and training required to fulfill the defined position he or she holds
- Be able to identify and make immediate use of specific skills and knowledge sets to achieve those tasks
- Understand and value the purpose of both the institution's mission and his or her position's assignment within that institution as a part of fulfilling that mission

In addition to these basic requirements, the person who provides reference service work *may* be required by the employing institution, as its governing body and administrative management judges appropriate, to:

- Have a specified credential, such as a master's degree or certification as having achieved completion of a designated preparatory course
- Supervise the service efforts of other staff members, or serve as consultants to them on complex matters
- Shape and manage the resources, and the budget accorded for such maintenance, of the reference collection

In any library context, there are characteristics of reference service work that require that staff performing the work demonstrate the following:

- Intellectual curiosity
- Open-mindedness
- Healthy personal boundaries

Intellectual curiosity includes the staff member's awareness that there is much to learn beyond what he or she already knows, and to be interested in finding out how new information can be acquired. Intellectual curiosity opens a person to new ideas, reconsideration of currently held beliefs, and interest in pursuing questions of "why" in his or her own life as well as applying that interest to his or her work. A staff member who is open-minded does not allow his or her own biases to intrude into his or her work. Like intellectual curiosity, open-mindedness usually is a characteristic of a person, whether in the workplace or going about other aspects of his or her life. Being open-minded doesn't mean someone can't or won't make decisions about values. It does mean that the person has a willingness and an aptitude to suspend judgment until all the facts are discovered. Healthy personal boundaries are important in any work climate where a staff member is available to clients and sometimes even other staff members who may be confrontational, unable to maintain their own personal boundaries emotionally or socially, or in need of services that fall beyond the institution's mission. Such healthy personal boundaries allow the staff member to be able to refer clients to more suitable agencies for some needs, to maintain behavioral standards in public areas, and to recognize situations in which unreasonable demands are being made on their capacity to deliver appropriate services.

REFERENCE WORK ADDS LIBRARY VALUE TO YOUR COMMUNITY

Knowledge is power.[2] You have heard this brief phrase often both inside and outside your library work. Library reference service is what transmits the power of knowledge from books, databases, web sources, and other authoritative media to community members who seek to have answers to the who, what, why, when, where, and how questions in their lives in a manner that provides both knowledge and understanding. Throughout this book, the terms "community members" and "clients" will be used when describing the people who are recipients of your reference service efforts. These terminology choices indicate the scope of reference work's value, which should go well beyond serving "patrons," who may be limited only to taxpayers. In some libraries, the terms used to describe the recipients of reference services include "customers," but we will not use that term here because the expectations of best practices in contemporary reference work are based on a model different from the marketplace.

The performance of valuable reference services should increase the health and vibrance of the community the library serves, whether individual community members apply directly for individual reference guidance. Think of this according to the paradigm of good community health. Not everyone in the community may identify a need that requires a visit to the hospital. However, the hospital that creates and maintains best practices plays a role in the overall health of the community: patients are not discharged with infectious diseases that can threaten others in the community; family physicians can make arrangements for more desired treatments knowing their patients will be able to receive the required care; health information is readily available and promoted throughout the community.

Years ago, reference services were conducted more like emergency rooms. The client/patient had to recognize a need for help, go to the designated facility, and receive services that might or might not lead to lasting results. By contrast, public health practitioners entered the community and provided what community members recognized as necessary for healthier living, and then were provided with further guidance toward health and the maintenance of healthy neighborhoods. Contemporary reference services borrow from this community-centered approach to practice. Instead of focusing on piecemeal applications of information help as they are brought to reference staff attention by individuals, the goal is to extend the means for acquiring the best possible information needed to improve knowledge gaps in the community.

Reference Service as Authority-Based

Library reference service provides information that is derived from sources that have been evaluated for their authority, accuracy, timeliness, and appropriate fit to the needs and capacity of the person who seeks or needs the information. Reference work is not relying on your own store of factual information and/or expert opinion to guide someone else, something you might do when responding to someone at your dinner table who asks you to recommend a good furniture polish or whether it would be wiser to buy a new car or lease one. While you undoubtedly hold a vast and valuable store of knowledge, your reference work as a library staff member must be guided by objective authorities. Books from reputable publishers have their editors' stamp of authority as well as the credentialed or experiential expertise of their authors. Many online resources can be determined to be authoritative as well, as we shall discuss in depth in Chapter 9. An authoritative source may even be the firsthand exchange you can arrange with a local community member who has professional expertise, such as a jeweler or a symphonic composer.[3] By referencing an authority in providing guidance to those with information questions, the reference service staff member connects individuals with the value of accuracy, relevance, and a level of certainty in the answers.

Reference Service as Lifelong Learning Support

Lifelong learning refers to the activity our brains must undergo in order to adjust to changes in technology, culture, and even the daily news. While the work of the youth or student includes a variety of formal education situations and exercises, lifelong learning may occur in informal as well as formal settings. Supporting someone's effort and capacity to find out the who, what, where, when, how, and even why of a vast array of daily life's facets supports his or her lifelong learning.

Factual questions arise from many sources. Perhaps the easiest type of reference question for anyone to recognize is the *imposed question*, a term that names the kind of question asked of the person by someone else and who, in turn, has brought the question to a reference staff member's attention. The information need arises due to someone other than the person responsible for acquiring the answer making a requirement on the person asking about the knowledge need. You probably needed to address imposed questions throughout your elementary and secondary school years. For example, children may need to know the name of the 14th state to join the United States because their teacher assigned that question in history class. Not all imposed questions are school-related. A new neighbor has asked your client about summer programs for teenagers and the client has never had teenagers nor has any interest in such programming. The client brings the question to you because she wants to help the new neighbor, not because she wants to learn for herself about such summer program opportunities. However, in all cases, the need to find the answers to imposed questions arises due to someone other than the party needing the information stating that this question must be answered.

Questions that arise because the person posing them generated them from his or her own need and desire to know, on the other hand, lead to that person's lifelong learning experience. Here are some questions that require lifelong learning support, rather than resolution, because they have been imposed on the person and about which they have no internalized interest:

- A young man who moved from South Africa to the United States several years ago wants to find out how to get a fair price for the car he first acquired upon arrival so that he can upgrade
- A grandmother concerned about her grandchild's healthcare because her daughter has been worried about having the child vaccinated
- A 70-year-old with no previous need for digital skills who wants to preserve the slides she's found when cleaning out her recently deceased father's apartment
- An 18-year-old who wants to self-publish a book

While it may seem that each of these factual information needs differs in complexity, lifelong learning support is delivered through library reference service when each one is handled by showing the client how to approach the question, which authority to consult, and what next steps are needed. As you read this book and practice performing reference service, you will continue to learn how reference work provides this support; and you will be supporting your own lifelong learning concerns as well by learning how to think about questions, information needs, and potential resources for authoritative help in finding answers!

Reference Service as Supporting Civic Engagement

While reference tasks often involve the information needs and expectations of individuals, more and more reference service provided by library reference guidance strengthens social and cultural connections at the community level. By working to provide authoritative information by which community members can plan, make decisions, and take part in civic affairs, the value added to community life includes the following:

- Growth in the number of community members participating in government, including as informed voters, occurs when high-quality information and improved evaluation skills extend throughout that community
- Communication and collaboration among community agencies who share community sectors receiving or eligible for services, with each individual agency's knowledge and awareness base enriched, when they all have access to the most recent and most extensive data resources, including each other's missions and goals
- Strengthening intergenerational ties through interest and ability scaled services over age demographic assignments allows for greater access by many to resources and activities they value
- Capacity building of local government, educational institutions, and individuals in the development of awareness of resources, and access to those resources beyond those present in the community orients the community toward higher goals of achievement

Perhaps as you first read the list of lifelong learning questions in the previous section, you imagined four specific individuals who decide that they need to come to or call the library to ask for reference assistance. That is certainly the model reference staff assumed as good enough service 80, 50, 25 and even a dozen years ago. However, there are many other models and many are community-based, whether the community served by the library is municipal, academic, or industry-based. We will discuss a variety of reference service delivery models in Chapter 11.

RECOGNIZING FORMAL REFERENCE QUESTIONS

Formal reference questions are those that clients articulate as requiring library-supplied information. They may not always be presented to the "right" staff person, if they are being presented in person at all. However, all library staff should meet any inquiry without judgment as to its importance or the importance of the person asking the question, whether the question is informal, or operational, or is in fact one that requires reference staff attention as discussed next. We will examine these matters in depth in Chapter 10. Here, however, let's discuss how we recognize a "formal" reference question, since often it comes to our attention without the obvious hallmarks of a stated factual query.

Whether the need for information has been imposed on the client by another party, such as a teacher, or has been generated by a need to resolve a situation, curiosity, practical demand, or other concern, a formal reference question can be answered through consultation with authoritative sources and good communication skills. That being the case, questions posed about directions within the building, weekend service hours, or fine structures are informal or operational, rather than being formal reference questions. While informal questions should be resolvable by staff members who do not need to access resources beyond signage or the policies of the institution that they represent, formal reference questions do require evaluated resources in order to resolve.

Let's consider the lifelong learning needs that brought community members in search of reference assistance previously. Here's how each of these needs might first be expressed:

- The young man who wants to find out how to get a fair price for his used car may inquire about whether there are laws or rules about selling used cars, or how to know if he's offered a fair trade-in price on his car. It will take some negotiation to come to the formal question: "What is my car worth?"
- The grandmother concerned about childhood vaccination controversies may ask whether it's true that vaccinations cause any specific child disability. Her formal question is unlikely to be frankly stated as: "Where can I find sound data on the relationship between vaccinations and childhood disabilities?" or "Do I have a right to intervene in the healthcare choices being made regarding my grandchild?"
- The 70-year-old who wants to preserve old photographic slides may ask about the possibility of using the library's photocopy machine to make copies of the slides, while the formal question has nothing to do with that piece of equipment, and is really: "How can these old photos be preserved and made accessible for future viewers?"
- The 18-year-old may ask if she is old enough to get a book published, while the formal question is: "What steps do I need to take to self-publish a novel?"

Recognizing each of these types of encounters as revealing a formal reference question takes communication skill. How that is achieved is the subject of our in-depth discussion in Chapter 2. For now, let's take a bird's-eye view of what needs to be in place before such questions are fielded and what, in broad strokes, takes place upon the question's recognition by staff.

RESPONDING TO REFERENCE NEEDS

Before any reference questions can be entertained professionally, the appropriate staff needs to be acquainted generally with the resources they have with which to respond to questions from the community. These include both materials and virtual resources, as well as a host of relevant skills to employ in making effective and efficient use of them. Each type of resource, as well as protocols for accessing and sharing it with clients, requires lengthy discussion and so we will look at ground level at each of these in Chapters 4 through 9. In our bird's-eye view, however, it is sufficient to note that reference staff must be prepared to make use of appropriate resources *before* any questions are presented.

Different communities are likely to have different areas of general and specific information needs. Determining how to scope reference resources and staff skill to the local community is also necessary to both preparation and ongoing work within the community. The ground-level details of this reality will be the subject discussed in Chapter 3.

With resource planning, knowledge of access means, and trained staff in place, what actually happens once a reference question emerges from the community? The following are the general steps that must occur in the performance of professional reference service.

Communication

The first and most critical phase of the reference encounter involves skilled communication. Staff may need to bear the burden of maintaining and modeling the necessary components of communication if the community member cannot share that burden. In Chapter 2, we will discuss a wide range of skills for in-person, online, and third-party communication success. Although these modes may seem like different means of providing reference service, they are actually different communication situations. Rather than being service models, they are simply communication situations. Communication is essential to reference service, just as essential as authoritative information. Communication isn't just about talking; listening and evaluating details presented in ways other than words alone are even more important.

Resource Awareness

As noted earlier, reference staff must be aware of the resources available to them, and that it is through reference staff use of those resources that community members with information needs find worthwhile guidance. Beyond being aware of what is available generally, staff charged with reference work must be able to think while communicating with the community member about his information need, keying mentally into what areas of the resources available are suited to the subject matter and also to the skillset and subtle facets of capacity this particular information needing client presents.

Resource awareness before the fact of a live question is one thing. Being able to make appropriate connections between the specifics of each encounter and the resources is subtly different.

Have you ever asked a friend or family member for input about, for example, a gift you are selecting for someone else, only to have the person you've asked tell you something along the lines of "Oh, Susie doesn't need anything" or "You should give Susie an elephant (or something realistically unavailable for you to give)" or "You should sew her a jacket"—except you don't know how to sew? These are examples of the person you've asked failing to meet the question where it is and then failing to match resource awareness with the person asking. We'll discuss this in depth as part of Chapter 3 because this facet of reference service remains essential no matter the mode of communication, the type of library, or the general demographics of both the community as a whole and the individual information seeker.

Question-Specific Evaluation

In order to undertake this cross-referencing of person, information need, and available resources, reference staff practice many types of question-specific evaluation. Here is a summary of the most important of them:

- What's the essential question or information need?
- What is the best means by which this person can understand an authoritative resource that will fill that need?
- Which authoritative resources that fit this person's access needs and skills have that information?
- How should we proceed so some measure of success or benefit is acquired by this person from this encounter?

Just-in-Time Teaching

Reference staff working in educational institutions may have the duty to instruct community members (students, though not faculty and staff) in methods just in case these means of research are needed. However, in public libraries (and with faculty and staff in academia and schools), the most effective point at which to teach skills related to information retrieval and evaluation happens just at the time that the community member needs that guidance.

Do you remember having to memorize dates of specific historical events or state capitals or how to compute percentage rates? When taught in a vacuum devoid of practical need, what is learned is either frustration, if one lacks a gift for rote memorizing, or incidental nuggets of fact unattached to value except maybe a transitory high mark on a homework assignment or exam.

Just-in-time learning, on the other hand, connects the need to know something with what or how to know. Knowing about how used car value can be computed using authoritative tools is most readily learned by someone who needs to be able to do this. Understanding the copyright process, as well as copyright's actual protections, requires a fair amount of research and specialized reading, all of which is more likely to be pursued, perhaps with step-by-step guidance, when actually needed than at a time when there is no apparent application to one's daily life.[4]

Providing reference services is a provision of just-in-time learning opportunities, with reference staff serving as tutors, guides, or teachers. While there are many situations in which complex research matter may not be deconstructed with the persons needing the information following closely, let alone participating beyond the periphery, each encounter should offer the just-in-time learning that interests the community member, including whether reference staff, and thus the library, can deliver value to their lives by helping to resolve the information need.

Such just-in-time learning is not limited to interactions involving library staff. As we will discuss next, reference service provision is not limited to responding to actively presented requests for information. In passive as well as active reference service provision, that just-in-time value should be present as it is that which engages the client and supports the transmission of resources into the stuff of knowledge.

PASSIVE AND INDIRECT REFERENCE GUIDANCE

One area of reference service that becomes increasingly significant with the penetration of casual factual inquiry being undertaken privately online is passive guidance from reference authorities. Instead of mediating any search for what was, in the last century, called "ready reference" or quick facts such as event dates, birth places, directory information, and calculation formulas, good reference service assures that community members can locate authoritative resources to find such data independently and virtually. We will discuss this at length in Chapter 8.

Indirect reference service is essential to develop as well. Instead of limiting reference tasks to one-on-one encounters that address individual (or a group's singular) information quest, indirect reference services allow community members to acquire authoritative guidance without asserting their specific information quest's particulars. American libraries have provided for this, to some degree, by supporting circulating collections of books and other media, which community members are welcome to use without explaining the parameters of why one or another was selected for perusal and study.

However, reference guidance in the contemporary library should be developed beyond this rudimentary indirect service of a collection to include connections for community members to more varied authoritative resources that address local information needs and interests. Here are some examples:

- Providing, through both scheduling and hosting, for navigational assistance regarding various government programs, such as the Affordable Care Act or Veterans Services
- Maintaining authoritative web pages for community members concerned with local history, genealogy, homework help, or other popularly shared information resource-based expectation
- Flexible and technically trained staff who can and do respond to technology training needs as they appear, recognizing that access to what is needed is germane to fulfilling the need

We will discuss these aspects of contemporary reference work in Chapter 11 explicitly. However, in each chapter throughout this book, the implicit understanding is that reference work in contemporary libraries should not be limited to responding solely to community members who present themselves to staff who, for the staff's part, are simply waiting for such specific questions to be brought to their attention. Contemporary reference work has moved beyond the emergency room model of service toward the public health model: we are concerned in maintaining and supporting excellent community information health and information access, not just in treating clients who visit us with an information cavity.

NOTES

1. The American Library Association's *Code of Ethics* (ifmanual.org/codeethics) speaks to all library work and workers. There are additional reference-specific ethics as well. Ethics will be discussed in detail in Chapter 3.
2. This assertion originally dates from the late 16th-century work of philosopher and statesman Francis Bacon, *Sacred Meditations* (1597), and has been deployed by such luminaries as Thomas Jefferson and organizations, including various state library associations.

3. Placing someone in contact with a specific physician or lawyer as an expert to respond to an information need, however, is not ethical. If such services are needed, the expertise of the local medical association or bar association should be offered. We will discuss this in more detail when we discuss the special handling required by medical and legal questions presented to reference staff.

4. There are, of course, many who enjoy learning for the sake of learning. They, too, are learning to a purpose—the joy they receive from the learning experience. Law students, too, learn about copyright, not in a vacuum, but rather in practical preparation for applying the information, or the structure of law, in practice that they plan to pursue.

CHAPTER 2

Communication and Reference Work

The consistent identifying mark of reference work across decades, cultures, technology use changes, and library types is communication of authoritative information. Communication takes many different forms and, of course, relies on multiple parties for it to happen at all. In this chapter, we will examine all aspects of communication relevant to providing reference service. As we discuss the topics here, remember to keep an open mind about the reference service model or models with which these skills and processes are used. Everything here can be applied to the traditional, and now generally outmoded, in-library reference desk model *and* to community models, virtual service models, and any other service delivery model designed for providing reference guidance.

We will discuss service delivery model types much later in this book, in Chapter 11. That is because such service models are not so much about how to include best practices, but rather how best practices are currently rolled into contemporary delivery models. No matter what models may emerge, like service models of the past and present, they must be based on making best practices operational in the context of community realities and technology standards of the time. On the other hand, communication practices transcend service model choices.

Consider how thoroughly communication tactics are part of your world in every context. They include the wayfinding choices you are provided and which, in turn, the library provides its community. They include sharing both facts and opinions in a manner that allows someone else to understand them.

SIDEBAR 1   REFERENCE INTERVIEWING COMMUNICATION IN DAILY LIFE

The communication skills used in the library reference service context are practiced in other areas of your life, too. Sometimes considering how you encounter these situations—both as an information gatherer yourself and as an information guide for others—can help you to identify and understand the effective use of these skills more clearly. How do you use reference-style interviewing in the following contexts?

- Discussing a new diagnosis with your doctor
- Working with a real estate agent to find a new home
- Assisting your adolescent child in finding and establishing her first bank account
- Obtaining an old family recipe from your grandmother
- Interviewing potential babysitters for your children
- Meeting with the lawyer who is executing your great-uncle's will

In each of these situations, one party (sometimes you) is seeking authoritative information from another party who understands how to acquire that information and can guide the information seeker to the appropriate information. You might find it helpful to construct an outline applying the steps of the reference interview to one or another of these situations to see just how the process unfolds in practical terms.

COMMUNICATION IS DYNAMIC

The communication involved in guiding community members in need of reference services involves a variety of behaviors and sensitivities. Each of these is an aspect of communication, and all must remain in your awareness with every communication interaction:

- Listening or, in the case of written communication, thorough reading
- Body language, including facial expression and posture, whether the communicating parties can see each other or not[1]
- Tone of voice, whether in speaking or writing
- Language and vocabulary choices, both when speaking and writing
- Appropriately audible speaking voice where those communicating are in person or on the phone or other telecommunication device
- Gestures or examples appropriate to both the situation and showing mutual respect between communicating parties, whether in speaking or writing

Take Responsibility for Good Communication

As the professional in the communication process, you may find that sharing the communications burden equally with a client doesn't happen. And that's okay! It's your job to keep the communications channel as open, flexible, and effective as it can be in the situation. This is true even upon our initial encounters and before a formal reference interview might begin. Check your posture to make sure that it shows you are approachable. Remain aware of your surroundings rather than becoming absorbed in a project with your head bowed, if you are assigned to being available to being approached. Be sensitive to those who seem hesitant to engage while also demonstrating facial or gestural evidence that they would really appreciate guidance and being approached.

Trying to be helpful, some people may phrase a question or assertion in a way that makes it seem more complex or difficult than you know it to be. Clients may think they must use special "library" vocabulary and, barring their knowledge of specific terms, find themselves at a loss to explain with confidence what they want. Think about how you try to use the technical language of another person's profession when seeking assistance with your own issues. Because we are each limited in expertise and technical jargon to just a few areas of endeavor, the chances are high of us employing an inaccurate term in someone else's field. We are trying to "meet the expert halfway" in order to get them to understand why we are bringing the problem specifically to them professionally. Unless community members really want to know library or information science jargon, there is little to be gained by correcting and nothing by rebuking someone for using the wrong terminology.

Most people do not understand how information is organized, and they shouldn't have to! However, you may need to help someone to understand where specifically to look in the stacks or how long it might take to get an authoritative answer. They may think, for example, that all the information on one topic will be in one place and pretty easy to find if only they had the magic word or access to higher powered technology. As you know, this isn't true. Information on a specific matter may be in a book near your desk, in one across the room, in books that are located a floor away, on a website, or in an online database. In order to help, you need to find out more specifically what the person really needs to find.

Information resources, in any physical or virtual format, can be complex in their architecture. Sometimes community members may ask only very general questions, or state black-and-white assessments of whether they think their information need can be met. The reference interview, which we discuss below in depth, is used to probe their specific questions or information gaps to determine exactly what is being asked.

Community members can unwittingly provide poor quality information while believing they are expressing themselves clearly. They may anticipate that finding the answer can be done quickly. They may believe that if you would only hand over a simple URL, the just-right book, or other resource, the job of reference has been done and they can continue on their own rather than considering there may be a need to dig more deeply to find their answer. Knowing that they need help can feel disempowering, so even if they don't know how to dig further independently, they may be unwilling to state that fact directly to staff.

Communication skills you employ help guide clients to be more specific. Be on the alert for overly broad requests like "Do you know a good website on baseball trivia?" or "I wonder if I can get a birth certificate that's official." Such openings require investigation on reference staff's part in order to even find what each of these people really needs to find: a particular baseball fact? Someone else's certified birth certificate?

Perhaps the most under-investigated presentation of a need for reference guidance within a library building is the question "Can I use the Internet here?" or "Do you have the Internet?" Those asking it may believe that once they have access to the web they will be able to locate the information they really want to find. Notice when persons appear frustrated or disappointed with a web search they are undertaking in the location where you are providing reference support. You might be able to direct them to a specific website or print resource that can provide the information right away; but first you will need to conduct a reference interview!

Tips for Optimizing Successful Communication

In the Library

While all of the items in the aforementioned bulleted communications list are critical to good reference service, there may be times when staff attention is necessarily divided due to various activities and requests for service happening at once. More than one person may make the need each has for assistance known in one moment. If you are providing reference services in a busy situation, you may need to juggle a variety of questions and people while you work. Here are some hints on the art of juggling:

- Instead of asking if someone has a quick question, ask, "Does anyone need directions?" People may well believe that they have a quick question and many of these indeed turn out to be long and complex.
- Acknowledge the people waiting. Let them know that you are aware of them and will help them as soon as you can.
- Be frank with them. Let them know that this is a busy time and that you will be glad to do what you can now, but that if they contact you at a less busy time, you might be able to provide more in-depth assistance. Let the client decide.

It may well be necessary to work with some community members for a while in order to find out what they really want to ask. Working through to the "real question" saves time in the end because it prevents you from looking for information they don't really want or need.

On the Telephone

Of course, you know perfectly well how to communicate by phone. However, talking with people whom you don't know and whom you are trying to guide can take some special effort. Here are some tips to remember:

- Talk to the caller as soon as you pick up the receiver; don't make the caller wait to hear from you. Listening to silence or to your conversation with someone else can be disconcerting.
- Identify the library and yourself clearly; don't speak too fast.
- Your initial greeting sets the tone for the rest of the telephone interview. If you sound rushed or harried the caller will feel that he or she has bothered you.
- Offer service (unless you already have your attention filled by a previously presenting reference matter with which you are dealing): "How can I help you?" is better than being silent after your initial greeting.
- If you know you won't be able to attend to the caller's need immediately, let him or her know this *and* offer a couple of options: they can call back at a time the two of you agree is good, or the person can call again after the passage of a block of time you suggest is needed for the current situation you are already handling to dissipate. In both cases, be specific with the caller as to the window of time that would work for you and pay attention to what his or her timeline is as well.
- Keep in mind, and act upon your awareness, that a phone caller is making as legitimate use of your reference services as is someone visiting in physical person the library or other venue in which you are providing reference support. Some callers cannot get to the reference staff and collection physically. Treat the community member who tries to

acquire reference guidance by phone with as much effort on your part as the ones who are physically present.

If you have to leave the phone to find an answer:

- Tell callers what you are doing so that they don't think that their calls have been dropped.
- Put callers on hold to protect the privacy of anyone in your location who may be speaking near the telephone.
- Never let a question drop because you can't find an answer right away. If the caller doesn't have time to wait for the answer, get his or her telephone number and tell him or her you will call back after working on it. This gives you time to look or even to call another source for the answer.
- Make sure that callers are told where you got the information you are providing; cite your source(s)! Also, make sure that callers understand your response and that the response meets their information needs.
- Give people on the phone time to write down the sources and information you are providing.
- Check to see if they have any questions about the citation. It is frustrating to a caller to be left with incomplete understanding of how the information applies to the question and the need to know where to find that information if it is needed at another time.

In Text Chat–Based Communication

Providing reference services through text and other online chat software requires some communication skills specific to the protocols of that medium. Terseness, in order to save keystrokes, is standard. However, disregard any temptation to forgo asking open-ended questions as a way of minimizing words. Community members who are served by text-based reference services are due the same scope and quality of satisfaction as those who work face to face with staff or speak with staff by phone or other voice-based telecommunication.[2]

Among highly effective attributes of texting available to the reference interchange is the transmission of hyperlinks to specific resources and screenshots. Unlike those with whom staff communicate by phone, text users can be shown and can show images that address or clarify the information gap.

Be Sensitive to Sensitivities

Trying to discuss something with a stranger or casual acquaintance when the subject concerning you is of a highly personal nature, perhaps a medical or legal problem, can make communication awkward, especially in a face-to-face exchange in a public area. Community members in these situations may be embarrassed to share their questions, or they may feel guarded about revealing too much for either their own safety or your comfort. You need to use a lot of tact to convey the idea that you are trying to be helpful rather than just being nosy.

You can be on the alert for when this kind of sensitive communication might occur and take some practical steps to help ease the communication process. If a matter seems likely to be personal in its nature such as interest in finding bankruptcy assistance or drug rehabilitation laws, move the client and yourself to a quiet place away from others. Let them know that you need to gather additional details in order to find the specific information needed.

For example, you might say, "If you can tell me more about what you need, I will be able to find the best sources to help you."

If the person has sent a text message, but seems reluctant to ask more, perhaps he or she could be asked if a telephone call would be better. If the telephone call can be made, from your side, immediately, this may allay the community member's anxiety about continuing a sensitive exchange. If, on the other hand, you seem to be putting off a sensitive text query to a much later phone call, the person may well feel dismissed.

Body Language

People notice and are influenced by body language as well as words. In addition to the important body language of smiling, here are some tips:

- Use physical actions to show someone that you are paying full attention. Stop doing any tasks and look directly at the person unless that is a cultural challenge.
- Be aware that different people may prefer different amounts of physical space around them. Some like to stand closer, some further away. Try to accommodate yourself to the individual community member's preferences, but don't let someone trespass into what you hold as your own safe space.
- Be aware that in some cultures it is impolite to make direct eye contact and respect that if the client appears to prefer avoiding your eyes.
- Be aware of nonverbal clues about how the other person is feeling by noting posture, distraction behaviors, and tone of voice.
- Use body movements that show you are interested in what the person is saying and feeling. Turn toward the person both when listening and speaking, rather than walking away as you begin a search.
- Relax your shoulders as well as your face.
- If you have an encounter that leaves you feeling enervated or anxious, change your own posture before continuing to work. This can be as simple as standing up, if you were seated during that exchange, or sitting down if you were standing or moving.
- Try to be at eye level with whomever you are speaking. For example, if the community member is seated, perhaps in a wheelchair, it is easier for him or her to talk to you if you are seated, too. Don't forget children; it helps to be at eye level with them, as well.

THE REFERENCE INTERVIEW

The reference interview is the process undertaken to find out what information is wanted or needed, through identifying appropriate resources to meet the information gap and then assuring that the desirable information is located and made accessible. The success of a reference interview can be measured by how efficiently and sensitively you gain the right kind of information to move on to helping to identify and find exactly what information is wanted and needed, in a format that fits the access needs of the person who needs the information.

Many people are uncomfortable approaching anyone for help, even someone with the job of assisting in the discovery of information. They may worry that you may think their question is silly, stupid, or too personal, or they may not know how to explain what they need in terms they believe can be understood readily or quickly. Good reference communication gets both of you past such obstacles.

Identifying the Information Gap: Establishing the Question

How you find out what information someone needs, what the question really is, and what specific kind of information is wanted and can be used is achieved by conducting a good reference interview. This can be the most difficult part of reference work. The information you may think a person wants will be off the mark with his or her real information need if you don't employ excellent communication skills to assure that there is a common understanding between client and staff about the specifics of the information gap. If you simply answer any questions as posed, without delving any more deeply, there's a risk of a failed interview and the person leaving with no information, incomplete information, or wrong information.

A reference interview is the mutual exchange of questions and answers in which you engage when you are working with anyone who is seeking information through library reference service mediation.

The communication that occurs during a reference interview allows you to learn more and more about the information gap at hand, including important details about the party with the question, such as their current knowledge base and language skills. Reference interview questions offer the opportunity to revise the way the information gap was originally presented and how it was initially understood. It is not unusual to discover, through the interview, that the real information need is quite different from what any initial presentation of it seemed to suggest. It's your job to help meet the real information need, even if the beginning point of the reference interview seemed to be going elsewhere.

SIDEBAR 2 THE FIRST QUESTION OR STATEMENT IN AN INTERVIEW MAY WELL BE JUST A WAY OF SAYING "HELLO!"

In American culture, we often begin any communication with another by asking a question or making a brief statement. At the beginning of what will become a reference interview, both the party wanting information and the reference service provider want to be sure the other person or persons know that there is some information need and that everyone present (and present, of course, may be online or via telecommunication) is approachable and willing to address that. Typical first questions are:

- Can you help me?
- Do I start with you?
- Can you answer a question?
- Would you like some help?

Sometimes instead of a question, the initiation of the process is a statement:

- I need to find a scholarship.
- Our teacher said you could help us find a youth hostel.
- Everyone else seems to know how to get an e-mail account.

These initial questions and statements are really just ways of announcing, "Hello. We might communicate about something specific, depending on how you respond to my initiation of communication."

Most reference interviews do not look formal. Two decades ago, the interview was generally placed in the library, at a staffing point and had a formal appearance and, often, could be less than inviting. This excluded many from asking for reference service, especially those who might be shy or lack knowledge of the purpose of the reference staff. As you read through the following section on the parts of the interview, it's essential that you consider each step as it might occur in a variety of settings and situations involving library reference staff and community members, rather than focusing only on a face-to-face model or even a single model.

The Power of Open-Ended Questions

When asked broad or general questions or told nonspecific information concerns, you need to find out specifically what is wanted and needed. The most efficient and effective way to do that is to begin with open-ended questions and invitations to express the need more fully. Open-ended questions are questions that can't be answered by a "yes" or a "no." Practice these examples:

- What kind of information on _____ are you looking for?
- Would you tell me more about _____?
- Could you tell me what you're working on?
- Is there something specific about _____ that you would like to know?
- What would you like to know about _____?
- Please give me an example so I can get a better sense of what we need.
- When you say _____, what do you mean?
- Please describe the kind of information you would like to find.

Encouraging those who need specific information, even if they don't seem to know exactly what it might be, is essential to finding out what is at the heart of the matter. Allow persons working with you on their information needs to use *their own words* to describe the information they want. Never assume you know their question. You can avoid putting words in their mouths; avoid yes/no questions at this stage.

Consider this example. If someone asks for information on World War I, ask, "Is there a particular aspect of World War I you are interested in?" rather than asking, "Is this for a school report?" or "Do you want books or magazines?" Suppose the person just wants to know how many people were killed in the war. If you've asked, "Do you want books or magazines?" the person with that actual information need is left to guess that the limit of forthcoming assistance is to show them where to slog through indexes or piles of paper or microfilm with no further guidance. The person with the question may have no idea at all if books or magazines would be useful to find the number of war dead. By asking leading or "closed" questions like these, reference staff actually slows down the whole process of finding out what's wanted, diverts the person with an information need from discovering an efficient and appropriate resource, and provides no library value to the exchange.

Offer choices between resource formats, such books or websites, only when you are clear about the desired information and the person with the question might be able to make a good choice among format options. People do tend to be agreeable, especially when they aren't sure about that reference staff's job to guide them to authoritative help that suits their need, so trying to be agreeable, they choose one and hope for the best. When staff offer leading questions, they are putting words in the mouth of the person who may have a very different real question. If the leading questions follow from an inaccurate assumption on staff's part about what the person really wants, the real question may never get broached. Asking closed-ended questions also puts the burden on those asking them to figure out what is wanted, rather than looking to the expert, the person with the information need, to help staff understand the real question.

At the beginning of a reference interview, you may need to ask more than one open-ended question. Later in the interview, when nailing down some specifics, closed questions can be used for clarification. With open-ended questions you need not know anything about the subject. Just asking some questions can help the community member share enough for you to identify appropriate resources. (Of course, this is posited on staff also knowing potential resources to tap for different areas of knowledge, which we address in the following chapters.)

Clarifying What Is Being Said

During the interview, you must engage in active listening practices. Questions and comments that establish whether you and the client have a mutual understanding of the desired information might include some closed-ended questions, but only when other aspects of the subject have been presented through open-ended questioning. Think of questions such as those listed here as clarifying dimensional aspects of the information need, rather than being the information that is needed:

- Where have you already looked for this information?
- Do you need a book you can take home, or can you use material that stays here?
- Is there a date after which you can no longer use this information?
- When you say you need recent information, do you have a specific time period in mind?

Once you believe you know what the real question is, there is one more step to take before beginning the actual search for information.

Verify

You must verify that you and the client agree on the essential information need. Glossing over verification with the assumption that you have figured out the question wastes time searching for something that wasn't really wanted in the first place. When you take the time and the opportunity to verify the client's question, you also establish that his or her information need is the center of your attention, and that is a signal of respect.

The best way to verify is by paraphrasing or by asking *neutral* questions. Putting the question you heard into your words ensures that both staff and client understand the real question. Neutral questions demonstrate active listening by staff. For example:

- "You need to know where to find a reputable trainer to teach your dog to protect your home. Is that what you want to find?"
- "What you want to find out is how to scan these slides into digital images. Is that correct?"
- "You need three scientific articles published in the last month about cell phone towers and health issues. Is that what you need?"

Sometimes you may feel certain that you know what the question is before it is even fully expressed. The man with the greasy hands who asks about car books is obviously going to want a repair manual, right? The 12-year-old who asks for a map of Wyoming is doing a school report, right? Maybe not. The man may be writing a novel and needs to know the kind of cars popular in 1920, and the 12-year-old may be taking a trip next month for which he is doing some research now.

During the reference interview, you must listen to the concern being presented all the way through before deciding what the question is and how to answer it.

Identifying Contextual Details

Best practices in library reference services go beyond plugging a desired fact into an information gap. The context in which the question or information need is presented and revealed must be recognized and the forthcoming information must be suitable to that context. Context for the situation includes a variety of details going well beyond a simple restatement of a factual question.

By the end of the reference interview, you should expect to have gathered each of the details described below. In most cases asking for these directly won't be necessary. Instead, the process of identifying the context of the specific information need will have been developed in the course of the interview. Asking open-ended questions, neutral questions, and appropriate clarifying questions should draw out the needed information for you to use even if the client may not see the connection between these details and eliciting the best possible information in response to the information need.

The following seven contextual details should have been revealed as you engaged someone in the interview:

1. **What is the question?**
   The client may make broad statements or ask general questions, requiring the need to determine the specific information gap(s). A child may say, "I want to know about some animals." You need to discover what particular aspect is of concern. The use of open-ended questions and clarifying statements helps both you and the child uncover the specific need. You may ask, "Is there a specific animal that you would like to know about?" The child could respond, "I am looking for information about whether giraffes are afraid of snakes," or "I am looking for information about which animals live in the tropical rainforests in Borneo." If you don't fully understand the specific information gap, the reference interview must continue with more questions. You should paraphrase, and verify that the specific question has been identified.

2. **Who is asking the question?**
   Is the person who is asking a medical question a nurse? If so, you would need to consider providing a different level of information than what would be useful to a young student doing a report. One word of caution here: again you must try not to make assumptions about what you think the person wants based on what the person's status appears to you to be. If a woman asks for car repair information, you should not assume she needs something very easy. She might be an expert car mechanic. You should be sure to ask what level of material is wanted when the topic is technical, such

as medical information or repair help. By using neutral questions information about the level of expertise wanted can be uncovered. Making assumptions, often done with the belief that such can save time, leads to unnecessary detours away from the real information gap.

3. **Why is the information needed?**

This can make a big difference in the type of information you provide. The information appropriate to a student working on a school report about the island of Borneo might be different from what is best for someone else designing a fund-raiser to publicize concern about the loss of rainforest habitat or to someone else who is preparing to vacation in Borneo. Where reference service is provided in a context such as a civic agency, the information need may be personal or it may be related to the agency work. While the reason for the information need does not qualify a question as more or less important, understanding the purpose to which the information will be put can add a dimension of understanding. Also you need to understand both the client's depth of knowledge of the subject matter and the skill sets he or she brings to incorporating the new information elicited by the question to that knowledge in order to provide the appropriate resources.

4. **In what format and amount is the information needed?**

The community members may need the information in a particular format, or expect that it can be obtained in only one of several that are actually available. What format is most useful, both for this type of information and to the person who needs it? Perhaps it would be easier to use in Japanese, or by referring to an infographic or a video than by reading narrative text. Does the person with the information need have low vision? Are illustrations important to the transmission of the information? Would one short article be enough, or does the person need extensive information?

5. **When is the need-by deadline for the information to be useful?**

If the person is preparing to give a speech, working on a report for school, or planning to travel, there is a specific deadline to meet. When asking a person when the information is needed, "as soon as possible" is the usual answer. Everybody would like his or her needs met as soon as possible. A better way to phrase the question is "What is your deadline for getting this information?" Careful listening throughout the interview may reveal the deadline for the information need, so asking for it explicitly may be required only if that detail hasn't emerged in the course of collecting other details about the information gap.

6. **Where has the person already looked?**

Knowing this can save everyone's time, but you should remember that some community members may be able to use library tools with greater skill than others. When specific resources already considered have been named by the client, some double-checking of what the person reports having done can be helpful. Pay attention to telltale expressions that indicate overly generalized searching on the person's part. When someone has "looked on the Internet," or has "done an Internet search," follow up by asking about the search terms that the person used. Finding out where this person has already looked for information can provide clues for working on the question. Neither of you wants to spend time gathering information already acquired, so the reference interview should focus on what else is needed.

7. **Where did the person hear about the topic in question?**
Knowing this can help gauge the reliability of the person's information. You will probably have less confidence in the information stated by the person if it was "heard from a friend" than if it was read in this month's issue of *Nature* magazine. The source of the question can often give you good clues on places to search. The article in *Nature*, for example, may include references to other articles, books, or websites. It may also provide the names of organizations or institutions whose websites may have additional information.

Among the subtle yet important details the reference interview allows you to collect are those related to literacy skills and any disabilities that may inhibit the client's successful use of some resources.

Learning to collect all these details is a matter of practice. As you become increasingly experienced both with reference methods and the community in which you are providing reference services, your observational and analytical skills grow and continue to develop with each new encounter, change in technology, and evolving community concerns.

Completing the Interview

Once you are sure of the question and the context in which it develops, you can proceed to find the answer. At times, the answer is handy. Perhaps referring to a current and authoritative news site, an encyclopedia, an atlas, or a dictionary is all that is truly needed. Other times you will need to show community members how to search the Internet or an information database efficiently and effectively. In still other cases the best answer may be found in the library's online catalog, another source that may require instruction to respond to the level of the expressed information need.

If the answer is not immediately at hand, you need to guide the community member or members to a place where the information has high probability of being found, whether in a physical or virtual location. This guidance may include walking with someone to another nearby location, making a written note of a URL or database name with the appropriate search terms, or providing a referral to another person or agency. We will discuss referrals next.

When you are busy with a variety of persons seeking information with different needs, or levels of need, responding to everyone at once isn't likely. During busy times or with a complex project, instead of being able to see the question's research completely through to resolution, you can help someone get started with the process by providing some relevant materials, guiding the person who needs specific information to a relevant online source, or showing the way to a section in the book stacks. When a reference transaction can't be completed at the first point of need due to conflicting demands, you must remember to communicate that there is more to be uncovered and you will return if necessary, to help further once time permits.

If you plan to continue to work on a question at a later time, you should make sure that three pieces of information are provided before you and the client break off your initial communication:

- The community member knows your name or whom to contact for follow-up.
- You have noted the name and contact information to get in touch with the person with the answer. Be sure to repeat any orally provided or handwritten contact information to make sure it has been accurately noted.
- You should provide clients placed in this situation of being asked to wait with a realistic idea of when they can expect to be contacted with the answer.

Follow-Up

Never assume that you have fully answered a question until you undertake some kind of follow-up. Whether in person or by remote communication of any sort, after you reach the point where you believe you have answered the question, check with the party who expressed the information need in the first place to make sure they agree about the completion. Asking "Does that completely answer your question?" is too global and pat to invite authentic feedback. Instead, you might ask, "Does this help with your concern?" or "Does it seem that we found what you hoped to discover?" In some situations applying newly acquired information must be undertaken before someone can confirm that the question has been resolved. In such cases, offer to contact them later, after the new information has been reviewed or placed into its planned context, to make sure the answer fit what was needed.

REFERRING A QUESTION

"Referring the question" means moving the question beyond the resources (staff or material) you have at the first point of question contact. When you can't find the answer locally, *always* offer to refer the question. Needing to refer an information need is not a reflection on your ability but one of training, familiarity with resources, and local availability of resources. The world of information is so vast that there is a good chance that even the most difficult–sounding question can be answered locally, in terms of uncovering authoritative data. However, it may be that the local discovery of that data doesn't suit the context for this particular reference situation. This can happen if you can locate only technical information for someone who needs more basic guidance, or resources in fine print or Spanish when the information needs to be found in a sound file or in English.

"No" Should Never Be the Final Answer

Many persons in your community are not aware that you can offer referral services. If you can't find the answer, you must be proactive in specifically offering to refer a question, and make sure that the community is aware that a referral is not going "above and beyond" reference service delivery available to them.

Before Making a Referral

Before beginning a referral process, you should check with other staff to see if any of them can help to locate the information locally. It is often helpful to get someone else's approach to a question, even when both of you are equally informed about local resources.

Just bouncing a question off a coworker can help you identify an approach you hadn't originally remembered.

You must perform a thorough reference interview about the question you are referring elsewhere so that as much information as possible about the need and its context can be passed along to the referral location. All the basic contextual information described earlier and a verification with the client about what is wanted should be included for anyone who will be performing further research on the question.

Types of Referral

The following types of referral possibilities may be available to you for questions that can't be answered with your own and your library's resources.

- Referral to the local consortial reference center
- Interlibrary loan (ILL)
- Referral to people and organizations in the community, including other libraries such as those at a university or hospital

Many questions sound impossible. Do not hesitate to refer even if the question seems very difficult. When clients look to your library for information, it is your job to acknowledge that the need is valid and you must help them get the information. Every question must be treated conscientiously, and that means locating a referral location even if it is one that is beyond the scope of your library.

You should be sure to inform someone with such a question that it is being referred and about the follow-through process, including the expected length of time to locate the information elsewhere and from whom the client can expect next contact if you are not going to be the one to deliver it. Will it be from the original reference staff or someone from the agency to which the question is being referred? Help the client stay in the loop of where his or her question is being handled and from whom he or she will hear about its conclusion.

Referring the question means moving a need for specific information beyond local resources because the resources needed to satisfy the question are not available where the question originally emerges.

One bibliographically oriented form of referral that has been traditionally used by local libraries is the interlibrary loan. This system dates from the era in which information was found through searching print resources and, of course, not every library contained every such print work locally. Interlibrary loans work between libraries, rather than between a library user and a library. The client's need for specific information, if it can be addressed through materials another library owns and an interlibrary agreement exists with the client's home library, is borrowed by his institution, for his use from the owning library.

How interlibrary loan requests were and are handled varies quite a lot between libraries, although many placed such a service with reference staff so that an adequate interview and evaluation of local resources and client needs could be achieved before a request from another library's collections was made. With increasing amounts of information being available through online sources, interlibrary loan is used less generally today to answer basic reference needs than to support special interests of isolated researchers or readers with specialized interests.

Providing the Results of a Referral, Including an Interlibrary Loan

A closing interview can be especially important when someone returns to collect information that has been sent for them from another agency. You should check to be sure that:

- The person understands the information provided. For example, if the referral has involved the interlibrary loan of a book, you should make certain the person retrieving it knows which part is relevant to the question or need posed.
- The information sent fills the need and answers the question. You may find that the provided information demonstrates a disconnect between what the person was trying to express initially and what you understood as the information need. You should not hesitate to "re-refer" such a question, first conducting aspects of the reference interview to make sure the need is now accurately recorded.

PERSONALITIES AND BEHAVIORAL CONSIDERATIONS

Human beings are highly complex and that complexity requires reference staff to be aware of and have the capacity to respond to a seemingly infinite variety of factors that influence communication and, thus, the provision of satisfactory reference service. As with any interpersonal event, both parties influence communication.

Culture, personal history, immediate circumstances, and other factors influence both staff and community members.

Personality facets that can and do influence communication in the reference context, whether these traits are perceived to lie in the client or the staff member, include:

- Demonstrative degrees of introversion or extroversion
- Shyness or pronounced boldness
- Pronounced pessimistic or optimistic outlook
- Self-involvement
- Naiveté
- Fear of failure or loss of respect

By being aware of one's own personality strengths and weaknesses and open to the reality that other individuals will include those with dissimilar and those with some similar traits, you can improve the communication quality in the reference setting, whether its location is in a traditional model or beyond a building setting. As with almost all matters related to providing reference service professionally, conscientious practice both improves performance and brings increased comfort to the staff members performing reference work.

RUSA Guidelines for Behavioral Performance

The American Library Association (ALA) includes a section specializing in Reference and User Services Association (RUSA), an important support and guide for anyone involved in professional reference work. Among the documents RUSA publishes online is the five-tenet brief on "Guidelines for Behavioral Performance of Reference and Information Service Providers."[3] Those involved in the provision of reference services in any library should take responsibility for familiarizing themselves with this document. Among the features of behavior it addresses are:

- Staff visibility and approachability
- Objective interest
- Listening and inquiring
- Searching skill use
- Follow-up

It is essential to note that these behaviors should be evident in all settings and with anyone to whom reference service is supplied. Some of these tenets require at least minimal planning of space or technology use. All require every staff member to be conscientious about their own perceived attitude and interpersonal comfort.

Guidelines for Specific Age Demographics

In addition to the tenets listed earlier, which are applicable to all, there are published guidelines that provide instruction and support for staff working with demographic groups who have inherent behavioral needs and concerns that should inform communication techniques.

RUSA, together with the Young Adult Library Services Association (YALSA), has published "Guidelines for Library Services to Teens, Ages 12–18,"[4] which, in part, speaks directly to reference service provision. Specifically, tenets three and four in this document discuss aspects of reference that are best designed for teen community members. The third guideline addresses the developmental attributes of adolescents that favor communication from anywhere and anytime. The fourth guideline emphasizes the need to recognize teen reference needs as including personal as well as school-imposed knowledge searches.

The document "Competencies for Librarians Serving Children in Public Libraries,"[5] from the Association for Library Service to Children (ALSC), addresses reference services directly in its section five. However, its section one is just as essential to any reference staff member who is interacting with someone under the age of 12 or 14. As with teens and adults, children present information needs that may be personal as well as those imposed by schoolwork. The communication sophistication of children at different ages and stages varies, as does the capacity of a child of any age to communicate with someone who is an official, a stranger, or who fits into any category the child deems unfamiliar. As with individuals of any age, reference staff should focus on the specific person, rather than a theoretical Someone Who Is This Age (gender, color, cultural affiliation).

As with youth, older adults may exhibit some age-related characteristics with which you should feel comfortable or, at least, of which you are aware. As with youth, older adults, too, are individuals, and the presence of white hair should not in itself suggest a general lack of technical prowess or other presumption.

However, older adults may move more slowly, suffer from degenerated hearing or vision, or have a reduced tolerance for taking on new and complex learning. The operative word here, of course, is *may*. While reference staff coming into first contact with someone who appears to be elderly should be alert to noticing any of these capacities reduced by advanced age, the individual might also be spry, unfettered by deafness or reduced vision, and deeply involved in learning new skills.

Age can indicate to staff members that certain behaviors and/or communication skills may be needed; however, it is appropriate to identify the capacity of the individual community member of any age, rather than to assume a curtailed capacity to participate in reference communication.

Whether much older or younger than a community member, you can make use of some specific actions to improve cross-generation communication:

- Try to be at the same eye level and maintain eye contact while interviewing in person. This may require you to seat yourself, or to have a chair available for clients to be seated beside rather than across from you in order to allow you both to engage with resources set before you.
- Don't assume all questions from children are school-related, but on the other hand, school is children's work, so treat school questions as real and important.
- Address the child who has the information need directly, even if the child is accompanied by a parent or a care provider. The companion's role is to assist you and the child, not to remove your attention from the child who is the client.
- Be sensitive to matching the information you provide with the reading ability of that particular client rather than assuming a capacity based on age or grade level.
- Remain open and nonjudgmental about the subject of the inquiry and listen as well as respond. Be careful not to agree or disagree with any particular opinion offered in an attempt on the community member's part to prove a social or political point. It is possible to acknowledge statements neutrally and that should be the tenor of your response.

Cultural (rather than linguistic) differences can also require awareness and conscientious approaches by reference staff:

- Silence on the part of the client to whom you have placed an interview question or delivered information should not be construed as misunderstanding or rudeness. Silence may instead indicate respect for staff authority, full agreement with what the client is being told, or fear of how staff might perceive the community member's accent.
- People from some cultures are not demonstrative. Smiling may hide emotions such as frustration or confusion.
- Verbal reinforcement such as "I see" or "Uh-huh" may not be part of a culture's mode of communication. Watch for nonverbal communication and prompt an acknowledgment of understanding by asking directly, "Do you understand?" or watching for a nod.
- Saving face is important in many cultures. You should allow for this by showing consistent respect to the other party in the discussion.
- In some cultures avoidance of eye contact is polite. Don't force it on someone who seems to want to avoid it.
- Personal name order may be different in some cultures. Ask for "family name" instead of "last name."

Guidelines for Specific Subject Areas of Inquiry

In many situations, reference service provision invites community members to interact with staff on a wide range of subjects. Even in what might be considered a setting where topics to be addressed are relatively limited in breadth relative to the universe of knowledge such as a library booth at a county fair, any topic can emerge at any time.

While you need not respond with detailed information on an endless array of possible questions, receiving some topically inspired questions does require special handling in the moment.

A person who presents a health information need to you when you are working in a highly public and busy location should be accorded the respect of helping him to maintain noticeable privacy. Instead of conducting a reference interview in the lobby of city hall, guide him to a quieter corner of the space where a reference interview can be conducted calmly and out of earshot of every passerby.

Students who have been given an assignment that brings dozens of what amounts to the same question to you each need to be accorded the respect they would have received had their question not been a repetition of the seventeen ahead and ninety behind each. To this student, this question is unique and has not been discussed with reference staff. You, then, must accord each iteration of the interview with the same degree of interest, engagement, and care.

By keeping in mind that good communication is sensitive and, when on the reference job, other-centered, you can maintain the integrity of clients' self-respect, and position yourself to be perceived as capable of lending assistance in their searches, rather than standing as a gatekeeper between what information they need and the most efficient way to access it.

HANDLING COMMUNICATION CHALLENGES

Even the best of skills and intentions as reference staff undertake communication with community members can be challenged by circumstances. Understanding best practices for coping with the most typical of these bumps in the communication road can help you to relax when facing the uncertainties that can arise unexpectedly.

Linguistic Challenges

In a nation of immigrants and a variety of social classes with their own communication styles and habits, linguistic challenges are bound to arise in nearly every community. As discussed at the outset of this chapter, it remains your responsibility to be aware of the need to reach further than halfway when such a breakdown occurs.

Among the variety of tools available to libraries and other agencies where community members need communication help to attain satisfaction in a shared language, Language Line[6] is one that should be explored and understood before the point of need. This service operates via telephone between speakers of more than 120 different languages and English-speaking service providers in libraries, hospitals, school departments, civic offices, federal bureaus, and other agencies. The service is via subscription with the subscribing agency entitled to place a call for professional interpretive assistance at any time. The key here, besides simple and pervasive availability, is that the interpreters are in fact professionally trained in their translation and communication work.

Why does that matter? While an ever-increasing number of machine "translators" burgeon online, translation and interpretation are not wholly synonymous. English and Spanish both have a large variety of dialects and regionally specific word uses, for example. While a machine translation may inform a Spanish speaker that an English language reference to a bonnet involves an old-fashioned clothing item for one's head, this becomes useless when the "bonnet" in question is a reference to a contemporary English automobile part.

Further, many subject areas use specialized vocabulary that must be perfectly interpreted language to language in order to impart technically correct information. A word-by-word translation for a doctor's diagnosis, for instance, could be deadly, needlessly upsetting, or just plain nonsensical. Professionally trained and credentialed interpreters don't translate. They also don't insert their own opinions or beliefs into the communication process between the two parties who need them to effect communication. This will be again discussed in more depth in Chapter 3's concentration on ethics.

In addition to Language Line, some libraries and other agencies employ bi- and multilingual staff who are tested and compensated for using their interpretation skills on the job on an ad hoc basis. You should know who those staff members are, their ranges of expertise, and how to contact them when needed.

A source of translation help that seems to be utilized, however thoughtless it is, requires specific discouragement here. Pressing children into the service of interpreter for parental communication, by library staff, is simply unethical. The adult deserves privacy, the child deserves to remain in the role of child rather than caretaker, and there is the high chance of this scenario becoming fraught with inaccuracies, however well intentioned both child and you may be.

Aside from the range of foreign languages, linguistic concerns in communication include local and social group argot. You should be familiar with the lingo used locally by English or any other dominant language speakers. Regional accents, idiomatic phrases, and more may take some degree of staff learning. As discussed earlier in this chapter, too, literacy skills vary and can require you to consider more or less basic written texts in the course of communicating written information.

American Sign Language (ASL) falls into the area of linguistic concerns as well. ASL is, in fact, its own language, not a word-by-word translation of English.[7] While this is a visual language used in the United States and some other countries, it does not necessarily have analogous visual language cohorts around the world. Signing in Latin America, for example, is not typical, so trying to find someone who can deploy "Spanish sign language" is not a sensible goal.

When reference staff are engaged with someone who speaks English well enough for the discussion to take place but who may lack the agility in this language a native speaker could demonstrate, the following tips can support successful communication:

- You should speak in short, simple sentences rather than long, complex ones. Avoid the use of library jargon.
- Instead of posing either/or questions, ask two questions.
- Speak slowly and articulate distinctly, without dramatizing.

- Repeat your own statement once, slowly, if you are noticing cues that it was not at first understood. If that doesn't work, try rephrasing instead of repeating more than once. Substituting words can improve overall comprehension.[8]
- When asking for clarification of your understanding of a pronunciation or an unusual term offered by the community member, keep the question short and specific and reword it, as needed, until the information is presented in a way that both of you understand.
- Allow time after asking or delivering information for the other person to translate mentally what you have just said. In other words, lack of immediate response is not an indication that no response is forthcoming or that immediate further prompting is needed.
- Avoid idioms and slang.
- Keep your voice level, rather than raising it, as many people do when talking with someone who doesn't seem to understand. Raising your voice will not help with understanding and it may be perceived as anger.

Communication Challenges Arising from Minimized Physical or Intellectual Capacities

While some physical challenges present little concern for altering best communication practices in general, others require reference staff to make use of tools and supports to bridge differences in capacity. Some challenges present an array of communication gaps to address, such as a stroke victim who has reduced mobility and speech disabilities. Others may not be quickly apparent and you may discover only after beginning an exchange that the client's physical or intellectual needs call on you to make adjustments in your communication methods.

Challenges to Hearing and Clear Speech Production

As discussed earlier, those who know and use ASL present a linguistic challenge. However, those who are hard of hearing and have access to no other language than Standard English, Spanish, or other language that relies on oral production and aural comprehension should not be subjugated to less than standard interviews and communications.

Among the tools that you should be ready to use are:

- Written notes in lieu of a spoken exchange. This can be achieved readily with pencil and paper or a keyboard and screen.
- Alteration in word choice. Some words are more easily lip-read and even heard than others, so using synonyms that differ in sound makeup can help to clarify spoken messages.
- Alteration in speaker. Different voice timbres may register better or worse with some listeners. If a low-pitched tone, spoken, for instance, by a baritone man, isn't audible, the voice of a woman with a contralto tone may work.

To minimize discomfort for those who have even marginally impaired hearing, and as a matter of courtesy in general, always face those with whom you are speaking and make sure that your face and mouth are unobstructed for your audience to use as support for hearing clearly.

In addition to freely available supports such as those listed immediately above, many states provide a relay system that supports both hard of hearing and speech impaired persons in communicating by a phone-based service. Similar in arrangement to Language Line, discussed earlier, such utility-sponsored services as California Relay[9] provide support between those who have standard hearing and speaking capacities and those with challenges in hearing or clear speech.

Challenges to Intellectual Development

Almost every reference service setting may see at least the occasional person with severe congenital or acquired intellectual delays. In some communities, reference staff may well see frequent and regular visits in the library setting by those who have such challenges. Often, in the case of regular library visiting, those with such challenges are accompanied by a care provider. In some cases communication itself presents no challenge different from those discerned with normatively developed community members. In others, the expert help of the care provider may be engaged to help guide the reference staff member. If that occurs, remember to address the person whose needs you are addressing, rather than speaking past him to the care provider.

As with anyone else, community members with such intellectual challenges require respect and deserve objective interest in their information needs, along with follow-through that would be accorded anyone to whom reference services are rendered.

If your local civic area includes a chapter of The Arc, reach out to it for staff training.[10] Whether or not there is a local chapter, The Arc's website includes many helpful supports for its community, as well as online training opportunities.

Community members for whom autism or other severe Asperger spectrum conditions are central to their communication capacities also require specific communication practices to best serve their information needs. A common communication-related feature of this syndrome is the literal interpretation of expressions. A key element in communicating well, then, is to use as idiomatic-free expression as can be accomplished and to note and address the likelihood of confusion arising from symbolic expressions.

Mental Illness and Emotional Distress

Communicating with community members in need of reference assistance even while delusional, in shock, or otherwise operating outside the normative bounds of psychological health can be stressful. However, it is the rare situation in which the sufferer of the psychological challenge is suffering less than the staff member with whom he is trying to communicate.

Empathy and boundary setting are both recommended strategies regardless of the details of the situation. Heroics are not a part of the reference service job; however, acknowledging that outside help may be required and then summoning it need not depersonalize the community member whose behavior seems to warrant intervention.

Reference staff should be able to recognize the differences between delusions and information needs, rather than consigning both to a kind of dumpster of what can be brushed aside without care. Contact the local mental health clinic, crisis intervention team, or similar office to engage a speaker to address staff information needs and concerns regarding exhibitions of poor mental health on the parts of community members. A proactive information and networking session with experts can itself boost staff confidence in appropriate communication practices to employ within the bounds of job performance.

A NOT SO FINAL WORD ON COMMUNICATION

Communication is such an intrinsic aspect of successful reference service provision that other areas of this book will include portions linking their concerns with the communication process. For example, in Chapter 11, reference service delivery models are discussed at length, and each of these includes a communication component. In Chapter 12, among the supporting resources discussed are those intended to address improvements in written communication for the web.

Since our very means of communication continue to evolve rapidly, discerning best practices for communicating in such media as text, visual telecommunication, and through other modes requires you and other staff members to develop skills and strategies that make communication as clear and accessible as possible with and for community members. Like all things reference, this aspect of service can never be fully achieved and yet always can be refined.

NOTES

1. While we are all aware of how seeing someone's posture and expression can influence how we understand his or her spoken message, posture and facial expression color our tone even when we cannot be seen, and also create or sustain a mood in the speaker. See Malcolm Gladwell's *Blink: The Power of Thinking without Thinking* (Back Bay Books, 2007), throughout.
2. See Allison A. Cowgill, Louise Feldmann, and A. Robin Bowles, "Virtual Reference Interviewing and Neutral Questioning," *Technology in Libraries: Essays in Honor of Anne Grodzins Lipow*, 2008, http://techinlibraries.com/cowgill.pdf for a full discussion of texting reference protocols.
3. Reference and User Services Association, "Guidelines for Behavioral Performance of Reference and Information Service Providers," *Reference and User Services Association*, 2016, http://www.ala.org/rusa/resources/guidelines/guidelinesbehavioral.
4. RUSA/YALSA Joint Task Force, "Guidelines for Library Services to Teens," *Reference and User Services Association*, 2008, http://www.ala.org/rusa/resources/guidelines/guidelinesteens.
5. Association for Library Service to Children, "Competencies for Librarians Serving Children in Public Libraries," *Association for Library Service to Children*, 2015, http://www.ala.org/alsc/edcareeers/alsccorecomps.
6. Language Line Solutions (www.languageline.com) is the interpretation service used by the federal government to ensure full public access to such initiatives as the Affordable Care Act.
7. Refer generally to the site maintained by National Association of the Deaf for an excellent introduction to the linguistic character of ASL, "What Is Sign Language?," 2016, nad.org/issues/american-sign-language/what-is-asl.

8. When speaking with someone whose linguistic background is Spanish (or another Romance language), careful word choice of synonyms with Latin roots can improve communication, for example, "avenue" instead of "street," "vacate" instead of "empty."

9. The California Relay Service (ddtp.cpuc.ca.gov/default1.aspx?id=1484) is one example of such a utility support in which both specialized instruments (e.g., TTY sets) and credentialed speech-to-speech interpreters bridge gaps between hard of hearing, speech disabled, and hearing parties. Check the health and human services, as well as the public utilities bureau, in your state for local contact information about such programs.

10. The Arc, formerly ARC, can be contacted at http://www.thearc.org/.

CHAPTER 3

Professional Ethics of Reference Service

Library work, like other professions, has a set of standards or rules guiding behavior. These standards are called "professional ethics."

Ethics are defined by the profession's members who conduct work in the specific field for which a specific ethical code is designed. Professions of all types, including medical professions, academic professions, trade professions, and political professions, subscribe to ethical codes. Ethics have a kinship with both laws and morals, but these three types of influential directives are derived differently and have different kinds of enforcement:

- Laws are created and enforced by a government. They describe acceptable and unacceptable behaviors as well as state-enforced punishments with which infractions are to be met. Anyone present in a location where specific laws are in effect is subject to those laws.
- Morals are personal values often, but not always, informed by religious tenets, schools of philosophy, or cultural norms. While failing to adhere to specific moral tenets can lead to censure by a membership body, such as a church or a neighborhood or a family, morals are internalized standards. As such, they can include wholly interior performances, such as thoughts or wholly legal social interactions, and thus may be judged right or wrong only by the person engaged in the thought or behavior.
- Ethics do not carry the force of law and, unlike morals, reflect only on external behaviors. Ethical tenets describe correct and incorrect treatment of others through the failure to do something or the doing of something untoward in the process of carrying out one's duty. Ethics are the standards by which practitioners share an identity and can measure their own and other practitioners' quality of professionalism.

35

PROFESSIONAL CODES OF ETHICS

The American Library Association (ALA) has been the official voice for all Americans concerned with library issues and ethics since 1876. Across that now nearly 150 years, this professional association has worked to define and refine the ethical guidelines shaping work in libraries and providing support for the exploration of new issues with ethical aspects as these appear with changes in technology and law. ALA publishes policies, white papers, and interpretations authored by field experts to keep its *Code of Ethics* timely, practical, specific, and comprehensive.

ALA's *Code of Ethics*

As with many other professional codes of ethics, ALA's is brief in spite of being both specific and comprehensive. An ethics code is simply the principles, not the interpretations or prescriptions, a specific library or library worker needs to make in order to breathe life into these principles. Like the alphabet and its 26-letter capacity to build words, the code supplies eight tenets that can help to create policies and procedures:

I.   We provide the highest level of service to all library users through appropriate and usefully organized resources; equitable service policies; equitable access; and accurate, unbiased, and courteous responses to all requests.

II. We uphold the principles of intellectual freedom and resist all efforts to censor library resources.

III. We protect each library user's right to privacy and confidentiality with respect to information sought or received and resources consulted, borrowed, acquired or transmitted.

IV. We respect intellectual property rights and advocate balance between the interests of information users and rights holders.

V.   We treat coworkers and other colleagues with respect, fairness and good faith, and advocate conditions of employment that safeguard the rights and welfare of all employees of our institutions.

VI. We do not advance private interests at the expense of library users, colleagues, or our employing institutions.

VII. We distinguish between our personal convictions and professional duties and do not allow our personal beliefs to interfere with fair representation of the aims of our institutions or the provision of access to their information resources.

VIII. We strive for excellence in the profession by maintaining and enhancing our own knowledge and skills, by encouraging the professional development of coworkers, and by fostering the aspirations of potential members of the profession.[1]

The influence of these principles touches reference services directly in several ways that are broad and deep, and inform best practices regardless of library type or community setting. Ethical guidelines direct reference services staff to preserve library users' rights to privacy as well as the rights of members of the community to fair and equitable treatment and equal access to the information they need. Whether providing reference services inside or outside a library building, you and other staff members should abide by the ethics guiding professional reference behaviors.

In general, the principles shape the following essential aspects of reference services:

- Reference staff members' obligations to uphold fair and equitable treatment of all library users
- Reference staff members' commitment to present as many points of view as possible in as fair a way as possible, regardless of challenges to any of those views
- Library users' rights in the area of privacy and confidentiality
- Respect for intellectual property balanced with the information needs of the community

The *Code of Ethics* is related closely to another ALA document and set of standards, the *Library Bill of Rights*.[2] This document shows how ethical library service touches the information needs of the library's community through such resources as informational material, library spaces, and access to services. It also gives notice to libraries that they play a significant and required role in defending intellectual freedom.

While you are guided by the *Library Bill of Rights* in performing reference tasks, library staff who work in specific library settings may need to consider exactly how these rights are addressed in their work. For example, a small public library staff may have a fairly clear view of how the library should, can, and does uphold every listed right in this *Bill*. An academic reference librarian working in a departmental library, however, may need to become more consciously aware of the (academic) community served and how its members hold such rights as that of service inclusion and intellectual freedom. In school libraries, staff may need to work with other teaching staff to increase mutual understanding of how multimedia resources can address diverse information access needs different students' learning styles require.

You need to be aware of the application of guidelines enumerated in both these documents and act according to them as they are inserted into your library's own policies and procedures. ALA has published, and will continue to publish, a complement of documents providing carefully researched interpretations of the principles and rights addressed by these two documents. "Interpretations of the *Library Bill of Rights*" (ala.org/advocacy/intfreedom/librarybill/interpretations) include discussions of the specific rights of various demographic groups including children, prisoners, and those seeking access to digital information, among many other specific topics.

Enforcement of the *Code of Ethics* isn't the responsibility of any governing body other than your employing library. Instead, the enforcement of the *Code*'s mandate of behaviors in the workplace is assumed as a standard guide in the formulation of the library's own policy adoptions. In many libraries, the *Code of Ethics* as well as the *Library Bill of Rights* is explicitly quoted in the institution's published policies, or referenced as the grounds for similarly worded guidelines. Performance appraisals of employees, then, are where ethical infractions are documented. In serious cases, such as a staff member refusing to provide service due to a community member's gender or withholding information that reflects an opinion the staff member finds personally distasteful, such documentation can lead to disciplinary steps by the employer.

ETHICS AND REFERENCE SERVICES TO SPECIAL POPULATIONS

The protection and upholding of intellectual freedom is made explicit in the second principle of ALA's *Code of Ethics* and the fifth item in ALA's *Library Bill of Rights*. This protection of the rights of library users requires thoughtful guidance because the wide range of persons seeking reference services may conflict with the "protection" some believe is warranted of some community members, or the misguided belief that controversial subjects can be addressed adequately from a single position's documentation.

Probably the group most likely to be the focus of denial of intellectual freedom in the use of libraries and the information available through them would be children and youth. This is addressed in the interpretation "Access to Library Resources and Services for Minors" (ala .org/advocacy/intfreedom/librarybill/interpretations/access-library-resources-for-minors) and "Access for Children and Young Adults to Nonprint Materials" (ala.org/advocacy/ intfreedom/librarybill/interpretations/accesschildren). Questions concerning intellectual freedom and the right of this population to search for and access information are common in many communities where parents or groups challenge materials they feel are harmful to children. ALA specifically states: "Every restriction on access to, and use of, library resources, based solely on the chronological age, educational level, literacy skills, or legal emancipation of users violates Article V [of the *Library Bill of Rights*]."[3]

Librarians have the ethical charge to meet the information needs of all library users[4] without exclusion and without censorship. In a public library situation, it is not the duty of library staff to assume the responsibilities of parents and guardians in regard to minors' access to library materials or ideas. School library staff, like teachers, may act in loco parentis, but school library staff cannot assert their personal beliefs when providing information assistance to students; that would not be ethical:

> Although the educational level and program of the school necessarily shape the resources and services of a school library, the principles of the American Library Association's *Library Bill of Rights* apply equally to all libraries, including school libraries. Under these principles, all students have equitable access to library facilities, resources, and instructional programs.
>
> School librarians assume a leadership role in promoting the principles of intellectual freedom within the school by providing resources and services that create and sustain an atmosphere of free inquiry. Major barriers between students and resources include but are not limited: to imposing age, grade-level, or reading-level restrictions on the use of resources; limiting the use of interlibrary loan and access to electronic information; charging fees for information in specific formats; requiring permission from parents or teachers; establishing restricted shelves or closed collections; and labeling. Policies, procedures, and rules related to the use of resources and services support free and open access to information. . . .[5]

Another population that has its right to intellectual freedom questioned both generally and in specific instances of attempt to exercise it is that of prisoners. The *Library Bill of Rights* interpretation "The Prisoner's Right to Read" (ala.org/advocacy/prisoners-right-read) does provide both context and a clear statement of ownership regarding ethical information decisions made by prison librarians:

> Libraries and librarians serving individuals in correctional facilities may be required by federal, state, or local laws; administrative rules of parent agencies; or court decisions to prohibit material that instructs, incites, or advocates criminal action or bodily harm or is a violation of the law. Only those items that present an actual compelling and imminent risk to safety and security should be restricted. Although these limits

restrict the range of resources available, the extent of limitation should be minimized by adherence to the American Library Association's "*Library Bill of Rights* and its Interpretations."

Other populations at risk of receiving ethically inadequate service due to their perceived status include undocumented immigrants and homeless people. In both situations, library requirements of government-issued identification indicating address in exchange for in-house use of information sources challenge the rights of such community members.

Having gained some familiarity with the ethics with which reference services are to be provided in the library context, let us now turn to examining touch points between reference tasks and ethical guidance in undertaking them.

ETHICAL REFERENCE PRACTICES

Where reference service providers are employed by institutions, these staff members must be aware of the institution's policies regarding services. Reading the texts of either the *Code* or the employing library's policies is not sufficient: reference staff members must follow the precepts and principles named in them and conscientiously use them in the performance of their work.

Useful Resource Organization Is an Ethical Matter

Resources used for the performance of reference work should be organized and maintained in a manner that allows both the staff member and any information seeker working independently of staff oversight to discover either specific information or a logical and efficient path to pursuing it. While this addresses such library practices as cataloging physical materials by subject matter, it extends as well to the presentation of resources that are virtual. We will discuss this at length in Chapter 11 and elsewhere in future chapters. For now, it's essential to recognize that maintaining and presenting information in an organized fashion has an ethical component because organization itself, whether oriented around a published classification scheme or an online site map, supports the library user's right to locate information within the library's resources.

Equitable Service Policies

The word "equitable" means *just, fair,* and *reasonable.* While all these terms may invite subjective application, ethical reference services require staff to apply them as honestly as they can in good conscience. Such policies as those governing use of resources, including staff, should be presumed to be fair to all who are members of the library community. In practical terms, the procedures that follow from such policies do not allow staff to discriminate by age, gender, sexual orientation, religion, race, or other defining terms that can be applied to individuals or groups.

An example of such equity can be found in a case in which staff agree to host a class or other group visit to the reference department for a presentation by reference staff. It is fair, and thus equitable, to require the group make an appointment so that others in the space where the group will meet with staff can be made aware beforehand of possible disruption and know how long that disruption may last so that they, too, can use the space effectively. Fairness also requires that staff committing themselves to the group not neglect other reference duties requiring their attention, or choose to host the class while leaving other users neglected. Equitable service policies call on reference staff members to balance demands, rather than to favor some or slight others.

Equitable Access

Fair and just access as an ethical stipulation calls upon reference staff to ensure that all community members have practical means of gaining information staff can provide or guide in discovering. Physical barriers in buildings or furniture arrangements, the need to make communication possible in languages, including American Sign Language, in which community members function when obtaining information, and responding to information needs at literacy levels that fit the abilities of diverse clients all flow from this ethical principle.

In the previous chapter, we discussed communication needs and strategies that may need to be deployed with specific populations. Note that the need to provide expert interpretation accommodations, rather than relying on accompanying children or other library users to broker cross-language communication, speaks to equity of access.

Accurate, Unbiased, and Courteous Responses to All Requests

Reference staff should note that this final phrase in the first ethical precept in the *Code* refers to responding, not submitting or acquiescing, to all requests for information. Facial expressions and posture can communicate a lack of respect. That does not mean that reference staff should believe they must be subject to verbal (or physical) abuse in the line of service. Reference staff members should be provided suitable training and be aware of how to cope with exchanges that become less than civil.

Accuracy being an ethical mandate, reference staff must be mindful of citing sources, consulting up-to-date information, and ensuring that those seeking specific information have acquired satisfactory guidance in finding it. As will be discussed more fully in Chapter 5, bias cannot be erased from human endeavors because we are subjective beings. However, reference staff can make a real effort to balance any specific biases resources show by providing resources that balance biases. That is why libraries maintain collections, whether material or virtual, from diverse viewpoints.

Intellectual Freedom

Intellectual freedom is an internal as well as implicit human right. In the United States, speech is protected, although there are limitations when it is used to incite specific illegal acts such as sedition or life-threatening panic in a crowded place. In terms of reference work, the need to protect and celebrate intellectual freedom requires that opinions not be labeled as right or wrong, orthodox or not. The expectation remains that facts are not opinions and may be termed "true" until otherwise proved.

This ethical position regarding intellectual freedom requires reference services staff to potentially pursue all manner of information with which they may disagree or find disagreeable. This is not limited to high-profile social issues but may be something as seemingly inconsequential as guiding a client through finding the address for sending fan mail to the president (an activity you believe wastes time) or learning how to access online auction houses (which you believe removes potential business from a local company). Whatever you may or may not value personally about such pursuits, everyone's intellectual freedom legitimizes them as potential content for reference assistance.

Questioning the appropriateness of a resource for children or access to a resource by children is probably the most commonly recognized breach of intellectual freedom in North America. However, more subtle forms of attempts to erode intellectual freedom should be recognized as such as well. Determining that reference staff and resources may not be accessed for specific purposes, such as researching an unpopular viewpoint or participating in popular culture information retrieval, can also be a matter of impinging on intellectual freedom. Trite as it may sound to some, there are libraries of all types in which reference staff refuse to answer questions if the questions are determined to be about crossword puzzles, document formatting, or how to use the index in a religious encyclopedia. Each of these is an example of failing to support the intellectual freedom of the community in general and the specific clients seeking specific information.

Library policies and procedures should spell out exactly what process is to be followed if either a staff member or a community member questions whether ideas, or any recording of them, in the library's collections should be removed or kept from the access of any other community member group (such as children). All communications between reference staff and community members, including other library staff, who present suggestions for minimizing access to ideas should be in the form of respectful, sincere, and honest presentation of institutional documentation regarding intellectual freedom and the prescribed path for bringing a concern to administrative attention.

The concept of intellectual freedom in the library context is further discussed and articulated in ALA's "Freedom to Read" (ala.org/advocacy/intfreedom/statementspols/ freedomreadstatement) statement.[6] It's important to note that private libraries (including those affiliated with private universities and colleges) may have alternate provisions that contravene the global ethical stance taken by ALA. However, working with scholars and with administrators in academia, library staff have a professional duty to champion intellectual freedom over restricted access to unpopular ideas.

Privacy

Privacy speaks to the capacity to search for, access, and use information without intrusion by any other person, whether using print or multimedia, or online resources. Reference staff members preserve the privacy of information seekers by affording sheltered spaces in which to conduct sensitive reference interviews and ensuring that those making use of reference resources are not tracked in a manner that can be attached to the individual's identity. While it is ethical to note that middle school aged youth seem to compose a large share of the reference room population late on Sunday afternoon, it would be an invasion of privacy to ask each of them the subject of the work that brings them to this place at this time.

Monitoring public use computers in a manner that forces each user to contribute his or her name to a log of users, or forbids lawful access to some sites, such as games or e-mail, and enforces that by looking over computer users' shoulders are all invasions of privacy. When reference staff make notes of contact information for those whom they will call with more information in response to an information need, those notes, and any interview notes, should be appropriately discarded after use to ensure the person's privacy is retained.

Confidentiality

Confidentiality is a near-relative of privacy. Reference staff members may not discuss the identities and information needs and interests of clients, repeat rumors based on expressed interest in specific topics, or share the names of who accessed what information. Confidentiality obviously is an ethical concern in some legal situations, discussed below. It is also at the root of some innocent requests that cannot be honored without breaching this ethical principle, such as a teacher turning to the reference staff to obtain a list of students who have made use of reference materials to complete a class assignment.

In the last chapter, we discussed the need, from time to time, to refer a client's question or seek assistance from another staff member in responding well to it. These actions do not breach confidentiality because the client remains in control of sharing information with yet another party. However, it can be helpful to tell the client directly that, although someone else is being added to the discussion, confidentiality will be maintained. And, of course, no matter how tantalizing the issue presented may be, it is essential that the multiple reference staff who work to resolve the information need respect the client's confidentiality in the aftermath rather than discussing it as gossip to which they are privy.

Respect for Intellectual Property Rights

The concept of intellectual property ownership is legal as well as ethical. "Owning" authorship of a published work, a creative endeavor such as a piece of music, or photos you have taken are all examples of intellectual property. Copyright protection of published materials (and therefore ideas or intellectual property) developed in the early 18th century, with the interests of book printers, rather than authors, at its forefront. We currently face a highly complex copyright and intellectual property environment with the electronic publishing technologies that moves expression of idea ownership from material expression, in print, to an online venue that, additionally, may cross international boundaries. On the international scene, different laws are in play. This may help explain why you cannot access some online resources, such as videos and audio recordings, outside the countries where they have been published.

The ethical principle of respecting intellectual property rights then is one that requires attention to detail, upkeep of changes in both law and publishing technologies, and the capacity to serve as a facilitator for less informed or observant potential abusers of those rights. We have moved well beyond the era in which posting a notice on the reference room copy machine is sufficient acknowledgment of this principle.

However, the ethics and legal issues of copyright and intellectual property require the reference staff member to be more diligent in exploring licensing requirements and permissions of specific published works. While copyright law carries a host of legally specific limitations on content use, which we will discuss in the section on reference services and following the law, in this section we need to spend some time with Creative Commons licensing and the concept of creative sharing, as well as noting the need to balance content user needs with content owner rights.

Creative Commons (creativecommons.org) is organized around the principle that published contemporary intellectual and artistic creations can be both shareable and open to participatory engagement. Instead of seeking copyright protection of work, those who value this approach to more open content availability can license their works at several possible levels, from fully available for change and distribution to more limited access for noncommercial uses or for use without changes. Creative Commons licenses are applied to images and multimedia recordings as well as written texts.

A popular social medium in which you can find different levels of Creative Commons licensing applied are photo sharing services. With no licensing, or ownership claim, made at all, photos you upload to such a site can be used by marketing companies as free illustrations for commercial campaigns in which you want your work to play no part and for which you receive no credit as the photographer. By applying a licensing level that requires other users to give you credit, or a stricter level that allows sharing only for noncommercial purposes, you are claiming different degrees of ownership.

Reference services staff should have an understanding of licensing levels and recognize international Creative Commons licensing as a type of intellectual property establishment in order to perform ethically in the role of balancing intellectual property ownership with information seeker's needs. This is an excellent area to explore with community members who are engaged in small businesses that have need of illustration, video, or soundtracks to accompany their own original work. Like you, clients are likely to find the topic complex, so helping them find a clear path through discerning who owns what intellectual property and how to make use of other people's intellectual property fairly is likely to come up in all types of libraries, from school to public to academic and even corporate or business ones.

Whether considering copyright or Creative Commons licensing, the important thing to remember is to recognize intellectual ownership by the content's creator and balance the client's need fairly. Often, this will lead you simply to finding an alternative source to fill that need, a source that can be used without infringing on copyright, or helping the client to use the intellectual property of another as the basis for his or her own original work. This is often the case in teaching students about how to avoid plagiarism: to avoid plagiarizing another's work, you must put the ideas into your own words. Or give the original author full credit for what you quote.

Treatment of Coworkers

In the previous chapter, we discussed best practices for referring questions and information seekers beyond the library and staff with whom the search began. These practices embody appropriate treatment of coworkers, according respect to those to whom staff refer issues they cannot resolve internally, rather than simply dumping a client and his or her question on a coworker with no explanation of what has been undertaken already and why the second staff member is being contacted.

In several other specific aspects of the reference staff member's work life, this ethical principle should serve as a guide to practice. In situations where individual staff safety or comfort is threatened, other staff have the ethical duty to assist. This may mean placing a call for safety officer intervention, if a weapon is present, or simply stepping up and asking mildly if you can help, if you see your coworker struggling to understand a community member's speech impediment. Obviously, the level of concern must be judged accurately in order for the appropriate support to be offered to your coworker. Individual library policies and procedures should spell out exactly when and how to lend aid to coworkers in a moment of need. At the very least, staff should be aware of each other's whereabouts and potential needs in the execution of their mutual work and lend aid when appropriate.

Distinguishing between Personal Convictions and Professional Duties

Here is the point at which we distinguish between ethics, which guide work behavior, and morals, which guide personal beliefs and concepts of right and wrong, and good and bad thoughts and actions. We make moral judgments; we behave ethically.

> The key to resolving what could be a dilemma is the recognition that reference staff have the ethical duty to withhold acting on a personal judgment about an information need.

When serving in their professional capacity, reference staff can and should believe what they find just and right. However, these judgments are theirs personally and do not belong in the reference work they perform for the community and their employing institution. Learning to withhold judgment can in fact be a growth experience at a personal as well as a professional level. Withholding judgment allows reference staff to pursue open-ended questioning more scrupulously, as we discussed it in Chapter 2, because staff assumptions about purpose, potential use, and correctness of the question are let go. This opens the encounter to one in which the focus is truly on the client's need rather than the staff's presumption.

There may arise situations in which an individual reference staff member's moral compass is so sensitive that he or she realizes that conducting this particular reference encounter cannot be executed ethically. When that occurs, the staff member must seek support from another staff member, and without informing the community member of the interior struggle the first staffer cannot surmount. The situation then becomes one in which the ethical principle discussed in the previous section on coworkers comes to the fore.

SIDEBAR 1   HOMELESS COMMUNITY MEMBERS AND LIBRARY ETHICS

Libraries, especially those open to the public, see many homeless people, both those taking shelter and those who have specific library service needs, including reference questions. When performing reference services outside a library building as well, homeless individuals and groups may be among those in proximity or even the demographic chiefly served at that staffing point.

It is never appropriate to judge someone's question based on what staff might guess or assume about his or her social or economic status. As with all others who present a need for information, reference providers should take the time and effort to perform the reference interview, and treat with dignity those who seem to be lacking in access to what we think of as standard living arrangements. The staff member may need to refer questions from this population group as from any other. In the case of a homeless person, however, care should be taken to discuss how she or he can be contacted once the appropriate response to the question can be developed. Even though many homeless people (especially youth) may have access to cell phones now, staff might suggest the user check back on a certain day, as an alternative to requesting a phone number.

Privacy and confidentiality concerns can be paramount to some who appear homeless, and the further apparently invasive, although well-intended, request for tracking information can feel insensitive. Community members who have left abusive situations and minor runaways who fear being returned to families who will not accept aspects of their being, such as sexual orientation, are among the vulnerable homeless population.

Practicing Professional Development and Supporting It in Others

The nature of practicing any profession includes the need to continue to update knowledge sets and rehearse skills that may fall into disuse after they are learned initially. Certainly reference staff members are ethically beholden to remaining current about:

- New information and evolving changes in fact
- Technology and its use in information and knowledge management
- Community changes
- Changes in law
- Best practices and learnings from them

Professional development may be supported monetarily and/or through release time by your employer. However, even if it is not, reference services providers are still under ethical obligation to obtain it. The plethora of available options for doing so include abundant online courses from reputable library and related professional educators, professional reading available in journals and books, professional association membership offerings and events, and local events that highlight community information interests and concerns.

Supporting the professional development of others includes communicating about the availability of development resources, sharing information gained through your own training attendance, and encouraging those whom the reference staff member supervises to participate in ongoing development.

REFERENCE SERVICES AND THE LAW

Practitioners whose professions require a license or certificate of practitioners must respond to both legal and ethical standards. For example, a medical doctor who behaves in a certain way, such as prescribing a narcotic for a patient without evaluating the patient's medical need for it, may be in a breach of medical ethics and law breaking. The state granting the license can punish the doctor for breaking the law. The ethics infraction, especially if a law was broken, may also lead to his or her suspension from the medical association of which he or she is a member. In some states, including Virginia and New York, professional librarians must be legally certified in order to hold public librarian jobs, so law as well as ethical tenets defines their work identities.

Many states certify librarians who work in public schools, allowing them to hold such positions legally. However, a compelling legal distinction, whether or not a state requires librarian certification, is found between librarians serving in public libraries and public schools. The distinction is one of in loco parentis issues. In public school districts in the United States, teachers and teaching staff (of which library staff are identified) serve, during the school day and in school-sponsored activities regardless of site, in the role of minor children's guardians, that is, in the place of students' parents. This means that school librarians have legal responsibilities that public library staff do not and can make decisions—as we will discuss next—about student access that public library staff has no legal standing to perform. However, acting in loco parentis does not mean that school library staff may practice their personal moral code in place of their professional ethics in matters of intellectual freedom.

Children's Internet Protection Act

Occasionally, national laws directly affect library work, including reference service delivery. One that can come into conflict with professional ethics is the Children's Internet Protection Act (CIPA) (ifea.net/cipa.pdf). How does a reference service provider handle such a dilemma? You are obligated, ethically, to be aware of CIPA's requirements and how those requirements affect your specific situation. To do that, you should examine the Federal Communications Commission (FCC) publication "Guide to CIPA" (fcc.gov/guides/childrens-internet-protection-act). This guide clarifies an essential matter straightaway: CIPA applies only to those libraries and schools that receive federal discounts for Internet access or in-house connectivity under a program known as the E-rate. Libraries (and schools) that do not receive E-rate discounts are not addressed by CIPA.[7]

Knowing that, you must also make yourself familiar with whether your employing library benefits from the E-rate. If it does not, then CIPA has no role in your work practices. However, if your library does benefit from E-rate funding, and filtering has been invoked in keeping with its mandate on computer access by children, you then need to:

- Become familiar with the filtering software used locally and how it affects searching
- Prepare non-web-based resources that appropriately address information queries by children that would be blocked should they attempt a web search with the filter in place
- Step in to perform some web searches yourself, on unfiltered equipment if a child's information need is such that it cannot be resolved through his or her own use of filtered access
- Provide specific URLs and search terms for the child to search at home or on unfiltered equipment available to him or her elsewhere

In fact, reference staff's ethical obligations to child clients may be more complicated to perform where computer filtering is in place, but filtering does not relieve reference staff of the ethical responsibility to provide full information services to those same children.

The Current Status of the USA PATRIOT Act

For just over a decade, one particular federal law—the Uniting and Strengthening America by Providing Appropriate Tools Required to Intercept and Obstruct Terrorism Act (USA PATRIOT Act)—and the regulations arising from it stood as problematic when considered from the ethical viewpoint of librarianship. Institutional practices and policies in thousands of reference services departments have had to address the demands of this law and educate service providers in how it affects their work.

The renewal of the law in 2011, and enforced in that version through the first half of 2015, continued to carry the threat to library computer user privacy.[8] In May 2015, parts of the act expired without renewal.[9] What is essential for reference service providers in libraries to note is that laws such as these can and do occur and have implications on both services and ethics. Librarians must work within the law while trying to abide by professional ethics. It is essential for reference services staff to keep apprised of current laws that affect ethical as well as practical service procedures. In the final chapter of this book, ongoing education needs and best practices for reference staff will be discussed.

LAWS AND ETHICS WITH MUTUALLY SUPPORTED ENDS

In some cases the law and professional ethics address similar service concerns while underscoring kindred expectations from librarians. In two major areas, eliminating barriers to access and protection of intellectual property rights, law and ethics support and inform best practices in important and distinctive ways:

- Barriers to access by those with disabilities are recognized by the Americans with Disabilities Act (ADA) as requiring correction and are viewed by professional ethics as inappropriate.
- Protection of intellectual property rights is addressed both in copyright law and by professional ethics.

In these two areas, legal issues and professional ethics mesh so that what is ethical happens also to be legally enforceable.

Disability as a Legal Status

Those with disabilities are protected from omission of services under the Americans with Disabilities Act (ADA) (ada.gov/2010_regs.htm), including reference services and other library services provided to the disabled person's community, whether in a public library, a school, or through an institution regulated by federal access laws. As we discussed in Chapter 2, community members may function with disabilities related to mobility, sight or hearing disparities, cognitive challenges, and environmental diseases. Some disabilities are permanent. However ADA protection also touches those with temporary disabilities, such as a broken leg that makes it impossible to use a staircase to reach a public building without a ramp or lift.

For reference staff, the following issues addressed by ADA regulations are most likely to have library service components:

- Building design
- Furniture layout
- Computer access software
- Presence of service animals
- Provision of equitable service without prejudice related to disability

While the first of these areas is well beyond the portfolio of reference service functions, staff should be aware of construction issues because they can hamper movement and access by community members, especially those with mobility and sight disabilities. Staff must be alert to facilitating access to information when such obstructions may hinder persons from accessing library services others can reach independently, such as materials in a stack area where no elevator or lift is working.

Furniture layout may be driven in part by building design. In addition, it is usually influenced by planned uses and users of the space. Reference staff should consider such elements as shelving heights, chair and stool placements (to avoid blocking an area or making passage through it in a wheelchair or without good vision dangerous), and desk heights that create walls for those in wheelchairs, or unreachable spaces for those with diminished capacities to stoop or reach above their heads.

The variety of accommodation software packages in current use addresses protected disabilities ranging from mobility and sight issues to hearing, intellectual capacity, and ergonomic needs created by some disabilities. Where public access computers are available to those in the reference services area, appropriate software should be installed to allow equitable access to information for community members with protected disabilities.

Fortunately, all of the design and equipment needs just reviewed are discussed with guidance for resolving at Information and Technical Assistance on the Americans with Disabilities Act (ada.gov). This site offers such immediate support for reference services staff, and others, as legal interpretation of Frequently Asked Questions about Service Animals and the ADA (ada.gov/regs2010/service_animal_qa.html), documentation of Effective Communication (ada.gov/effective-comm.htm) that addresses such matters as the presence of companions to perform such functions as reading (for the blind) and free telecommunication supports for information transference with those who are hard of hearing, and Project Civic Access (ada.gov/civicac.htm) that provides access to information about federal cases designed, as it notes, to "ensure that counties, cities, towns, and villages comply with the ADA by eliminating physical and communication barriers that prevent people with disabilities from participating fully in community life."

Reference staff members should be aware of any agencies or training facilities in the area where a significant number of disabled community members may require reference services with accommodations such as schools for the blind, sheltered workshops for those with intellectual disabilities, and housing for those with mobility support needs. Such co-location of community agencies with disabled populations should further influence how library services are presented locally, including staffing patterns to support high-volume reference access that may rely upon large print resources or shelving heights that take frequent wheelchair access needs into consideration. Acknowledgment and planning to include those with accommodation needs is an ethically principled, as well as practical, approach to service planning and staff development training choices.

Copyright and Fair Use

The U.S. Copyright Act (17 USC S 108) provides a set of rules regarding reproduction of copyrighted materials in the library. In December 2014, expiring provisions of it were reauthorized. In general, a library open to the public will not be liable for copyright infringement based upon a library user's unsupervised use of photocopiers located on its premises, provided that the equipment displays a notice that the making of a copy may be subject to the copyright law. The notice must appear in a specific form, as seen here:

Warning concerning copyright restrictions
    The copyright law of the United States (Title 17, United States Code) governs the making of photocopies or other reproductions of copyrighted material.
    Under certain conditions specified in the law, libraries and archives are authorized to furnish a photocopy or other reproduction of copyrighted material. One of these specified conditions is that the photocopy or reproduction is not to be "used for any purpose other than private study, scholarship, or research." If a library user makes

a request for, or later uses, a photocopy or reproduction for purposes in excess of "fair use," that user may be liable for copyright infringement.

This institution reserves the right to refuse to accept a copying order if, in its judgment, fulfillment of the order would involve violation of Copyright Law.

Even if the library provides photocopies from materials in its own collections, a notice is required. It usually consists of a stamp placed on the first page of a copy and it reads:

NOTICE:

This material may be protected by Copyright Law
(Title 17, U.S. Code)

The legal concept of "fair use" is the reason that library staff and users can make copies of portions of copyrighted works without having to obtain permission from the author; this concept is written into the law as the Fair Use Clause. Fair use allows the limited use of copyrighted materials for certain purposes, such as criticism, comment, news reporting, teaching, scholarship, and research. There are four factors to be considered in determining whether or not a particular use is fair:

- The purpose of the use, including whether such use is for commercial purposes or is for nonprofit, educational purposes
- The nature of the copyrighted work
- The amount used in relation to the copyrighted work as a whole
- The effect of the use upon the author's potential market for or value of the copyrighted work

Your library should have a specific and explicit policy that sets forth how it will handle copyright and copying requests. Reference staff should be familiar enough with the policy to be able to explain its requirements and purpose on an as-needed basis.

OTHER ETHICAL CODES OF INTEREST TO REFERENCE STAFF

While this chapter delves into principles affecting reference staff at any type of library, there are additional codes available that address ethics many reference providers need to consider in their work. Reference services connecting clients to members of the bar for pro bono legal assistance should be aware of the ethics related to legal practice and to pro bono work at least to the degree that appropriate referrals are made. Reference staff working with health and wellness information, whether employed in a health sciences library or working with healthcare consumers in a public library, should review and attend to the *Code of Ethics for Health Sciences Librarianship* (mlanet.org/p/cm/ld/fid=160), published by the Medical Library Association.

Like communication, ethics are an essential skill set to know, practice, update, and monitor throughout a reference services staff member's career. Newly visible ethical issues can arise with changes in technology, law, and best practices development. While ethics themselves are principles that do not change, their interpretation in practice requires understanding how to apply the principles in current situations.

NOTES

1. The ALA's *Code of Ethics* was first published in 1930. The text here, the current, was adopted on June 28, 1997, by the ALA Council and amended on January 22, 2008.

2. Adopted June 18, 1948. Amended February 2, 1961, and January 23, 1980; inclusion of "age" reaffirmed January 23, 1996, by the ALA Council.

3. "Access to Library Resources and Services for Minors" (ala.org/advocacy/intfreedom/librarybill/interpretations/access-library-resources-for-minors).

4. In Chapter 11 we will discuss in detail how newer models of reference services recognize "all patrons" rather than the more limited "all library users." Reference services are presumed throughout this book to address the needs of the full community the library serves.

5. "Access to Resources and Services in the School Library Media Program" (ala.org/advocacy/intfreedom/librarybill/interpretations/accessresources).

6. Child pornography is illegal in the United States and most other nations. That is the only "information" to which a library user has no right of access. Child pornography is defined at 18 U.S. Code § 2256.

7. In 2014, fewer than 5,000 U.S. public libraries applied for, let alone were granted, e-rate discounts, according to the government-appointed body administering the application and administrative processes (Universal Service Administrative Company, 2014 Annual Report, page 3) (universalservice.org/_res/documents/about/pdf/annual-reports/usac-annual-report-2014.pdf).

8. Brett Williams (quora.com/What-is-the-current-status-of-the-Patriot-Act-in-relation-to-libraries-turning-over-lists-of-readers-on-Terrorism), December 28, 2011.

9. Read the updates as the expiration neared, reported by Eyda Peralta, National Public Radio, at "Parts of Patriot Act Expire, Even as Senate Moves on Bill Limiting Surveillance" (npr.org/sections/thetwo-way/2015/05/31/411044789/live-blog-facing-midnight-deadline-the-senate-debates-parts-of-the-patriot-act), June 1, 2015.

CHAPTER 4

Building and Maintaining a Reference Collection

In the 20th-century library, reference collection building and maintenance came to be regarded as essentially synonymous with providing good reference service to library visitors. While staff could be expected to engage helpfully with those requesting assistance, the provision and presentation of often costly, single-purpose reference books took large quantities of financial, physical, and human resources.

Many elements in reference work have now evolved beyond this model of service. In this chapter the contemporary reference collection dynamics and resource requirements are discussed, while keeping in mind that many libraries of every type are now implementing a 21st-century concept of the reference collection in today's library.

In order to place this discussion in the appropriate context, you must first recognize the many ways information resources are available to both you and the community at large. Now well-developed technologies have altered how information can be discovered and shared by reference service staff, who must also grow awareness of the community so as to understand how its constituents will be able to use these technologies independently and effectively.

While previous generations have been required to visit, telephone, or write to a library location in order to access a reference collection, this is no longer the case. It follows that the reference collection now needs to be developed and managed so that remote use can be made of it and clients can turn to it with minimal staff intervention. What both *collection development* and *collection management* now entail looks very different in practice, yet the resources needed to effect both so as to best serve the community rely on some principles that remain the same as they have been traditionally. The first of these is to know your community.

KNOW YOUR COMMUNITY

The contemporary reference collection is designed to meet the information needs and expectations of the community it supports. This requires reference staff to become and remain knowledgeable about the information and information access needs of the community. What does this mean in practical terms for you and your library?

- Reference staff must be familiar with the demographics of the community as a whole, not just with library building visitors. This requires study of such government statistics as census reports and school district reports on home languages. If the library or the state library publishes data showing circulation rates, program attendance, and other comparative library activities for similarly sized communities, these, too, should be studied for insights about the library's perceived standing as an information resource in the community.
- Staff must be aware of local opportunities and challenges to civic engagement. Such awareness can be built and strengthened through consultations with other service agencies, ranging from governmental such as social services to private such as churches popular with immigrants. Certainly reference staff should follow local news reporting and be familiar with small businesses surrounding the workplace. All of these measures reveal how the community feels about its own health and substance, the basis on which its members, both established and newly arrived, determine their own personal opportunities for safety, economic viability, and social connections.
- Staff must understand economic opportunities both generally within the community and reflected by any major industries present in it. To research this, you can work with the local chamber of commerce. To find out more about how a major industry presence impacts information needs and access, consider the job classifications of the industry's local employees: required education for job performance, stability of the industry and the job in the state and national economy, and customary benefits granted to employees in a specific industry all provide insights on community information needs.
- Staff should also consider physical environmental factors, such as weather and climate, quality of nearby natural resources and spaces, density of housing, and presence of geographic barriers to neighborhoods, such as major highways or secluded mountains. The geographic environment impacts community health as well as suggests alternative activities and visitor presence in the community. However, geographic features can also impact access to technology by cutting neighborhoods off from high-speed Internet connectivity through which information can be delivered reliably.
- Staff must keep up to date regarding private technology access within the community. While new connectivity attained in a neighborhood may make the general news, awareness of smartphone ownership patterns at the local level is likely to change more quickly and without a journalist to present regular updates to the librarian. Casual observation of access and capacity for learning digital strategies among library visitors is not enough and skews library staff's awareness of how these patterns are emerging in the broader community.

As this list emphasizes, reference services cannot be conducted independently of other library service efforts as they pertain to providing the community with the best services possible. Reference services require as much community knowledge as do children's services, adult programming, and even the development of a collection for adults. Reference needs do not occur in a vacuum that excludes local knowledge of whom and why the information needs are likely to occur and how they can be effectively and efficiently resolved. If your library does not conduct community scans and other studies of the community as a whole, not just library users, on a regular basis (at least every three years), your effort to improve reference services may present the impetus needed to begin this broader work.

With knowledge of the community, the reference librarian can anticipate demands. The collection's purpose is to meet the needs of the community, and so knowing the community first is essential to reference collection development. Once the information about the community is analyzed, the reference librarian must apply it to collection planning as well as to service performance.

BUDGET

One aspect of collection development over which you may have relatively little control is the amount of money available to you for maintaining a healthy collection. However, that does not mean that you should scale your efforts to create a good collection; instead, it means that you may need to be more creative in locating no- and low-cost authoritative resources for the collection. Changes in technology and information access across recent decades have major implications on reference collection budgets of all sizes. While printed materials and databases have become increasingly costly, shared subscriptions to databases, when they are available in your region or through your state library, mean you may not have to invest only local budget in those. Online resources that can be reached without any or with very little cost also affect the budget you may have previously needed for print resources and speak to the potential for economic savings coupled with access to more up-to-date information.

In addition to costs associated with resource purchase, or subscription, social and technological changes impact budgets required for the housing and physical care, such as repair and cleaning of physical reference collections, in a positive way. Monies for bindery, microformat machine upkeep, and replacement of worn materials have been reduced as costs for computer hardware have also stabilized. The inclusion of Wi-Fi in many public settings, including where reference services are offered, has a cost, of course. However, the steep rise in personal computer and mobile access reduces the need to build increasingly large desktop computer farms as a correlative need of reference resource access.[1]

However, a library's reference collection does require a budget that fits:

- Scope of the library's reference service, such as community size, presence in it of other libraries with professional reference services, and degree to which local administrative decisions direct reference support of students, tourists, remote users, and other groups likely to present specialized information needs
- Needs and expectations of the community the library serves, taking into account that a successful reference collection may create higher expectations and reveal needs that have not been addressed by traditional print reference collections

- Prevailing costs of the specific resources available to meet the task of providing reference services, with the awareness that these costs can change radically when it is time to renew subscriptions or that new consortium efforts can promote more favorable pricing

The development of your budget planning you need to make for upcoming budget cycles should look to all three of these factors as guides to purchasing and subscription decisions related to the reference collection. To determine what that local budget should be, the full breadth and scope of collections and services undertaken by the library must be part of the equation.[2] The good news is that balancing cost and need is more easily undertaken in a world rich in authoritative web-based resources. In upcoming chapters that address specific subject areas there is care taken to make reference resource recommendations that include low- and no-cost web-based ones of high quality, as well as more traditional and costly commercial options.

REFERENCE SOURCES SHOULD INCLUDE A VARIETY OF FORMAT TYPES

Locating and making use of information requires the collection to be composed of resources appropriate to the expression of the information available. For example, if you want to know how a particular birdsong sounds, listening to a recording of it is more suitable than reading a narrative description. This is a major change in reference collection development since the days of resources being available only as print materials or in formats, such as microfilm and fiche, created to preserve images of print materials.

Now that reference collections can include print, commercial databases that are continuously updated with new content, video, sound, and even telecommunication connections with experts, resources can be selected to best serve a variety of information needs and gaps. Step-by-step directions that were once tied to a paper page can now be followed on video, where moving images can show exactly how simultaneous actions may be needed, as when one ties a shoe. Locating the most recent information on a legal, technical, or even popular topic can rely on authoritative resources that are or have been updated moments before. Maps that are online can be viewed with more detail and can include a view of traffic moving in local areas, significant improvements over relying on folding state maps or atlases that indicate roads but not traffic patterns.

The contemporary healthy reference collection includes multiple formats, with each resource making good use of its format and each format type managed according to the best practices developed to maintain its integrity. Let's take a look at what those practices entail.

Print and Bound Materials, Including Books and Pamphlets

Reference collections continue to require a few, depending on library type and scope, traditional paper resources. Those added and retained in the reference collection should represent titles that are pertinent to the community, available only in print form, and most accessible to potential users in the traditional format. They must provide the most authoritative and accessible information on the topic they treat. In some communities, they may duplicate the authoritative content of resources found in other formats, if there are extenuating requirements for duplication of materials on a topic. For example, for subjects treated equally well in traditional print and database, clients who cannot access database sources due to disability are served by the print option. However, it is essential that reference staff make conscientious decisions about such needs, rather than making unsubstantiated assumptions about the community they serve.

The print materials brought forward into a contemporary reference collection, having been accepted as traditional inclusions in previous generations, must be proved as continuing to be authoritative when contrasted with online information. For example, bound books concerning prescription medications, even if updated with each new print edition, are rarely appropriate to the contemporary reference collection because their information necessarily is outdated at the moment of publication when contrasted with prescription information that is maintained online. On the other hand, an authoritative bound biographical dictionary of 20th-century literary authors may provide the kind of replication that is welcome by students and their families who want to browse potential subject assignment options and are limited in access to a correlative online database.

Managing the print reference collection requires both its physical maintenance and care with its informational quality. Avoid maintaining print materials of marginal use simply because they were published as reference books and make the service point in the library "look like reference." The books may better serve community members as circulating material, without impacting the strength of the reference collection. And obviously maintaining materials for the visual indication they may offer that "This is the reference room" indicates a problem with signage or staff activity, rather than providing a creative explanation for retention.

Among the print reference works that should be on hand are:

- Collegiate-size American English dictionary of the latest edition
- Bilingual dictionary where community members and staff communicate most comfortably in only one of the two languages it covers (e.g., staff is monolingual English-speaking and a large sector of the community is monolingual Spanish-speaking)
- Local directory of government offices, telephones, addresses, and officeholders
- Handbooks in any disciplines reference service users, including staff, expect to need on a frequent and ongoing basis, such as a general cookbook, or a volume of mathematics tables
- A local area map that clearly indicates street names, named buildings, transit routes, and any local highway interchanges

Subscription Databases

At this time, there are hundreds of databases containing reference resources available for library subscribers. Many of them will be discussed in subsequent chapters. Here, however, the discussion is of their general role and management in your reference collection.

By design, subscription databases provide access to both material and information formerly obtained only through books, journals, and multimedia resources. Many of these databases are commercial enterprises and thus are vulnerable to corporate changes that can impact their scope, stability, inclusiveness, and cost. For example, a database owned by one company with access offered through subscription to libraries may be found by the owning corporation to be insufficiently lucrative to maintain, in effect determining for subscribers that they no longer can count this database's coverage among their resources.

In order to mitigate costs libraries can seek out noncommercial databases such as those provided by the federal government[3] or develop cost-cutting arrangements such as joining a purchasing consortium. Some states, such as Idaho[4] and North Carolina,[5] make database subscription decisions at the state level. In other areas, formal regional consortia agree to specific database sharing packages. However librarians may choose to select and budget to maintain independent choices of database subscriptions when the community has specific and sophisticated information needs not reflected across regional libraries. For example, where a particular community evidences deep interest in genealogy and the library's consortium package includes nothing specific to this interest, the individual library might subscribe to the full Ancestry[6] database, rather than relying on only its free content.

The following database selection criteria[7] can be applied across content types of databases, and should be considered in the case of both paid and free database options:

- Content scope should be specific, supported by authoritative documentation, and clearly make a positive contribution to the local library's reference resources.
- Usability by both practiced staff and clients unfamiliar with this particular database should be functionally intuitive and supported by readily identified guides and user tutorials on the site. Responsive design, which allows users to access the database with positive results on mobile screens as well as desktops, is becoming standard.
- Quality of media integration should also be sophisticated to the degree that information is presented in the medium most appropriate to the content, sound and video files require no special plug-ins on the computer through which they are being accessed, and subtitles are provided for users who cannot access sound, due either to hearing disability or to environment in which access is being undertaken (such as a meeting during which the user is trying to locate information needed in that moment by those in attendance).
- Likely popularity with community should also be considered and speaks to the fit between community needs and interests with a database's offerings. This isn't about a popularity contest but rather the call to focus on why this particular database would seem beneficial by the community in general. How would you describe this database's worth in popular terms?
- Elegance in functionality can be evaluated by looking for unexpected roadblocks to searching and noting positive surprises, such as working internal links to related content within a resource page or search returns that are grouped according to reading level.
- Best buy evaluation requires you to balance the positives of this particular database against both its cost and its likely amount of use in your library's setting. To evaluate whether it is a best buy, you must contrast it with other resources already available to you as well as different potential purchases you might make instead of this one.
- Integration of external with proprietary content helps you to make a determination about whether this is a best buy as well as measure the elegance of the database's functionality. How does this database add its own proprietary elements, including style and explanatory material, to contents it funnels to its users from sources other than those it creates? Databases providing access to suites of magazine contents, for example, typically present all articles using a database-specific design that usually includes bibliographic details as well as article contents; the database presentation doesn't mimic the style of each and every magazine from which contents are funneled. It is this layer of design that we are evaluating at this step, noting whether the database as a database is designed so that it becomes almost invisible to the magazine article reader.

- Quality of original content must be evaluated as well to ensure that the database compiler has made wise choices that reflect high standards of information quality.

Multimedia Formats

Some libraries must maintain multimedia in specific physical formats to best serve community reference resource needs. For example, some communities have undertaken oral history projects that have produced audiotapes and even video that should be maintained, along with playback equipment, until such physical files can be digitized (a secondary project likely to require a budget and considerable planning).

Most reference materials in a collection now, however, that are made accessible as sound and image, are provided through Internet connections. Maintaining separate budget lines for multimedia reference such as instructional video is no longer warranted.

Where multimedia materials compose part of the reference collection, upkeep of playback equipment and preservation efforts both must be maintained. The assumption should be that if the material is worth presenting in a physical format, it must be kept in good and accessible condition.

Make Use of Standard Selection Aids

The reference collection's development requires use of standard, authoritative selection tools. In each of the subject and format sections in succeeding chapters, we will include a discussion of where to find standard selection aids for each area of concern. First, however, we need to explore criteria identifying a selection aid as a standard, or recommended, one.

Using standard selection guides in the management of the reference collection assures your community that care is being taken to locate truly valuable information for inclusion. "Valuable" here indicates accessibility and applicability as well as authority. Rather than predetermining that a popular reference source—that is, one the community knows by name—is really the best suited one for the local reference collection, due diligence should be taken to authenticate its appropriateness, and value, as part of the collection.

Because the World Wide Web is so expansive and expanding, selecting sites for inclusion as documented parts of the reference collection should also be pursued with standards for selection in mind. Rather than overwhelming the community with options that are more or less helpful reference resources, or expecting each information need to have to begin with a new web search, select sites for which there is documented evidence of their reference value. Websites for inclusion as reference resources, through maintained links to the library or reference department's web page, should deliver unique, readily searched information that supports community information needs generally, and can be presented as "first places to go online" in the absence of staff intervention with research.

Among the general standard guides to reference collection development, the following continue to be authoritative:

- American Reference Books Annual (ARBA) (arbaonline.com/factsheet.aspx)
- Best Free Reference Web Sites Combined Index, 1999–2015 (ala.org/rusa/sections/mars/marspubs/marsbestindex)
- Best of the Web: Reference (botw.org/top/Reference/)
- *Booklist Magazine Online* Reference Sources reviews (booklistonline.com)

In addition to these standard guides, *Library Journal*, *School Library Journal*, and other trade publications targeting librarians carry reviews of new reference resources, both in material formats and in online formats.

STRIVE FOR BALANCE OF SUBJECT AREA DEVELOPMENT

Some aspects of the reference collection are easier and/or less costly to build and manage than are others, such as those reflecting generalities and basic language usage and word definitions. However, within the scope of what is appropriate in reference resource terms for the community served by the library, care must be taken to develop and manage all aspects of the reference collection and to maintain balance in coverage areas and among format options. In practical terms, this may mean selecting the best resource to address one specialized area significant to only a few community members, such as an up-to-date business directory for small business owners and innovators, while making sure to select multiple resources, in multiple formats, for areas that are in general demand for different purposes and by those with information gaps who have different access needs, such as a health-related database for health consumers, along with directories to various health issue and syndrome support groups, and access to authoritative and up-to-date information on both prescription and nonprescription drugs.

We all have a tendency to find it "easier" to concentrate on improving access to topics about which we feel confident in our knowledge and which seem important to us personally. As a reference collection developer, you must strive to become aware of what your own subject preferences may be and take note of whether these preferences are leading to better development of those areas of the reference collection than others. An important use to which to put this book is to rely on its advice in those areas in which you feel less certain or interest so that your personal preferences don't lead to a lack of balanced access for your community.

Identifying Experts as Development Resources

Allowing an information area that is needed by the community to go unaddressed because you feel unsure of how to select and maintain authoritative resources in that knowledge area should serve as a prompt to reach out for assistance. You are encouraged in Chapter 2 to call in an expert for a question that seemingly cannot be answered from library sources. You should feel equally free to ask an expert for help in choosing a reference tool for your collection. Among library-based experts in the community, you may want to confer with academic, hospital, and/or theological school libraries in order to identify the resources needed at the public library reference resource level.

As discussed in Chapter 2, *referral* is undertaken when the library's own resources cannot meet the information gap. To permit efficient and graceful referrals, the reference collection should include, for staff purposes, a list for ready staff access of such referral options. Such a collection of community referral points (with telephone and e-mail information) can be housed in an intranet database or even a simple file on staff computer desktops. Such a referral guide must be updated frequently.

Other experts may have answers to queries that are more than an answer to a reference question. These experts have the kind of information about their organizations that community members need to support their daily lives, whether for assistance (such as shelters) or enrichment (such as volunteer opportunities). Such a collection of referral resources should include:

- Directory entries, including open hours and access policies, of all other local libraries, museums, parks, and other recreational points of interest
- Each city and/or county office with whom community members can expect to need to interact, such as those issuing permits of all kinds
- Public assistance and nonprofit social service venues, including emergency shelters, food pantries, and crisis hotlines
- School district offices, including contact points for alternative high schools, and adult education

One way to begin to generate such a list is by accessing the local 211[8] source. However, the records in the local 211 database may not be as up to date or as complete, as reference staff should supply during referrals. This is a starting point to explore for up-to-date information for the reference staff's referral directory inclusion.

MAINTAIN THE REFERENCE COLLECTION, NOT NECESSARILY ITS MATERIAL PIECES

Reference collections are in as much need of weeding care as any other part of the library collection. Weeding is critical to preserve the integrity of the collection's physical, informational, and community appropriate aspects. This is true of physical materials and resources in electronic, or virtual, formats; all require regular evaluation, and action must be taken to remove those that fail to meet these criteria:

- Up-to-date subject coverage, which varies by subject, as we will discuss in subsequent chapters.
- Accessible format(s) for intended resource users, including both physical access and linguistic access.
- Containment of duplicate coverage to those resources needed to balance access needs and to address diverse points of view

If your reference collection is composed of book and microform materials, you may have invested considerable budget over a period of time to acquire and maintain the collection. However, you need to be managing a contemporary collection, looking at the present and the predictable future rather than thinking about the costs incurred to purchase materials a decade ago. Your collection maintenance focus belongs on the reference collection that provides valid resources, in accessible formats, for current and future use.[9]

EVALUATING REFERENCE SOURCES

Evaluation, regardless of a resource's format, measures the authority and the accessibility of the reference source. Evaluation considers organization and ease of use of the resource, the accuracy and currency of its coverage of the topic, and the purpose of its use in terms of scope and audience.

Continual evaluation of available resources is an essential element of reference work. Like communication, the capacity to undertake it can be practiced without ever being perfected because both information resources and the means for applying information to knowledge need change and evolve across time. Every resource used must be evaluated, both when it is selected for the collection and with each use, on a regular basis and compared and contrasted with other resources available that provide similar information and query source support.

When using any information resource—whether a book, website, or another format—reference staff should keep in mind the following questions:

- **How is the resource used?** How does someone find information within this resource? How is it organized?
- **Is the information accurate?** Is the creator of the content authoritative and reliable? Is the information current and not obsolete?
- **Will it answer the question?** Is the source meant to provide the information for which there is a knowledge gap presented for bridging? Is the information in a form that is usable by staff or by the person seeking the information?
- **Is this the most expedient resource to use?** Would it be more efficient to consider something else? Does the time allotted to find the information fit the amount of time needed to make the best use of this source?

Specific formats have their own elements that should be considered in evaluating reference resources. Print, databases, and the open web are discussed next.

Print

In print books published specifically for reference purposes, the introductory section at the beginning of the book often describes the book's organization; authority; the years of data included; and the book's purpose, scope, and intended audience. You can check the introduction to find an explanation of the organization of the book and how to interpret the information it provides. If information about when the material was updated is not stated in the introduction or "How to Use This Book" guide, you should check the copyright date. Note that the information presented in the book typically is at least a year older than the publication date. Finally, the introduction should also state specifically what the purpose of the book is, what aspects of the stated subject are covered, and what related subjects are not covered.

Databases

Most commercial online databases open with a screen that briefly describes its authority, scope, purpose, and audience. Its currency is also usually noted. However, you may have to dig deeper to find out how frequently the online subscription is updated and whether *embargo* dates that delay inclusion of the most recent published work of some periodicals from third-party resellers. When commercial databases present, as a third party, contents collated from the original publishers, often the database's contractual arrangements with the original publishers state that the contents may not appear in the database for a period of hours, days, or weeks (and, in rare cases, months) after the original publisher makes these articles available for sale in their own magazines, journals, and newspapers. This practice is called placing an embargo on the content that the original publisher wants to sell before allowing the database company to earn a profit from selling it in the future. In some cases databases may be partially updated daily, while in other cases it may be much longer between updates. This, in part, has to do with addressing embargo periods and, in part, how the database company has decided to schedule its own work in uploading new content.

Because all this evaluative information is represented minimally on that opening page of many databases, you should check the list of help features linked at the top, bottom, or side of the screen. "About Name-of-Database" and "Guide to Name-of-Database" are among the headers that alert users to where documentation of the database's essential criteria can be found.

The Open Web

On websites, the *homepage* is often used to introduce the website to the user. Links like "about us" or "about name-of-website" may also offer information about its author(s) and about the purpose of the website. Typically a "help" link will take the user to information about how to use the website efficiently. Reviewing the "frequently asked questions" (FAQ) is an excellent way to become oriented. Because of the self-publishing nature of websites, there are many ways that this evaluative information may be provided, if it is provided at all. Those accessing an open web site, even one that has proved helpful in previous research, may have to be creative in finding this descriptive information.

The complex nature of the open web requires a much lengthier discussion of how to evaluate the contents of any website. This is taken up in Chapter 10, in which developing the necessary evaluation skills for yourself and for teaching your clients how to evaluate web search results will be discussed. For purposes of evaluating websites for inclusion in the reference collection, the following criteria must be measured:

- Website authority: Who or what agency has created this site? Are they experts in the content area it addresses?
- Website purpose: Why was this website created?
- Website currency and upkeep: Is it clear that the site is maintained, updated, corrected, and designed according to current web standards for ADA accessibility?
- Accessibility relative to information need and scope of need: Is it in the appropriate language, whether simple or sophisticated, to suit the information need? Are details provided in its content sufficient for the information need while also providing direct access to information without detailed examination?

Adding specific websites to the reference collection allows reference staff to make resources available anywhere they or community members have Internet connectivity. By providing curated web links, by placing them on the library or reference department's web page in a manner that allows clients to find them as readily available suggestions, information needs can be more quickly and accurately satisfied than if each time a staff member or a client has a need he or she must first establish the above criteria of each website before considering it as a resource with high potential for search satisfaction.

Standing Orders and Subscriptions

Many different types of information used in reference work require regular updating to maintain accuracy and authority. In the realm of paper-based reference publishing, this need has been addressed traditionally through a library standing order process so that each new edition of a reference work, such as the current telephone directory, the latest road atlas, or the newest used car pricing guide, can be acquired upon publication. Publishers have established internal schedules and criteria to prompt new editions that are delivered on standing order plans. In some cases, new editions may be available and delivered annually, or more frequently, as when the contents of the resource include significant amounts of directory data, market worth, or other information vulnerable to rapid change. Others prepare and deliver new editions when irregular events occur, such as changes in law.

Where a local reference collection includes standing orders among its contents, you should become familiar with:

- The schedule or event triggering a new edition for each standing order title
- The remaining worth of a superseded edition, if any
- The continuing value of such a print-based resource relative to its information coverage and the community's information needs in the topic it addresses

In many libraries, superseded editions of reference resources replaced through standing order arrivals of the latest edition have been passed down either to a circulating book collection or to another library unit within the system. This is, at best, a dubious practice because you are buying the new edition to get the best information. Giving outdated information to another librarian or sector of the community is not going to be helpful and, in cases of law and medicine, can be harmful. It is a better practice to respond to calls from other library staff or clients looking for the latest information.

Here's an example: A library places the older edition of a book about adoption law in its circulating collection when a new edition arrives on standing order for the reference collection. A member of the community doesn't question whether it is the most recent and believes this copy she can take home to study is factually accurate. However, the law has changed since this older edition and her efforts to acquire the proper credentials she needs to present to the adoption agency fail to include the newly required criminal background certificate from the FBI. Even if she works out the issue and reapplies correctly, she has lost valuable time and now finds herself in a new age category viewed less favorably by the adoption agencies.

If the expense of maintaining a standing order plan is what drives this postdated use of older editions, then the standing order plan itself should be reconsidered. It may be that two copies of the latest edition are actually needed, rather than one new edition and one older one. Maintaining older editions of books providing legal guidance to laypeople is both a disservice and unethical. Receiving legal information, through the use of such superseded editions, misguides the community member with declared superseded information. This hand-me-down practice fails the tests of both authority and currency when evaluating the superseded edition.

Other standing order plans supply book-based information that is cumulative and thus remains authoritative across time. For example, publisher works that contain literary criticism, such as *Contemporary Literary Criticism*, may arrive at the reference collection on a regular basis, through a standing order plan, to be added to the volumes of the same series, rather than to replace them.

Reference staff working with collections that contain standing orders need to understand the purpose of each work, each plan, and the relative space and budget needed to maintain such plans.

Multimedia

With the penetration of online multimedia resources, physical format multimedia, such as sound and image recordings, play a significant role only in the most specialized of reference collections. One related material type, however, is the microformat-dependent backfile of long-held journal and other subscriptions, as well as death records and sometimes building codes.

Microfilm and fiche were once a significant part of the resources maintained in reference collections as they afforded a means for both preservation and efficient storage of historical information sources. The local reference service staff must evaluate the relative needs for such resources to be retained in the contemporary reference collection. Among the questions to consider are:

- Is database and web access to the information provided by these microformat files stable enough to be reliable? Sometimes this is not the case, or the community wants and needs access to issues much older than full-text coverage in the available database(s).
- Does the community need and expect to access the information housed throughout the microformat collection, and in this material type? Usually, contemporary public library users have little expectation of referring to microformats except in the case of property records or death indexes. The local public library may not be the appropriate agency to house these if call for them is slight and they are locally available in another government office or through online searching.
- Is accessing equipment, including machine readers and their peripherals, kept in good repair and serviced regularly? This becomes increasingly difficult to assure as the popularity of the formats has dwindled. Especially in rural and other isolated communities, acquiring on-site repairs may not even be possible.

Making wise determinations about the retention or disposal of microformat files should be undertaken deliberately and with reference to whether the information the backfiles provide is both unique and necessary locally.

Community Agencies and Experts

Reference resources in the collection include people! Organizing and maintaining information about community experts, both individuals and public and private agencies, requires community knowledge and staff capacity to investigate the authority and accessibility of each such expert. It also requires staff effort to document where and why these experts should be found. Some libraries create local databases of community agencies that include hours, alternate languages they provide for handling inquiries, and scope of services. Building such a local database saves reference staff time when a local expert is considered to be the best resource the collection can offer in the pursuit of information.

In some information need situations, an expert who has not been previously identified may be warranted. For example, a community member may want guidance in selecting a reputable jewelry evaluation expert. Reference collection resources should include Chamber of Commerce and Better Business listings for such situations. Reference staff, too, can bridge such information gaps by coaching the clients in appropriate questions to put to a possible expert to evaluate his or her appropriateness to resolving the information quest:

- If the expert deals in valuable assets, is he or she appropriately bonded?
- Is the expert credentialed or licensed, if applicable?

- Does the agency keep up to date with changes in law?
- What is the preferred means for a community member to access this agency or expert?

This list of questions should form the basis of any locally constructed community expert file staff include among their reference collection options.

In the chapters following this one, resource identification for specific subject areas of knowledge, along with those specific resources staff generally should know and be able to access for specific settings and situations, is addressed. How to make effective and efficient use of search strategies with the variety of resource types discussed in this chapter will be expanded.

NOTES

1. See the Pew Report "Americans' Internet Access: 2000–2015," *Pew Research Center: Internet, Science and Tech*, 2016, pewinternet.org/2015/06/26/americans-internet-access-2000–2015/) and keep apace of developing trends in access by making ongoing visits to pewinternet.org.
2. See the American Library Association's Issues page "Best Practices for Creating a Successful Budget," *American Library Association Legislative Advocacy*, 2016, ala.org/advocacy/advleg/advocacyuniversity/budgetpresentation/bestpractices.
3. In the following chapters, various government-established and -maintained databases appropriate to reference collections will be identified.
4. See the Idaho Commission for Libraries, *LiLI Databases*, 2016, libraries.idaho.gov/page/lili-databases.
5. See the State Library of North Carolina, *Databases by Type*, 2016, statelibrary.ncdcr.gov/ghl/resources/bytype.html.
6. Ancestry (ancestry.com) is a commercial database with tiered access to its information, offering some for free on the web and placing a pay wall in front of deeper levels of research support for casual genealogists.
7. *Library Journal* runs an annual feature-length review of experts' top selections of best databases. The criteria employed to identify each year's selections for the list offer good tips toward local database evaluation as well.
8. The United Way underwrites 211.org (211.org), which is an online and telephone accessible directory that can be searched by city, state, or ZIP code. Reference staff should become familiar with its quality in their immediate area.
9. See Goldsmith (2015) for an in-depth discussion of weeding reference collections.

CHAPTER 5

Organizing Print and Electronic Reference Sources

This chapter will discuss resource organization. When evaluating a book, journal, database, or website, information should be accessible quickly and easily. Reference staff develop and practice skills for approaching resources with knowledge about how the organization of the resource supports its rapid and efficient use. Knowing where to look quickly to uncover the authoritative information needed is essential to effective reference service. Sometimes information is needed to respond to a question presented by a client; however, it may just as well be needed for staff to use to design information literacy opportunities for the community. When a staff member is asked to speak about government initiatives such as access and compliance for the Affordable Care Act or is planning to host workshops targeting amateur ancestry researchers, references will be needed to develop the presentations and to present to those in attendance as best resources on the topic.

UNDERSTANDING ORGANIZATION WITHIN TRADITIONAL BOOKS

Reference books, whether in paper format or electronic, are generally of seven broad types:

- Dictionaries, which define terms
- Encyclopedias, which discuss topics in context

- Indexes, which provide location information within other books
- Directories, which provide contact information and geographic or online location of entities
- Atlases, which bring together maps or other schematic images
- Handbooks, or manuals, which explain how to perform functions
- Collections of content from other sources, brought together in a volume or series of volumes for ease of research on an extensive topic

By the nature of the differences in content type, books cannot all be arranged uniformly. In addition to differences in book types, the purpose of a specific book, or the publisher's intended audience for its use, influences the arrangement of any specific book. The following guidelines, then, are not absolute. They suggest the most likely ways to begin exploring an unfamiliar reference book. Many reference books are organized alphabetically. For example, dictionaries almost always arrange words alphabetically, A–Z; encyclopedias usually are organized alphabetically by subject; print directories may be organized alphabetically or geographically or even by company or demographic size; and biographical dictionaries are often organized alphabetically by name. However, reference books can be organized in many other ways, including chronologically, by geographical region, or by scientific classification. By flipping through the text of an unfamiliar reference book, you can quickly get an idea how the book is organized. If this organization is not immediately understood, look for an essay or introduction with information on the book's organization.

At the beginning of most reference books there is important information about how to make the best use of the book in the "user's guide," including both *how to find information* in it and *how to interpret* that information. Trying to use a reference book without reviewing this guide presents the risk of overlooking something essential to understanding the information it contains and whether the information is of a depth and scope appropriate to the reference question at hand.

When the main content is not organized in a way that makes finding information intuitive, and you haven't taken time to read the user's guide, a secondary way of locating information within a book resource is the book's index. The index may supplement information found readily. For example, information about airplanes can be found in the "Airplanes" article of a general encyclopedia and the encyclopedia's index provides directions to more information that can be found in other articles: "Transportation," "Aerodynamics," and "Invention." Some topics in a general encyclopedia may not have an article written about them, but there may still be information in other articles. For example, there is no article on "San Joaquin Valley" in the *World Book Encyclopedia*; however, according to the index, information on that topic can found in the "California" article, under "Agriculture."

Some reference books, especially those that are directories, may have multiple indexes. Each index concerns a particular method of searching, such as a proper name index or a geography index. Where multiple elements are combined in a single index, a different typeface may be used to indicate which entries point to what kind of information. For example, a cookbook with a single index may indicate entries for main ingredients (raisins) by printing them in bold, while the entries for recipes (pies) are printed in regular font. Becoming acquainted with the organization and presence of the book's index(ices) not only saves time but also gives you the opportunity to consider approaching the question at hand from an angle other than what seemed to be the obvious or intuitively "right" one.

Journals provide up-to-date information on a variety of topics depending upon the subjects the journal covers. If you do not have access to a database of journals and still subscribe to a variety of titles that come on a regular basis, you will need to purchase a guide to the contents of these journals. For popular journals, the indexing tool *Readers' Guide to Periodical Literature* will be covered thoroughly later in this chapter.

SIDEBAR 1   ANATOMY OF THE BOOK'S WORKING PARTS

Print book resources used in reference work typically have specific parts that perform specific functions that aid the user in making efficient access to the contents. Here are words to know and functions to understand:

- Appendix—Relevant material that supports the main contents of the book by providing explanatory information, applicable research methods, sample forms, and other contextually enhancing data, the appendix appears at the end of the work's main content. Some books have multiple appendices (or appendixes), and many have none.
- Bibliography—Published works used by the authors to form the foundation of the assertions, factual inclusions, and historical context of the present work are arranged often at the end of the book; sometimes, however, each chapter includes a bibliography. The information included in each bibliographic citation allows the reader to locate the original work cited by providing author(s), title, work in which the article was published (such as a journal), page numbers, and date of publication. An annotated bibliography also includes a line or two describing the contents of the work cited in the bibliographic listing.
- Citation—The intellectual responsibility and published location descriptors of a work form a citation.
- Contributors—Volumes that are composed of writing and/or research compiled from multiple authors list these, with a brief description that validates his or her authority. Sometimes the contributors are arranged, often alphabetically, at the back of the book, while in other cases the contributors are enumerated after the title page.
- Copyright statement—Information that includes the year of publication, and revision, if any, the publisher's name, and the place of the publication form the copyright statement. This usually appears on the verso (back) of the title page. By noting the date of copyright, the user can judge the age of the content of the book.
- Editor—Books composed of works by various contributors credit an editor, or a variety of editors, with bringing the material together and assuring that the arrangement of the content in the book presents a cohesive whole. Some series have an editor in chief who oversees the series as a whole, while individual volumes in the series are the works of individual editors with expertise in the area of that volume's content.
- Footnote—An assertion made within the text of a book is supported by including information about where to find information to substantiate it. A footnote may appear at the bottom of the page where the assertion is made, or footnotes may be collected at the end of the chapter, in which case they may be called "endnotes." When a book contains a bibliography, the footnotes may simply list the author, page number, and year of the referenced material and the user can refer to the bibliography for its full citation.
- Foreword—Material collected in the beginning section of the book, sometimes called a "user's guide" or similar descriptive term, explains the purpose and intended use of the work as a whole. The foreword can be presented in a variety of ways, from narrative prose to a table showing keys to symbols and/or abbreviations used throughout the book.

- Index—The map of exactly where in the book to find specific information takes the form of one or more alphabetically ordered lists, usually found at the end of the volume. An index is created by specific rules so that every part of it is consistent. See Sidebar 2, "How an Index Works," for detailed information about the schemata employed by indexers to present these data.
- Plates—Although modern books rarely include these pages printed on special stock to show high reproduction of images, older volumes include them to provide more accurate publication of art works and scientific drawings. In volumes where they are included, the clay-coated paper on which plates are printed tend to be collected together in one or more places in the volume, rather than specifically at the point of text reference to them, so noting which plate number to reference is necessary for the user to do.
- Series statement—Publishers create series to allow users to explore a theme from a variety of approaches, angles, or across time. If the book in hand is part of such a series, the publication information will include the series title and information about the series as a whole, often including titles of other volumes within the series, where the series as a whole is indexed, and/or the frequency of volumes being added to it.
- Table of contents—Usually appearing at the front of the book, after the title and copyright pages, this chart lists the order of the volume's content coverage. Many such tables of content list only chapter titles, along with the page number on which each chapter begins, while others also list the chapter editor(s) with the chapter title. An analytical table of contents provides even more information, such as listing the major subjects addressed in each chapter.
- Tables—Graphs and charts that provide information through schematic renderings sometimes appear at one place in the volume, such as in an appendix; sometimes at the end of the related chapter; and sometimes within the text where reference is made to the concepts appearing in the schematic. Like plates, tables are generally numbered so reference can be made to the appropriate one and linked to the narrative content it explores. The locations of specific tables may be noted in the table of contents as well as in the index.

To save shelf space, paper, and repetition, reference books often include symbols and codes for many repeated data points or for information that is difficult to express in minimal printed words. A dictionary's pronunciation key, for example, explains in one part of the volume what various diacritical marks mean when used throughout the rest of the work. A collection of plot synopses for various plays may include a coded designation with each synopsis to note the anthology of plays in which the full work can be found. Maps in atlases of both geography and the human body print specific elements within each image in a color that provides information about the services or functions of that place.

Look in the beginning of the book for an explanation of any internal symbols or abbreviations.

SEARCHING PRINT REFERENCE SOURCES

Let's take an in-depth look at specific types of reference books and consider how to search them for helpful information. These include bibliographies; indexes; compilations of abstracts; chronologies; dictionaries; encyclopedias; almanacs; directories; handbooks and manuals; and atlases. A separate section covers reference books for children. These will be covered in depth with the understanding that some of the search procedures are similar to what you will do with a reference resource that is online as an electronic book or collection.

Bibliographies

Bibliographies are directories of other published works. They serve as tools for discovering where to find authoritative information published elsewhere. Many books that are composed largely of narrative text, as well as journal articles, may also include bibliographies to support the authors' assertions. By turning to an appropriate bibliography, you can find exactly where to go to locate specific discussion, research studies, and other authoritative published content that specifically addresses almost any information gap. You probably have noticed the bibliography at the back of a nonfiction book you have read about a topic in history or the biography of a famous person.

However, community members with a basic information needs are unlikely to need, or want, or often even be able to understand, the content of the specialized publication cited in a bibliography, unless that bibliography has been composed specifically for an audience with such basic knowledge needs. For example, a five-year-old who is looking for information about how a car's engine works is unlikely to have any use for a bibliography of published research studies about combustion engine efficiencies. However, she may be delighted to discover that an adult who looks at the bibliography in a nonfiction children's book about construction equipment can find other books like this one with even more information. In fact, bibliographies in children's nonfiction books can be great tools for uncovering detailed publications on the subjects they treat without requiring the researcher to have a sophisticated understanding of the topic.

Among the important purposes of the reference interview, discussed in Chapter 2, is that of determining the scope and level of the data that would best fit an information gap as you clarify what that gap is. It is through the interview, rather than through your assumption, that you can make sure the level of information offered is complete and suitable. The bibliography serves as an excellent case in point: it may be that you learn in the interview that the question arises from an academic assignment to find published critical essays about a work studied in a literature class. This will provide a just-in-time opportunity to show the person with the question how a bibliography provides exactly that type of material. You can explain the structure and authority of a bibliography while providing citations to essays that fulfill the assignment requirements.

Indexes and Abstracts

An index guides the researcher to a page or even to a place on a page where the relevant information can be found, while an abstract provides a brief synopsis of the information found at that location. Both may be published as reference works themselves or may be parts of other published works. Specific indexes that stand alone as reference books, instead of being a part of a book to which the index refers, are discussed later in the following chapter. Journal articles often include abstracts at their beginning, and these abstracts are frequently collected for publication together, along with the bibliographic citations to each specific article.

Abstract reading can prove efficient and effective because enough information appears to allow you to identify the topic treated as well as the approach and often even the findings of the specific article. While a bibliography or index listing simply shows you where to find the complete information, the abstract provides enough detail to make well-informed decisions about which resources to track down and consult in full.

While there are many types of *chronologies* varying in detail, length, and scope as well as by topic, chronologies that place news articles in time order can be helpful when deciding which journal or newspaper articles to consult to read about an event in order of original discovery and documentation. Such chronological arrangement of abstracts can show clearly when a particular news event first became public and across what period of time new information became published. For decades the print *New York Times Index*[1] was in fact a combination of index, abstract, and chronology. Arranged in alphabetical order by topic, and with directions to the date, section, page, and even place on the page of the article indexed, longer articles were also abstracted as well, with a sentence or two (and sometimes even more) detailing what that specific article covered. While the topics are arranged in alphabetical order, the specific index references appear in chronological order, so that by scanning the abstracts under a specific index listing, and before moving to consult the full newspaper article, the reader can see a news event unfolding across time and make an informed decision about which point in the story is of real interest.

Among the paper-based volumes of index resources you need to cultivate familiarity with are those series that provide access to the contents of older periodicals. Not everything has migrated to Internet databases that can be accessed without such a print index! These print indexes, like *Readers' Guide to Periodical Literature*, provide the service of cumulating the specific magazine or other journal contents from hundreds of different titles and showing exactly which page on which issue of which periodical an article addressed the topic being researched. In order to accommodate so much data between the covers of a volume, even if that volume covers a time span of only a couple of years, many abbreviations and symbols are used to express information. Each volume of such a print index includes the necessary key to these.

SIDEBAR 2   HOW AN INDEX WORKS

The arrangement of an index is codified so that the user can understand aspects of the book's content beyond the location of a specific piece of text. There are a variety of guidelines available to those undertaking the work of indexing content and different works employ different structures.

When making use of an index, it is not essential to know the specific rules of the index format selected for use by this indexer or publisher. However, it is essential to recognize patterns to aid in the efficient use of how those guidelines have arranged the contents of the index.

First, the user must note whether the book has more than a single index and then consider whether the information being sought within the book would be better documented in which specific index. For example, a work that contains separate indexes (or indices) for proper names and for all other terms allows the user to search through one index when what is wanted is a person and the other when what is wanted is a concept.

Within the index, the list of words, terms, and any other nomenclature is arranged alphabetically. A typical rule of thumb is that "nothing comes before something," which means that where a space appears between two words (the space being "nothing"), the index will file it before a term where another letter ("something") follows immediately on the word that began in the same way. For example:

- *Think* follows *thin*, because it has an additional letter after the first four the two words otherwise share in the same order.
- *Shelters* follows *shelter*, according to the same reasoning, *groceries* precedes *grocery* because the letter-by-letter alphabetical analyses of these two words mean that "I" precedes "Y."
- *Sandwich spread* precedes *sandwiches* because, while the first term may have more letters in all, there is a "nothing" after the "H".

The actual words and terms used in any index come from an authority file created for that index. The authority file provides the indexer with the specific term to use among possible terms or synonyms for that term. Because users of the index may well not know what the authority list contained and omitted, the indexer uses *See* references. The various popular synonyms are listed just once, in their appropriate alphabetical place in the index. However, instead of indicating the location of the information within the book, the synonyms are followed by "*See* (term chosen as the authority filing word). Here's how that looks:

> Capital punishment
> Counterfeiting
> Dalliance
> Death penalty. *See* Capital punishment
> Guards, prison
> Hanging, death by. *See* Capital punishment

The indexer also files the most important word in a phrase, inverting any phrase where a descriptive term appears before that keyword. In the example immediately above, the indexer uses the term "guards" and then adds the modifier "prison," rather than filing the term under "prison guards." This allows all locations related to the keyword to be brought near each other in the index.

Sometimes the book contains a main portion about a subject and also references the subject in other places that discuss other topics. The indexer indicates this by using a "*See also* reference":

> Animals. *See also* Dogs, Horses, Swine.
> Arabian stallions. *See* Horses
> Dogs
> Horses

Although the main purpose of using the index is to find the specific point within the book that contains the information needed, looking at the terms indexed can help expand searching possibilities both within the book in hand and elsewhere. For instance, seeing that the term "death penalty" is an alternative to "capital punishment" serves as a reminder that research on the topic can be pursued with multiple names. The index in a cookbook can provide ideas for using specific ingredients on hand.

Sometimes the index uses bold type to indicate which, among the various locations listed for information about a topic, is the main resource of subject-specific information in that book. Even when a book is arranged alphabetically, check to see if there is an index, because the volume's arrangement may not place every element about a specific topic within the main entry for it. For instance, a biographical encyclopedia may arrange the subjects in alphabetical order. However, the index may indicate that information about the marriage of one subject to another is discussed in the partner's entry.

Some indexes, including those that support research outside the limits of the volume in hand, provide lists of people, places, events, or concepts in thematic lists. For example, an index of stock exchange information may arrange stocks traded on each of several exchanges so that the index user can quickly discover which exchange is related to which stock.

Dictionaries

Dictionaries perform the work of defining words and terms, sometimes supplementing that data with pronunciation guidance or derivation of the word in question. Staff will need to understand the differences among several kinds of dictionaries so they can choose the dictionary which will answer the need of the question.

A monolingual or single language dictionary, for example, like *Webster's* or the *Oxford English Dictionary*, collects the vocabulary of a language and presents each word's common spelling, along with alternatives arranged in order of popular use. A pronunciation key allows the dictionary to provide diacritically marked sound renderings of the spelled word, such as where to place an accent and how to pronounce a diphthong. The part of speech and the denoted meaning or meanings of the word when used as that part of speech are arranged next, sometimes with an illustrative sentence or quotation in which the word is used correctly.

Bilingual and multilingual dictionaries also treat language. However, they may lack definitions or other elaborating elements of the monolingual language dictionary. Instead, a multilingual dictionary lists vocabulary words translated from one of its languages to the other, with each language having a section of the book arranged alphabetically according to the words reflecting that language.

Many specialized dictionaries provide definitions of specialized vocabulary, jargon, biographic names, geographic designations, and even images labeling printed terms. Depending on the needs and interests your collection serves, these specialized dictionaries may define meanings when words are applied to architectural features or the names for specific bones in the human body.

The common attribute of books that are dictionaries is that they supply information about what a word or term indicates. Dictionaries do not discuss the things themselves that the terms define, as do encyclopedias, which we will discuss next. The dictionary's purpose is to clarify word meaning.

Encyclopedias

Like dictionaries, encyclopedias are available to cover a wide range of possible topical areas. General dictionaries, whether in a single volume or in sets of multiple volumes, present discussions of general knowledge. General encyclopedias may provide basic or introductory information on a topic of interest. By reading an encyclopedia article, you gain contextual understanding of a term, how this specific thing or event might relate to others, and, usually, how the concept developed through history or related ideas.

Special encyclopedias also present articles discussing specific concepts, events, ideas, persons, concerns, facts, and so forth. A sports encyclopedia is the best route to finding a basic discussion of the development of basketball rules across American history, while an encyclopedia about world religions gives the researcher explanations about commonalities and differences, offers history and geography details that can further understanding of a religion's development and its practice, and treats each different religion with roughly the same fairness by staying with objective features, rather than arguing that one is right and another wrong.

Like dictionaries, encyclopedias are typically arranged in alphabetical order. Some encyclopedias may contain articles that are over one or two thousand words each, while others may present only a paragraph or two per entry. The purpose of an encyclopedia is to provide a context for the topic at hand, rather than a place to locate definitions of words. By consulting an encyclopedia at the beginning of a research project, whether general or specialized, you can develop a sense of important elements of the topic, such as events or persons relevant to it, as well as gain a broad understanding of the structure of the topic within the larger universe of knowledge, facts, or history.

Almanacs

Almanacs published in book format serve many purposes. Each volume contains a year's worth of information about something, bringing together many details related to that subject as relevant to the specific year. Generally, almanacs relate the recent past, as well as historic records; however, *The Old Farmers Almanac* purports to provide forecasting information; however, this prediction of the future is based on recorded trends in weather, climate, and so forth.[2]

Like dictionaries and encyclopedias, almanacs may be general or dedicated to narrow topics. Authoritative general almanacs, such as the *World Almanac and Fact Book*, compile such broad areas of information that backfiles of them can provide a balanced retrospective view of political, social, and natural changes across time. Specialized almanacs treat a wide range of focused concerns, such as *The Guinness Book of World Records*. Almanacs were much more useful and popular in reference collections before the Internet developed to the point that uncovering tiny facts became relatively simple to undertake on the web. However, they are still useful for confirming a "fact" found on the Internet, such as a 20th-century athlete's best score, or a list of the largest recorded earthquakes.

Using any almanac requires attention to its construction. Some have an index at the front, while others contain an index in the more traditional end of the volume. General almanacs typically are divided into thematic parts, such as "World events," "Rainfall in capital cities," and even the forms of government in place in each world nation during the period of the almanac's coverage. Details are brief in an almanac, and its best use is as a starting point to find specific dates or names of well-known people, details sometimes needed to help prepare the most effective and efficient direction that research on a reference topic may need to take.

Directories

Directories are among the print book resources that have undergone so much change in utility that few may be present in the contemporary reference collection. Most have migrated to online platforms, whether e-book or database. However, understanding the searching principles applicable to a directory can support learning web-based content structure and searching in general, as websites often have a directory underlying their structure.

The purpose of a directory is, as the word itself suggests, to aid in locating an entity (person, agency, corporation) as that entity can be found in the world, rather than within text. Directories supply the specific ways to access those they include, such as phone numbers, e-mail addresses, street addresses, or place in a corporate or government structure. Among the printed format directories most familiar to you is the telephone book. Here, the white pages are organized by name, whether personal or business, and the yellow pages are arranged in categories of business identity. In both cases, the arrangement is alphabetical. Telephone directories often include blue pages as well, which provide assistance in locating information about government office locations and contacts; today these listings may also include the government office web address.

Some directories offer much more extensive information beyond simple contact points for listed parties. A scholarship directory, for example, presents educational awards available and is usually organized both by awarding body and by attributes applicants must possess, such as grade point average or heritage. Such a directory's listings include a paragraph or more of information for each listing, usually in a combination of narrative and bullet points, detailing the specifics of each scholarship opportunity in terms of size, intent, and application steps. Directories of hospitals offer information about numbers of beds, medical staff composition, and other facts that allow the directory user not only to locate a hospital but also to note comparable data about this one among the other hospitals in the directory.

A directory may be arranged in any of several ways, as the telephone book example shows, and almost always includes multiple arrangements within it. Content may appear alphabetically by party name, grouped by area of business or organizational concern, geographically, or even according to a coded structure such as the National American Industry Classification System (NAICS).[3] Accessing the content of a directory requires an understanding of its system for arranging the listings within it.

The major reason book directories are falling by the wayside is that information about contact numbers and addresses, both online and on the street, changes more rapidly than standard book publishing can reflect with accuracy. Directories must be updated regularly, and any lapse between most print-based ones is greater than the ongoing maintenance that occurs online with directory information. However, the arrangement of some printed directories allows the user to browse listings such as viewing which restaurants have been able to afford the largest ad space in the yellow pages.

Examining a couple of print directories, such as the local telephone book and another that you can find that might be your state government's directory, is a good exercise for building awareness that you need to search the web effectively. Noting directory structure, multiple access points, arrangements within different content areas, and degrees of detail transfer as skills onto the much more complex world of the web.

Handbooks and Manuals

A specific type of reference book called a handbook or manual presents technical information arranged for practitioners of that skill or area of work. Manuals and handbooks deal in facts and how to connect things with processes in order to reach desired new states for the things. Applied technologies such as medicine and computer education are typically treated in this book format. Among the manuals and handbooks you may use in your personal life, or at least recognize from daily exposure, are cookbooks. A manual or handbook brings together a variety of data types in order to provide the user with information needed to undertake complex practical activities. In the example of a cookbook, the volume typically contains a variety of recipes presented as formulas and directions for combining and treating each set of ingredients; food storage may also be addressed, as well as menus, preparation tips, such as the handling and care of knives.

Repair manuals are organized according to similar principles: specific mechanical and body care and mending are described, usually with accompanying diagrams to make detailed parts and connections visually explicit; the steps in which a repair process must be followed are enumerated, just as the steps in a recipe are explicit; sometimes specialty tools or suppliers are listed to further aid the user in moving from manual to execution of its instructions.

Handbooks and manuals describe how to take specific actions, using specific tools, and upon specific materials or in specific situations. The books are designed for easy access to the specific page or chapter the user requires at this time and it is unlikely that most readers would consume a manual as they might a novel, from the beginning to the end. Both tables of content and indexes, as well as appendixes, usually appear in handbooks. Sometimes consulting the contents guide is more helpful, and sometimes beginning with the index is appropriate. The situation, as well as the quality of the manual and the user's degree of subject expertise, guides the potential user in this decision.

One of the strengths of the print manual or handbook is that it provides specific details within the context of a larger, but very much related, universe of information. The well-edited handbook generally can be browsed near the "almost right" place in the book to locate the exactly right place the ordering of content emulates practical knowledge. For example, a general cookbook's chapters treating different courses of a meal, with recipes for soups near the front of the volume and those for desserts toward the end, echo the practice of a meal unfolding first with soup and finally with dessert. Browsing is a good approach to take when reading an unfamiliar manual as that also informs you about the plainness or jargon of the language it uses, the layout of its approach to the topic, and how refined the indexing is.

Atlases

An atlas is a book that brings together a collection of maps or other schematics such as drawings of the human anatomy or how a science fiction author's world building might translate to visual representation. Often, geographic atlases are quite large, even too high, and/or wide to be placed on a bookshelf. When using atlases, you must understand the principles of map reading. These include:

- Interpreting coordinates expressed as a grid on the page allows you to locate a specific point on a map from a map's index, a finding tool that is arranged by place names and, instead of page designation (or page designation alone), the point on the map at which that place is shown. Coordinates use letters and numbers, one on the y-axis and the other on the x-axis so that when you draw the lines to where they meet, you have arrived at the desired point on the map.
- Noting and using the scale information accompanying the map is also essential to understanding the map's representation of reality. To be accurate, the map must show all distances in relative terms, so that an inch on the page at this point expresses exactly the same distance as an inch on another point of the page. In bound atlases, scale is usually noted on each page and there may be blowups, using a different scale, of dense

areas. For example, a map of Japan as a geographic entity may be represented at the scale of 1 inch to 50 miles; however, a blowup included of the downtown area of the city of Osaka is shown with 1 inch representing half a mile. This difference in scale allows greater detail to be shown where there is deemed more need for that.

- Discerning what any symbols used actually mean in order to gain a clearer understanding of how the map relates to the space it depicts requires you locating the map key. In an atlas, this may be at the front of the book or it may be on each page. This aspect of map reading remains important, whether you are looking in an atlas, at a folding paper map, or a map online. Symbols are used to represent such ubiquitous features as the location of railroad tracks, major interstate highways, or public buildings, on a map showing a town, neighborhood, or countryside. A map depicting an area such as a park employs symbols for the locations of picnic areas, washrooms, and trail heads. Rather than guessing what a symbol might suggest, checking the key assures you that you are interpreting the map correctly.

Geographic atlases may show regions depicted with their names at the time of the book's publication, as is the case with a road atlas intended for travel use. Other geographic atlases show maps from specific periods of time such as maps of the United States during the Civil War, or maps of railroads throughout the United States. Yet another atlas may show maps of places that exist in works of fantasy literature. Making sure a geographic atlas is up to date, then, varies with what it presents: you need to have a road atlas that is current, while an atlas of Civil War battles has a much longer shelf life (unless, of course, some momentous new discovery is made by archaeologists!).

In addition to geophysical maps, atlases can contain other kinds of schematized, two-dimensional representations, such as the systems in the human body or other animals' anatomies. Instead of showing accurate physical details, maps and atlases may also represent comparative charts, such as an atlas of languages that depicts both where and how many people speak which language.

Approaching any atlas for the first time requires noting what the foreword or user guide lists as methodology for interpretation of the maps and schemata within it. When using an atlas that purports to depict current reality or knowledge, it is essential to check the copyright notice. An out-of-date map that one intends to use for guidance, of course, derails the whole purpose of consulting an authoritative resource.

Like handbooks, the advantage of an atlas is that it brings together many different parts of a larger whole—Chicago, or Irish whiskey—so that the use of the atlas allows one to gain context readily. Because a book can be turned at an infinite variety of degrees, viewing a page can be undertaken readily from many angles.

Using Children's Nonfiction as Reference Resources

A rich contemporary book source of basic reference information can be found in quality children's nonfiction. Popular publishing trends across the past couple of decades bring an increasing variety of books that address many areas of concern and would be of interest to people of all ages, with illuminating illustrations, vetted facts, and clarity of prose. Like encyclopedia articles, these books can offer information on specific and narrow topics that help introduce the researcher to terms, history, and other context within a style that engages interest in the topic quickly. An adult who understands nothing about magnets, for example, may welcome the simple text and illustrations in a good children's book about magnets and magnetism.

While such books typically remain in circulating collections, keep this resource in mind when pursuing information that is both accurate and suitable to anyone needing a basic introduction to a topic. Users can begin their research with these books simply because the texts tend to focus on highly specific facets of large subjects allowing the adult reader to acquire a cogent overview with correct vocabulary.

ONLINE RESOURCE STRUCTURES

Searching online is divided into two distinct types, reflecting differences between searching databases, accessible through the Internet, and finding and using sites on the open web. The requisite skills for most efficiently searching in either milieu share traits in common with searching printed resources, too, such as understanding how to use a directory, what an index can and can't do to support your search, and how different presentations of information are designed to call attention to the uses expected to be made of them: defining (dictionaries), describing in context (encyclopedias), mapping relationships (atlases), instructional guidance (manuals and handbooks), and suggestions of other resources to consult (bibliographies)

Databases Accessible through Internet Connections

Databases are resources the contents of which are closed and curated; new contents are added by humans and fit criteria specific to the database's scope. A database may be available for free on the web or by subscription. Databases provide all kinds of data types, including images, sound recordings, and text narrative from thousands of third-party publishers including books, journals, encyclopedias, dictionaries, and records that address chronological events or collections of intellectual property on a particular subject, like literary criticism essays.

Many of the authors and publishers who provide reliable information in book formats also provide reliable information that can be accessed through database subscriptions. However, such commercial databases don't arrange their records exactly the way the parts of the publisher's books tend to be arranged and may not include illustrations found in print materials. It might help to think of a database as a park in which you can follow a variety of trails that cross each other, rather than a highway where you enter and exit according to the traffic engineer's and the law's requirements. However, you follow certain rules wandering the paths that you do traveling the highway: you move, probably facing forward; you stay to the right if you pass oncoming traffic; you watch out for signs of irregular events around you. In other words, you use similar skills in both settings.

For reference work, the common skill set is the evaluation process. Evaluating the authority, currency, purpose, and scope of a specific database is straightforward:

• What body organizes and maintains the database? Reputable reference resource publishers, governmental bodies, professional associations, and field experts are likely to include contents in a database that meet strict authoritative criteria for inclusion.
• How frequently and regularly is the database updated both to reflect new content and to withdraw content that is no longer authoritative? This information is included in the database's "About" or "How to use" pages, which are almost always available on every screen.

- What is the purpose of the database? This information often is *not* spelled out in so many words on its opening screen. As a library staff member, you have access to the subscriber information supplied by most commercial database publishers. However, to find the database's purpose described when you are at the resource itself, you need to check the "About" or "How to use" page mentioned above.
- What is the scope? This is valuable for understanding the intended audience and is also described in the "About" or "How to use" section of the database.

By their nature, databases are working with a closed set of records, but those records can each be described according to different fields a user might want to search, such as names or places or areas of fame for records that describe the lives of celebrities. Many databases provide a quick search box and also indicate the availability of an advanced search function. You need to know what is included in the advanced search because setting up several parameters at the outset, such as name plus date plus nationality, may recover the desired information more quickly than taking a broad approach at the outset. Think of this as related to the reference interview, in which you find out what exactly is needed before launching into a search.

Different databases differ in the default field to which the quick search is set. If the quick search is actually searching author names, then looking for a specific title using the default index wastes time. If the quick search actually defaults to keyword searching, so that all fields are being searched for matches to the terms you set, the user must be specific about the keywords entered into the field in order to receive results that are immediately useful. For example, a keyword search in a biography database where the searcher enters the keyword "Adam" could retrieve many records for people with the first, last, or even middle name Adam, as well as titles of works in which the word "Adam" appears. Some online databases include pages that allow the user to choose to browse alphabetically or chronologically, as can be done within a print book organized in either of these ways. While browsing in a printed book can turn up some useful information, it's less likely to be an effective way to find something specific in a database or other electronic file. However, if the searcher isn't exactly sure which topic he or she wants to choose among the universe of famous Asian Americans, for example, browsing can offer the opportunity to see a range of possibilities, along with some details that may pique specific interest for further consideration.

Websites

Like books, most professionally developed websites conform to certain conventions of organization that make finding information in their web pages easier. Here are some of the conventions commonly used:

- **Homepage**—The homepage is the first page of a website, or the entrance to the site. It typically functions like the title page, table of contents, and introduction in a book. From this page the user should know where to go next (which link to follow) to find the information needed. If a search engine link has brought the searcher to a website page that is not the homepage, it may be easier to navigate the website by first going to its homepage. This can be done by clicking on the site's title, often embedded in a logo or image, usually at the top of every page of the site. The homepage commonly includes links to administrative information about the site, like contact information ("contact us"); information about the website and its authors ("about us"); and an organized list of all pages at the website ("site map" or "site index"). Often there is also a link to another page of the website that lists links to other websites with related content. These links may lead to even better sources of information on the topic being researched.

- **Navigation Bar**—This is a group of links to the basic sections of the website, similar to the table of contents in a book. Navigation bars are usually found on most or all of the website's individual pages; this way the searcher can easily navigate the website from any of its pages. The navigation bar usually appears along the left side, the bottom, or top of a web page. The first thing to do when entering a website is to scan the navigation bar for the section that seems best suited to the information the searcher wants to locate.
- **Site Map**—A site map lists all the major pages of a website in an order that makes it easy to locate a specific page. If the searcher is not able to find information by following the links provided on the homepage, using the site map may prove helpful. If the website offers a site map, it will be linked from the homepage.
- **Search**—Sometimes a website encourages the search of its full contents, using keywords, from a search box that resembles the structure of a search engine search area. This function, or a link to it, is typically found on the homepage.

Because of the open nature of website publishing, the site attributes listed earlier may or may not be included in a specific website. Site authors who have less than optimal understanding of information architecture may overlook including essential guidance points such as these. The first judgment you can make of a website's likely authority is based on its unique website address, or Uniform Resource Locator (URL), which reveals the host name which provides access to the site's information. The next detail to note is whether the site's structure supports good access to its content.

Locating Websites for Reference Work

While locating potential print and database sources in a search requires that you understand the library's fairly stable resources, or at least how to locate appropriate ones efficiently through use of the catalog, the open web comes with no guarantee that what is here this morning will still be available this afternoon. Websites can change rapidly in quality, become unfindable if coding mistakes are made by their webkeepers, and can be hacked if the website owner has not taken appropriate precautions. In other words, web contents are not stable, as are physical materials in your collection or curated databases to which your library subscribes. Instead, they are open to immediate change. That doesn't mean, of course, that they will definitely change all the time. It does mean, however, that their fluidity must be kept in mind as you search for and evaluate them.

Open web resource identification can be pursued from a number of unrelated and more or less reliable means. Print materials in your reference collection may have website Uniform Resource Locators (URLs) noted as citations in the bibliography or an appendix. Obviously, such links may go away across even a brief span of time so that the address isn't necessarily accurate. However, such printed resource lists include the names and purposes of the websites included so you could use those terms to search for a possible new location of a defunct web address.

Another means for identifying potentially useful web resources is through hyperlinks that give direct passage between one web-based resource and another by embedding the second web source's web location in code within the text within the first source. Like printed web addresses, hyperlinks, too, can degrade over time. Because the link sometimes connects from text that is no more descriptive than "here" or "as So and So notes," the researcher may have less solid information about the source noted to search for its new address through a web search engine.

Search engines stand as the premier way to locate web-based resources for which you have no online address. Search engines are mechanical means of identifying web pages that fit the criteria a user inputs into their search box(es). While each search engine has a website that contains information about it, search engines are not sites; they are computer programs. The search engine program is designed by humans; however, the collection of pages searched according to that program is undertaken robotically and according to visits repeated at different points in time. That means a search executed in a particular search engine, when reconstructed exactly six months later, may result in different retrievals or in a list of retrievals ranked differently from the initial search.[4] Effective web searching requires that you understand how search engines differ, the basics of how they operate across the ever-growing fields of data they search, and how to invoke advanced searching processes in at least two or three different search engines because each search engine's proprietary program has its own specific scope.

SIDEBAR 3   CURRENTLY NOTEWORTHY COMMERCIAL SEARCH ENGINES

Within proprietary databases, it is a search engine that interpolates terms input by the searcher to identify the results with fitting criteria. Commercial search engines operate in the same manner, except that they invoke the search against the World Wide Web's open content instead of inside a given database.

Every web search engine has particular strengths and at least a few particular weaknesses. Choosing both the right search engine and the right deployment of a search in it is an essential skill for the contemporary reference staff member. Here are some general rules about search engine best practices:

- Establish the parameters of the information gap to be addressed through locating information on the web before beginning the search: perform a reference interview and evaluate the information seeker's knowledge base, literacy level, and other details that help to define the scope and depth of information that is needed.
- Select the search engine that best suits the specific area of knowledge about which information is sought. A table of search engines follows this sidebar.
- Search as specifically as possible. This often means using the "advanced search" function supplied by the search engine or at least considering some of the criteria suggested by the advanced search template as delimiters.
- Scan the results to determine whether the ranking in which they are presented may be useful, or whether the ranking doesn't really help to determine the specific information need in hand because that need is specialized or has other criteria attached to it that cannot be associated with either popularity ranking or link ranking. (Popularity ranking places the retrievals in order of most accessed, with retrievals for paid placement near the top, while link ranking presents retrievals according to the number of other websites that link to each of these.)
- If the retrieval set is more than eight or ten pages, the search terms used are likely too broad to make an efficient use of the search engine. It's time to limit the search further.
- If no results are found or too small a number to find a resource that passes critical evaluation (discussed further in this chapter), then it's time to broaden the search terms.

- Results on pages after the first one may be exactly what is needed, so if the staff member is satisfied that the search terms are exactly the right breadth, then the results on all returned pages should be considered as potential for evaluating fit to information need.

At the time of this book's publication, the most important search engines for reference staff to learn and use are:

Search Engine	Search Engine Help Page	Search Strengths
Google	support.google.com/websearch	Breadth of coverage; support for both search and search engine optimization; detailed advanced search options
Bing	help.bing.microsoft.com	Searches patents
Duck Duck Go	duck.co/help/results	Privacy of search habits
ixQuick Metasearch	support.ixquick.com/index.php	Results pulled from multiple other search engines' responses

From Analysis of the Information Need to Web Searching Structure

Analyzing the information need should occur before turning to the open web and a search engine to find suitable resources there. To achieve this, and in light of the reference interview, which includes the gathering of subtle as well as explicit details, you should think like an indexer:

- What is the main concept underlying the information need?
- To what knowledge area, or subject, does it belong, in the context this community member presents? How does this facet fit within that subject area's larger whole?
- What are the most specific descriptors that can be employed to identify the topic as the question challenges aspects of understanding it?
- What expertise would be needed in order to address the topic with authority? Who has that expertise?
- How time-sensitive is the knowledge that responds to the question?
- Are there specific parameters related to comprehension, accessibility, or other constraints that the scope or breadth of the needed data should respect?

With these details in mind, you can more wisely select the most appropriate search engine and web searching techniques to suit the situation. It may be that the exercise alerts you to the likelihood that the needed information can be found most quickly through limiting an advanced search to files other than web pages, such as images or videos, that explicitly show how to build a model ship in a bottle. In other situations, this analytical reflection helps you to realize that broadening a detail in the question will increase the likelihood of finding authoritative results in a written style better suited to the general knowledge of the researcher. The intention of the reflective pause between clarifying the question and turning to the open web is the space needed to become aware that perhaps the open web is not the first most efficient place to search, but rather a database or even a book resource like a vintage bibliography of journalistic reports from an era long past may be more straightforward.

Search the open web when that large and changing universe of information makes good sense for the question's scope, the abilities of the researcher, and efficient use of time and resources, not just as an automatic first place any question is taken.

Evaluating a Website's Authority

Anyone can publish online, and anyone can pose as an expert on any subject. That doesn't mean that only government and commercial sites are authoritative, or even that, by contrast government and commercial sites are more authoritative. Instead, it means that site evaluation is an essential reference service best practice.

Websites created by amateurs and hobbyists can be the most comprehensive sources of information available, and they can be a lifesaver when looking for information that is too marginal to attract the attention of a researcher, publisher, or government agency. However, deciding when to turn to experts who publish only what they put on the web themselves requires much practice.

A website's address (URL) includes a convenient clue about the producer of its information. The first part of a web page's address, called the domain, will end in something like ".edu," ".gov," ".org," or ".com." These two- to four-letter endings indicate the type of organization that produced the website. These are some of the more common ones:

- **.edu** Example: www.stanford.edu is Stanford University. Website domains ending with ".edu" are hosted by an American institution of higher education, often a university. Typically a website affiliated with a university can be trusted to provide reliable information. But be aware that educational websites are also hosts to web pages produced by inexperienced undergraduate students, who are free to put whatever they want on their personal student web pages.[5]

- **.gov** Example: www.dot.gov is the U.S. Department of Transportation. Website domains ending in ".gov" are hosted by U.S. government agencies, at the federal or state, or even city level. Federal sites use only.gov, while domains for smaller government bodies in the United States incorporate the state or city name in the URL as well. Both government websites and commercial websites carry indicators of the nation in which they are published. U.S. federal government sites do not, for now, include "us" in the domain and are simply ".gov." The state name or the two-letter postal abbreviation for it immediately precedes ".gov" for each U.S. state's website. For example, ".ca.gov" is used by California government websites, and ".michigan.gov" by Michigan state websites. Government agencies are almost universally regarded as authoritative and are the sources of much of the statistical and research information that we use. The only thing about which to be cautious is political bias on party-member pages. Work reflected on agency pages is undertaken by employees of those offices, including a wide variety of professionals with applicable knowledge and skills, so typically their information is not politically biased, although it can be employed for political purposes.

- **.org** Example: www.ala.org belongs to the American Library Association. Website domains ending in ".org" are assigned to nonprofit organizations such as trade, industry, and professional associations; libraries and museums; and health organizations. All normally are excellent sources of reliable information. Keep in mind, however, that a host organization is not required to be a nonprofit to use this domain, and nonprofit organizations, just as for-profit and government sources, can have biased points of view.

Become more familiar with the organization using this domain before judging the reliability of the information it provides. Look at the "about us" page, and do a basic check: How long has the organization been in existence? How many members does it have? Who belongs to it?

- **.com** Example: www.amazon.com is Amazon's U.S. corporate site. Websites using ".com" are usually commercial. The primary purpose of such a website is to make money for the company in some way. If the website provides quality information, it will often be for a fee: magazines, newspapers, historic deed records, and so on. A company website can often be a good source for information about that company and its products, but in general you should approach it with the same skepticism as you would an advertisement. When such a site serves as a sales point, there may be abundant information about its products that can be accessed for free. However, bias is a necessary facet of such "free" information, even when that bias amounts to a limit on exposing information about competitors' qualities.

SIDEBAR 4 BIAS

One of the most important facets of evaluation of any resource, in any format, is the recognition of its bias. Bias itself is not a bad thing. In fact, as subjective beings, we all approach any understanding or expression with bias. What is necessary to achieve, however, is the recognition of how a resource's bias affects both the authority and the usefulness it can supply to filling an information or knowledge gap.

The evaluation questions discussed in this chapter and, in more detail, in Chapter 10 should detect the specific bias of a resource. By recognizing who said it, why they said it, what entity may have sponsored (paid for) their pronouncement's publication, when it was said, and to whom the message was addressed, specific bias becomes discernible.

Sometimes a reference question actually requires resources to reflect specific biases, such as when a community member is researching position statements or preparing for a debate. Other times, resources with different biases when brought together can help a researcher find and clarify details in one or all that aid in understanding the complete picture, as when someone checks multiple news sources to better understand an event.

Among the more subtle biases too often ignored on the web are those related to why the content has been presented, apparently for free to users. This often arises in e-commerce sites where there is a wealth of content, such as book reviews or cleaning tips, that can be accessed without charge. However, advertisers are in fact paying for the presentation of the material, so these advertisers have a stake in what is being published. The information may well be, and often is, perfectly sound. However, reference staff need to explore whether the bias compromises the information's authority.

Domain protocols are approved by an international body, the International Corporation for Assigned Names and Numbers (ICANN).[6] Other domain endings important to reference work include .net, .biz, .tv, and .info. URLs, or web addresses, for personal web pages often use the ".com" or ".net" domain endings, since these are available to the Internet service providers that host their subscribers' websites.

Each nation also has a specified URL domain. Government websites have the two-letter designation for the nation, along with clarification that the site is the official government one, noted as the domain. The codes used to express "government" are not uniform as they reflect different national languages' words for "government." Here are some examples:

- *.gc.ca*—Canadian government
- *.gov.uk*—United Kingdom's government
- *.go.jp*—Japanese government
- *.gob.es*—Spain's government
- *.gov.gh*—Ghana's government

Websites of commercial enterprises outside the United States can be formulated in several different ways. Some may have just the corporate name and the national domain (the German arm of Amazon is just amazon.de). Others use the domain ".co" or ".com" with no geographic designation. And many combine the national domain with an indication that the specific URL is a commercial enterprise:

- lawtons.ca—the URL for a Canadian drugstore chain
- costa.co.uk—the URL of a British coffee shop chain
- kodansha.co.jp—the URL of a Japanese book publisher
- cervezasalhambra.es—the URL of a Spanish beer brewer
- jumia.com.ng—the URL of a Nigerian online general retailer
- patrickroger.com—the URL for a French chocolatier

Using the URL to assess the authority of the information found on a website can be taken much further than simply checking the domain. If a site doesn't include an "About" or "Who we are" link with sufficient information to make an authority judgment, reading the URL in chunks, stopping just after each slash mark (/) can reveal the necessary insights. By looking at the root page and the subsequent pages that are layers up from the page that requires evaluation, the author or the origins and nature of the site providing the information come into focus. When uncertain about a page's authority, looking at the URL chunk immediately preceding the domain reveals the page's server, the equivalent of a book's publisher.

Here's the URL for an article titled "Exercise + Class Work May = Better Math Scores": healthfinder.gov/News/Article/708329/exercise-classwork-may-better-math-scores

The information after the final slash (/) indicates the title of the article. Moving to the next chunk to the left, we have a series of numbers, which isn't really very informative if we don't know this site (it's the record number attached to this one article in the site's articles database). One more step to the left tells us clearly that this is an article; we know from the URL, then, that what we are going to retrieve is probably a narrative piece. What kind of article is revealed by the next step to the left: it reflects news (rather than history or another type of article). Before the slash to the left of the word "News," we find the domain name and see that this is a U.S. government site, based on ".gov" here. At the far left, we see the name of the site as a whole: Healthfinder.

Let's look at another example. Here, each part of the URL being identified is in *italic* when we determine what it means and we will work left to right, as we read in English:

johnlewis.com/browse/special-offers/toys-special-offers/_/N-ei7
First we have the name of the body affiliated with this site.

johnlewis.*com*/browse/special-offers/toys-special-offers/_/N-ei7
The domain indicates that it is a commercial site.

johnlewis.com/*browse*/special-offers/toys-special-offers/_/N-ei7
Here we know we are going to look at lists, perhaps of categories this commercial site sells.

johnlewis.com/browse/*special-offers*/toys-special-offers/_/N-ei7
Instead of looking through all the categories, we are looking specifically at "special offers" or sale items.

johnlewis.com/browse/special-offers/*toys-special-offers*/_/N-ei7
Of all possible items this commercial entity might have right now, we are looking for specifically at those that are for toys.

johnlewis.com/browse/special-offers/toys-special-offers/*_/N-ei7*
These last two sections of the URL don't tell us much unless we know all about the underlying structure of the John Lewis Department Store's stock management coding. And that's okay, because we know from the parts of the URL to the left of these what we might find on this page, at least generally: toys on sale at a department store.

Recognition of the site's domain is not the end of site evaluation. Other important evaluative steps to take include the following:

- If the website provides a list of "related links" or "additional sites" look at those. Do they work? Are they well chosen? Are they annotated? Do they include other viewpoints? Do they indicate a particular bias?
- If there are hyperlinked numbers or text, which function on a website as footnote designations on a paper page, check for the documentation to which they lead. What kinds of publications or sites are they? Reputable? Scholarly? Are they real? On the web (where most pages go without any or very little editing and fact checking by a third party) it is possible to create fake references that lead nowhere.
- If locating a resource that is clearly authoritative seems unlikely, due to the nature of the question (not to time constraints), compare multiple resources. If they seem to agree on the facts, then the information can be provided to a client with the caveat that the data are not completely reliable.

RESOURCES INTENDED TO GUIDE REFERENCE STAFF TO MORE RESOURCES

With a foundation in measuring value and making the best use of resources in any format, you are ready to locate the highest-quality resources to fit your community's needs. In the next chapter, discussions of union catalogs and trade and subject bibliographies follow upon learning how to use the local catalog as a resource in itself.

Everything we have discussed to this point, including communication skills, collection dynamics, and resource evaluation criteria, ties to the how and why of catalog practices as a structural backbone of reference negotiation.

NOTES

1. Morse (1980).
2. In print as a very elaborate advertising platform, in the manner in which newspapers and the yellow pages rely on advertisers and advertisers rely on their ubiquitous distribution, for more than 200 years, *The Old Farmer's Almanac* (almanac.com) speaks to the interests of those who pursue traditional interests from canning to stargazing to fishing. While it is hardly a scientific authority, it does provide a wealth of information of use to gardeners, folklorists, and those just beginning to consider such hobbies as birding.
3. See the NAICS tables at naics.com/search/.
4. See Google's informative page "How Search Works" (google.com/intl/en_us/insidesearch/howsearchworks/index.html) for an accessible tutorial on its own tools, policies, and practices.
5. To discern whether the webpage is a personal one hosted on the university's server, check for a tilde (~) followed by a name at the end of the URL. That indicates such a personal page. It may be that of an undergraduate student, a full professor, someone no longer associated with the university, and so forth. Seeing the tilde should alert reference staff to evaluate the site further.
6. ICANN's own website (icann.org) provides a lot of instructive and informative information about the development of the recognition of websites, including policies, practices, international agreements, and how registries (URL groups) are constructed. The Internet Assigned Numbers Authority (IANA) oversees the top-level domains, such as those used by international treaty organizations and those used for mapping Internet Protocol (IP) addresses. See www.iana.org/domains for details.

CHAPTER 6

Library Catalogs and Bibliographies

This chapter explores the library catalog as a database and other resource searching tools that give both library staff and the library community access to information locations. The library catalog both lists the library's collection holdings and gives details that can take catalog users to more information in places beyond finding works to consult from the local collection.

THE ONLINE CATALOG IS A DATABASE

No matter which integrated library management system (ILS) supports the database that is your local online catalog, it operates according to some general principles shared by all such catalog systems. Understanding the fields and functions in the local online catalog helps reference staff improve search skills that will be applicable to other online databases. If your library does not yet have an online catalog, you can access WorldCat (worldcat. org), the international union catalog facility available from the Online Computer Library Center, Inc. (OCLC). Both WorldCat and most local library catalogs support and display records for resources in all formats, including e-resources such as commercial databases and e-books. While WorldCat can provide local record information that reflects only holdings in its member libraries (but does not reflect circulation status for them), exploring it as a database may prove a valuable source for availability of information beyond the local collection. It is built for library staff from all over the world to use and has excellent tutorials. You can also set it to reflect your geographic area first in any search results.

The online catalog database, and any database, is like a deck of playing cards: each record in it is different and yet each shares some similar attributes that allow a player to use specific elements of each one to bring them together according to the rules of any of various games. In some solitaire card games, a player pulls cards together that share color and ranks them according to suit. In poker, cards have specific values that are relative to each other. Even the children's card game of fish calls upon the player to make what amounts to a search command to acquire card faces with some matching elements. Searching a database, including the catalog, is abiding by the rules of the "game" you choose so that you can bring together things that match according to criteria, such as title or author, and allows you to rank the records' value, or worth in terms of your current information need. Unlike a deck of cards, the catalog may grow (or even shrink, if a major weeding is undertaken) across time in number of records.

While manipulating playing cards in an almost endless number of defined functions is required by specific games' varying rules, using the online catalog calls on the user to manipulate search strategies and terms to bring together sets of records that match expressed criteria. Like playing card games, however, "finding" each record can be undertaken by various methods, not just a single route. These include author, title, and subject search; delimiters; and keyword searching. What the searches can reveal, however, go beyond finding a record that fits the search method, which is why the catalog can be a rich source of reference support.

Searching the Catalog

Database architecture connects fields within all of its records so that a particular field search results in uncovering all records with contents that match it. A catalog database search of the *author* field for contents by someone named Johnson, for example, returns all records in which the name Johnson appears in the *author* field, regardless of whether that one name is used as a surname, first name, or middle name, as long as it is in the author field. A *title* search, for example, "All about Cars," retrieves every record reflecting that title regardless of format or location. A *subject* search, say, for "trees," pulls results matching that subject term if that subject has been entered into the record. From these examples, you can see why knowing both more precise catalog searching and awareness of where the contents in the searchable fields are found on various works to create the records boosts your ability to make stronger use of the catalog as a tool.

Author and title are assigned from the title page of the book they describe. For other formats, this information reflects title of the work and the person or body responsible for creating it (such as a film's title and its director, or a symphony and its composer as well as the orchestra who recorded it), as those names are presented in authoritative resources, such as film credits, recording inserts, and even the catalog records of other libraries owning the item. You don't have to figure out what makes an authority to follow when creating these catalog records; you do have to be aware of the fact that their contents are drawn from specific places either on the material itself or from authority files. This might explain why the title listed for a book doesn't seem to match the title on that book's cover: the information in the catalog comes from the title page, and the cover's design may have included altering "and" to "&" or omitting the subtitle, for example.

The subject, or subject tracing, applied by catalogers to each record in the catalog is limited to the standardized list of subject headings, a subject authority source.[1] This is pointed out here because a keyword search, discussed later, moves beyond the limits of a subject search. This may be the most difficult point to explain to new catalog users who do not have much experience with databases generally: "subject" and "keyword" are not interchangeable terms when applied to searching. The subject field in the catalog, no matter which list of subject headings has been used as the resource to assign these tracings, has to be limited in order to allow a subject search that can bring together returns that would be overlooked if synonyms, different abbreviations, or other nonauthoritative subject tracing terms were applied in the subject field. If you search for the subject "furniture finishing," an authoritative subject heading, and a cataloger has instead decided to call the subject of one book in the collection on this broad topic "refurbishing furniture," it would not be found in your subject search. The whole purpose of strict subject headings is to apprise catalog searchers of where in the collection information on the specified topic can be found.

Delimiters in the online catalog allow the searcher to do more efficient retrievals by applying filters to a search. If you have shopped online, you probably have experience with delimiters: these allow you to narrow results of an initial search by specific criteria so you don't have to wade through records that, while matching in author, title, and/or subject tracings, won't fit the information need at hand right now. Most online catalogs have the following delimiters:

- Format: Is this a book? A CD? An e-book?
- Status: Is the material available and on the shelf? Has it been noted as missing? Is it unavailable due to repair work on it? Is it in transit from one site to another? Is it on a hold shelf and available only to the party whose request that it be held is current? Is this the only request or is there a queue awaiting this item when it is returned?
- Language: Is the work held in a specific language? Which language(s)?
- Collection: Where in the library system is the material or item "at home"? Is it part of the children's or reference collection? Knowing the collection suggests the material's intended use.
- Location: Where can you locate the item in a library system? Related to Status and Collection, this delimiter provides information about in which building of a library system the item can be found, including which sites own copies.

Beyond delimiters, many online catalogs support searching records by *keyword*. This can be a powerful searching strategy because it moves the user beyond the rigid subject heading list used by catalogers. However the keywords selected for searching should be carefully chosen in order to ensure efficient and effective searching. Making use of keyword searching can turn up records not found using the official subject headings, but it can also leave unfound records where a subject heading search might have found both more complete and more specific information. Therefore, using both a subject search and a keyword search may be necessary in some search situations, and choosing which of the two might be a better starting point becomes a skill improved through practice of both.

Here's an example:

A keyword search using "science fair" may retrieve over a hundred records. However, if the searcher's intent was to locate instructions for building science fair projects, a more useful retrieval list is returned with a subject search "science projects" or a subject search with the type of science, such as chemistry, within the list of authority terms: "chemistry—experiments." That latter subject heading in a search (by subject) returns fewer than 25 records in the same collection. However, none of them are fiction books about science fairs and all of them are specific to the type of information being sought.

One keyword search that can aid exploration in many ILS catalog structures is a search that seeks a specific descriptor of the material that may be recorded only in the record note fields. For example, while a keyword search such as "illustrated" on its own across an entire catalog may retrieve a useless number of records, including that keyword in the catalog's advance search along with author or title or subject can be productive. Seeking a closed caption video in the collection, if that term is not a subject heading, can be undertaken with a keyword search once the collection has been limited to material type (such as DVD). Keyword searching is an excellent way to gain access to any content notes or synopsis included in a record where the keyword of interest is highly unique and unlikely to be included in the author, subject, or title fields of the record. For example, "moral imperative" is not a standard subject heading, but it is an expression likely to have been used within a few materials within the collection, and may be recorded in the records for them in notes fields that list anthology contents or a synopsis of the work.

Becoming fluent in the functions of the catalog is an essential skill for reference staff. In many libraries, staff and the public are provided with interfaces that differ not only in appearance but also in functionality. When engaged in work with the community, reference staff need to be mindful of guiding them in the public-facing catalog, which means you need to understand how it works as well as understand how the staff interface may work differently. If staff find that some operations necessary for community work are not functioning in the public mode of the ILS, refer this as a problem to be resolved to the appropriate administrative division or leader. Differences in appearance are fine, and there are many ILS functions (such as user records) that should not be exposed to the community. However, the functionality of the catalog should be optimal for both staff and the public to locate records reflecting available information resources.

Documentation of e-Resources in the Local Catalog

The documentation of available e-books, subscription databases, and third-party services that provide access to e-content, whether downloadable for a loan period or via streaming in real time, is complex. How well this is accomplished varies according to local cataloging practices. For reference staff, this is significant when local cataloging practices obscure specific records except when viewing the titles directly or accessing a third-party connection, such as another library's catalog, in favor of the local catalog.

Ideally, a library's resource content, regardless of format, would receive representation in the local catalog that allows someone using the catalog to discern such elements as availability, subject, and location markings in the way that call numbers provide these descriptors for content identification purposes. Both staff and the public can be frustrated by the inability to narrow a search for e-resources according to delimiters that are permitted with material resources. At this time, many small libraries, for example (and even larger ones), use the term "e-book" as the only subject heading for any title held in this format. Further, the call number for all the e-books in the collection is the same, regardless of where that e-book content would be placed if it were a paperbound book. How useless it is to be unable to search for a specific subject knowing you will not locate any of the library's e-books in that subject search or even by call number search!

Using the Catalog as an Information Resource in Itself

While the use of the library's catalog typically relates to the search to locate specific items in the collection, the catalog's bibliographic records themselves can answer a wealth of questions. Whether the item to which a record corresponds is physically available, the record remains accessible and complete. The catalog record supplies the following:

- Correct spellings of proper names
- Full names of authors and illustrators
- Correct names of corporate authors
- Contents notes for anthologies, which may include the correct titles of individual poems or other short literary works
- Publisher's name and the place of publication
- Publication dates, including that of the currently held edition and often previous and original publication dates
- Length of the work, in page numbers, running time, or other measures that fit the medium of the title
- Links to pseudonyms associated with an author so that all of his or her works can be located regardless of which name he or she used for which publication
- Authoritative (or uniform) titles of works translated to English
- Original titles of works originally published in another language
- Current Romanization authority of proper names and titles translated from languages using Cyrillic, Chinese, or other writing system

In addition to finding resources in your own catalog, many libraries belong to consortia with shared catalogs. Having instant availability to such record information as appears in the aforementioned list for contents that may be in another library expands the information pool reflected in the catalog records even further. Knowing that another resource is available in a nearby library is useful. Even more useful, however, is having access to such facts as those listed earlier even if your own library doesn't include such information in the local catalog. Having such details can help you to create more accurate web searches for information beyond your collection.

OCLC WorldCat

Moving beyond the local consortium, you can access OCLC's WorldCat from anywhere that is web-enabled, including your computer or a mobile device such as your phone. This database is a massive compilation of records with a sophisticated, user-friendly database function, and OCLC allows anyone to set the geographic proximity from which you do your usual searching so the results of your search also indicate how close the actual item may be in a library collection. WorldCat includes items in every format currently collected by libraries, including books, periodicals, film, sound recordings, e-resources, and other electronic files. It even allows you to search for specific articles, although you won't be able to read them without accessing the library where they are part of the collection. Because OCLC serves libraries throughout the world, any language in which collected items have been published is included in the catalog.

Because OCLC's development of this database is authoritative, WorldCat makes good contemporary use of such new discovery strategies as user tagging. User tagging is a record annotation that indicates a user's suggested terms for identifying the resource's content so this can supplement and enlarge upon formal subject headings supplied by catalogers in preparing the formal records for each item. Tags are presented in their own field and identified as such so there is no confusion about what is an authoritative subject heading and what is a user tag.

Reference staff should first train themselves in good database searching methods before they can exploit any catalog to its full potential. WorldCat offers a great way to pursue this personal staff development as OCLC also provides a suite of tutorials and documentation (oclc.org/support/home.en.html) to help the new searcher.

In some libraries, reference staff are responsible for initiating interlibrary loan (ILL) requests, for which they may make use of WorldCat. However, even if you are not looking for a title to borrow for a client through WorldCat's records, this resource is essential to know for spell-checking unusual and foreign names, whether newer materials are available on a very narrow subject, the pseudonyms under which authors have published (if your own catalog doesn't include that), and even the names of research institutions that seem to be doing a lot of publishing about certain areas of information, such as clinical drug trials in which a client may be interested in participating. If your library has limited access to periodical indexes, you can also use WorldCat to search for articles by keyword, author, or subject, and further delimit the search by journal name if there is a preference for a specific publication source, such as one in your collection.

OCLC regularly shares experiments in knowledge management they are undertaking. At the time of this book's writing, the WorldCat Identities Network (experimental. worldcat.org/idnetwork/) offers the possibility to see and create visual aids to show connections between and among subjects. This offers reference staff quick and free access to learning about how infographics and other maps of related concepts can advance understanding of which pieces of information may be important in a search and how they might be connected to other subjects. This can prompt you to double-check possible alternative subjects and keywords to employ when a catalog search leaves you feeling stuck.

Teaching Others Efficient Use of the Library Catalog

Learning the fields and functions of the catalog is an essential skill not only for reference staff but also for the public your catalog is intended to serve as a resource to finding information and collection items. Your library mission may not directly suggest reference staff act as teachers (although many public libraries do include lifelong learning for their clients in the library's strategic objectives), but many who are unaccustomed to library organization of knowledge and collections may need a direct lesson in catalog data retrieval. Online literacy continues to grow in importance in contemporary communities. Online catalogs provide many more entry points to a contents search than did the old card catalogs (and searching the card catalog was not a skill that every library user had learned or could use a second time if the period of time between learning the first time and a later use was years apart). What you know about your community's online comfort with activities like banking and shopping can help you to determine how comfortable they may be, in general, with database searching. However, there will always be outliers, those who don't have online experiences like these as well as those who work in jobs centered on database building or manipulation.[2]

Union Catalogs

Many librarians make use of a union catalog to find resources that can be obtained through ILL. Some such union catalogs, such as Link+ (csul.iii.com/screens/linkplusinfo. html), which offers coverage of member library collections throughout California and parts of Nevada, and OhioLink (ohiolink.edu/content/about_ohiolink), which does the same for many academic libraries in that state, can be utilized directly by community members for ILL delivery. Requests for the transference of a desired item to the user's local library is initiated by the person who wants it, rather than by local library staff intervening to make the request. These two serve as excellent examples of union catalogs that are truly public and allow the public to interact with the actual collections libraries belonging to that union hold. Other union catalogs require library staff intercession for ILL and may, through that, create abridgements to such broad access as paywalls for ILL requests.

In either situation, reference staff members should be able to provide guidance to community members who cannot find needed material at the local library and want to try to locate it elsewhere. In the situation where the client's home library charges for ILL or does not even provide ILL services, you as the reference service staff must explore whether the requested item contains information that can be found through another means, such as searching the web. Even if your library supports staff-initiated ILL, a delay until the item can arrive may be a problem for this particular client in this particular situation. Make sure that your reference interview addresses the expected delay and goes beyond identifying an ILL solution to, perhaps, a way of resolving the information need through the resources your library does have, including your web searching skills.

BIBLIOGRAPHIES AS INFORMATION FINDING AIDS

While catalogs provide access to collections of content in the library, bibliographies provide collected citations, which, in some ways, are much like catalog records because they describe resources and indicate where to locate them in the publishing world.

In the previous chapter, the information construct of the bibliography was discussed. Both reference collection development and reference information searching make use of two types of bibliographies: those that are constructed and published by trade publishers to show what is available commercially and thus available for inclusion in a collection, and those that are collected and published to reflect research sources related to a topic. Both types of bibliographies may be published in paper format or online, and both may reflect contents gathered from many different publishers. Reference staff make use of both types of bibliography in order to identify where to find, or even acquire, appropriate content addressing a particular area, whether it is the need to cover a subject, or perspective on a subject, or to complete a collection of works by an author.

Trade Bibliographies: What's Available to Acquire?

Bibliographies from publishers and businesses that sell to libraries[3] have recently been joined by multimedia services that provide e-content to libraries as well.[4] While typically used as general collection development tools, such commercial bibliographies can supply reference service staff with additional information as well.

Information sources available for reference work will always be greater than what one library has on hand. Trade bibliographies offer the means of identifying additional and alternative resources for librarians to consider including in the collection or referring clients to access elsewhere (such as through ILL or as a less expensive e-book the client may want to purchase independently). Trade bibliographies also inform reference staff of alternatives to traditional reference standard texts, which may be less than ideally accessible to community members, with titles that do provide linguistic, visual, auditory, and other communication refinements to better reach community needs.

Specialty publisher bibliographies, such as those developed by publishing houses and delivered as promotional catalogs, provide early awareness of new publications that may not appear in review sources for months or even more than a year. As quality information becomes increasingly time-sensitive in nature, knowing today that a work has been published, with its content description and authors noted, can be important for tomorrow's question: even though the new title isn't available yet, you now know the names of some authors who seem to specialize in that area and can search databases and the web to find information they have already published on that topic. Such specialty bibliographies can also help you plan reference budgets more accurately as they show how much new books in a certain field are costing. Prices may seem too high to warrant your library ordering these materials; however, you now know that older information on the topic is outdated and should be examined in your collection and that up-to-date information should be sought through web and other low-cost resources.

Subject Bibliographies

Unlike bibliographies that are provided to promote publisher sales, subject bibliographies provide reference staff and other researchers with information unrelated to sales or prices. In the previous chapter, we discussed bibliographies as they relate to a book or journal article's parts. Here we are turning to volumes, online lists, and publications of subject bibliographies in library literature like *Library Journal* and *Booklist*. Subject bibliographies include both new and older resources, as long as the older ones are still available and exemplary.

If your library's reference staff are charged with reference collection development, you are likely to face the need to explore knowledge sectors with which you are relatively unfamiliar. You can find reliable guidance in subject bibliographies prepared by subject experts, which, if not present in your own collection, can be obtained for use through ILL. For example, a bibliography of science experiments and projects can guide your development of the collection with wise choices for inclusion that reflects this area of information. The most useful subject bibliography is annotated so that each entry in it is described with sufficient, although concise, detail to allow you to decide whether the listed work may be appropriate and helpful to an ongoing information quest. Like the bibliography attached to a book or journal article, the subject bibliography's entries include formal citations listing the following details:

- Party responsible for intellectual content of the entry, such as author(s), corporate, or others
- Title of specific work attributed to this author at this entry

- Location of that work, if within a compilation or journal or other collection such as papers presented at a specific conference
- Place and date of publication
- Other details specific to the type of content, such as whether it includes maps and illustrations
- Annotation

Subject bibliographies may be grouped into larger bibliographic works that a librarian would reasonably consider as a coherent and focused collection. An example of this is the picture-book bibliography *A to Zoo*, which, as its subtitle notes, provides *Subject Access to Children's Picture Books*. The thousands of entries here are arranged into a number of different bibliographies, each arranged by subject addressed by the picture books included in it. Subject bibliographies provide guidance for topical inquiries in virtually any realm of knowledge. Consider the following examples:

- Biblical translations—*Catalogue of English Bible Translations: A Classified Bibliography of Versions and Editions Including Books, Parts, and Old and New Testament Apocrypha and Apocryphal Books* (Greenwood Press, 1991)
- Authors fitting specific identity criteria—*Caribbean Women Novelists: An Annotated Critical Bibliography* (Greenwood Press, 1993)
- Authors and/or books contributing to a specific literary genre—*Academe in Mystery and Detective Fiction: An Annotated Bibliography* (Scarecrow Press, 2000)
- Civic and planning studies—*Compact Cities: Everyday Life, Governance and the Built Environment, An Annotated Bibliography and Literature* Review (University of Auckland, 2009)
- Social and political issues keyed to a time and/or place—*Children and Youth in Africa: Annotated Bibliography, 2001–2011* (Council for the Development of Social Sciences Research in Africa [2014])
- Science and scientific history by discipline—*Astronomy: A Short List of Books for Beginners* (State Library of Louisiana, 2009)

Subject bibliographies located in narrative books treating specific topics also point you to specific titles to seek for subject development. For instance, a narrative book that presents theories and reports events concerning the Great Depression should contain a bibliography of primary sources as well as citations to books written by others. It would include newspaper articles, locations of pictures used to illustrate the text, and perhaps lists of films depicting this period of history. These resources in the bibliography offer a writer who consults the bibliography with many ways to find additional information. Biographies of politicians, philosophers, and other theorists who may themselves have written extensively often include valuable bibliographies of that subject's publications.

Increasingly, subject bibliographies can be found on the open web. As with any web-based resource, due diligence must be undertaken to evaluate the authority of the source providing a subject bibliography.

Because the word "bibliography" is itself a subject term, WorldCat can be deployed to search for subject bibliographies by using the advance search. State libraries also provide subject bibliographies on matters that are specific to the state, such as all the publications known about its indigenous Native American groups or titles to suggest to families with children in public Individual Learning Plan programs. If sent from an agency like the state library to all libraries in that state, whether in paper or online form, there may be no record in the local library's catalog noting such a bibliography is available.

Needing to keep subject bibliographies that are part of the reference collection up to date varies with the bibliography's scope. In the case of a bibliography reflecting current picture-book choices available, the need for maintaining the latest edition is obvious. However, in the case of bibliographies that reflect publications of a specific historic period, the need is less, and some masterful bibliographies appear only in a single edition so that, while they reflect publication only to that point in time, they nonetheless provide valuable background to future information gatherers.

WHERE WE GO FROM HERE

In the next three chapters, we will discuss particular types of reference materials, and core titles reflective of each. Best practices in the collection development, maintenance, and reference use of these resources will be illustrated through drawing connections between knowledge needs and authority identification.

In the chapters ahead, the titles mentioned should be viewed with awareness of one's own community needs and concerns. In addition, the methods and venues by and through which reference services are provided influence the suitability of specific material and resource types for the reader's situation. These next chapters rely on your having acquired a deep understanding of the essential best practices related to communication, resource evaluation, and community awareness at the local level. Reviewing the earlier chapters may be helpful before moving forward.

NOTES

1. Standard subject heading authorities in widespread use in North America include Library of Congress Subject Headings (LCSH) (id.loc.gov/authorities/subjects.html); Sears List of Subject Headings, which is available by subscription from EBSCO (ebscohost.com/public/sears-list-of-subject-headings), as well as in print format; and the Book Industry Study Group (BISAC) Subject Headings (bisg.org/complete-bisac-subject-headings-2014-edition).
2. See Pew Fact Tank (July 28, 2015) "15% of Americans Don't Use the Internet. Who Are They?" (pewresearch.org/fact-tank/2015/07/28/15-of-americans-dont-use-the-internet-who-are-they/).
3. Sometimes called "jobbers," companies that work with libraries to provide publications from a variety of publishing and production sources include the likes of Baker & Taylor, Ingram, and Mackin.
4. Such platform distributors include OverDrive, Hoopla, Zinio, and others that typically concentrate on specific media types, including audiobooks, video content, and magazines.

CHAPTER 7

Understanding the Role of Serials in Knowledge Publishing

Serials include a variety of titles published across time and with the publisher's expectation that volumes and issues shall continue to be presented into the future. Many are published at regular and stated intervals, including daily, weekly, monthly, several times a year, annually, and at intervals measuring several years. The most common serials include the following:

- Newspapers
- Journals
- Magazines
- Yearbooks or annuals

Serials as a resource developed between the arrival of relatively broad access to the printing press, accompanied by affordable paper stocks, and the transformation made by online publication to the capacity to produce renewed content more quickly and without regard to physical distribution requirements. Serials continue to play an important role in many areas of knowledge publication and so continue to be important for reference service providers to recognize and use effectively.

SERIALS AND REFERENCE CONCERNS

Many different types of information, including travel guidance, local to international news, and even directories like phone books, and many publishing entities, including government agencies, trade publishers, and schools, can be identified within the broad class of serials. Each serial type has specific attributes that reference staff should recognize, such as frequency of likely new editions (such as a yearbook appearing, we expect, annually). Like other bibliographic terms, words related to serials publication describe important details; they aren't jargon. Each type of serial also offers a specific type of research help, ranging from newspapers' coverage of current events to journals that provide research articles.

Newspapers

Newspapers, so named in English because of their broad content subject and their affiliation with publication on stock that could be printed and distributed with relative ease, provide reports of contemporary events and are usually supported through advertisers' funding. Newspapers typically have editorial direction from a publisher and utilize the work of both staff and freelance contributors. Syndication has developed as an element of content acquisition by many newspapers; syndication is the means by which the publisher acquires specific content (although not usually feature stories that are developed locally or by freelancers) on an ongoing or an as-needed basis.

What this means for researchers is that indexing of newspapers often won't include "everything" in any issue. Staff-written articles are indexed; syndicated contents may be indexed elsewhere. Interviewing someone who is seeking specific newspaper content can be thorough and still does not identify the content the person believes was contained in that newspaper.

Another element of newspaper production detail is the advertising content as a source of information. While advertising is a major part of the funding for newspapers, this isn't and hasn't been indexed. A few ads may be available in book collections published as curiosity browsing volumes showing reproductions of historic newspaper advertisements. Other books may have references to information gleaned from studying both the major advertisements and the classified notices[1] in a newspaper from a particular time and place. Classified notices can have great value to researchers looking for genealogical, economic, and other historical social information. They present accurate pictures of housing costs, job market trends at a specific time and place, ads for grocery stores detailing food costs and availability of specific foods, and so forth.

Another area of poor to nonexistent indexing concerns vital records. Birth notices, marriage announcements, and obituaries in local newspapers receive less than ideal indexing attention from major publishers. To locate these, a hand search of the actual newspaper, or examination of its digitized images, is probably going to be necessary. Some excellent online resources for some communities can be located through the Newspaper Archives, Indexes & Morgues site maintained by the Library of Congress (loc.gov/rr/news/oltitles. html), which includes links to digitized collections of such newspaper contents from a variety of U.S. newspapers. Depending on the age of the locality served by a newspaper and local interest in its history, indexing these contents of historic newspaper files can be enormously satisfying as a reference service if no such resource has been created already. While you and your library staff likely don't have time to do this directly, you can help the community identify an appropriate grant opportunity and agency that could expand the worth of the historic local paper or microformat newspaper files you have in the library's collection. In a later chapter, we will discuss digitized and digital collections of all kinds as reference resources.

Magazines

Magazines are a type of serial that is "periodical" in their publication and distribution. In this context, the term *periodical* indicates the scheduled publication of a serial, usually on a weekly, monthly, or bimonthly basis. Magazines provide content focused on specific areas of interest or concerns, from hunting, fashion, housekeeping, and spirituality to computer repair, video-gaming, and many others. Like newspapers, the contents are created by staff employed by the publisher and directed by editors, with some inclusion of freelance material. Also, like newspapers, most magazines derive their income from paid advertisers, who typically represent commercial concerns allied with the focus of the magazine's editorial content. For example, a magazine concerned with muscle cars and targeting car enthusiasts is more likely to rely on advertisers of motor oil and automobile cleaning products than on those promoting vitamins or high-end formal wear.

Magazines have been in publication for a short time in comparison to newspapers, with the first published in America appearing about 50 years before the American Revolution. Indexing the contents of English language magazines has been fairly good since *Poole's Index to Periodical Literature* began publication early in the 19th century (and now covers content back to 1802). For a century, the *Readers' Guide to Periodical Literature* continued *Poole's* work. Today, EBSCOhost provides the *Readers' Guide* as a subscription database, with indexing reaching back to 1983. Like newspaper indexes, these general magazine indexes cover only published content and specific volume, issue, and page numbers on which to find them. Like newspapers, too, advertising in magazines can be a valuable research tool for historians and those examining social and even technical histories. Databases providing the contents of contemporary magazines do not provide any coverage of the advertising, so a researcher would have to find print or microformat copies of the titles to pursue locating the information found in magazines' advertising content.

Journals

Like magazines, journals are periodicals, reaching publication on a calendar-specified basis. Unlike magazines, journal contents are the work of contributors whose draft submissions undergo evaluation by a board of their peers. Journals typically provide access to professional and research writings, which can range from scientific to literary. Some journals carry a few advertising pages. However, financial support for the journal does not derive exclusively or even in more than a small part from third parties. The financing of journals comes from the hosting professional or academic organization that publishes it, or from an endowment concerned with the discipline the journal represents.

A few journals are indexed in general serials indexes noted in the Magazines section previously. However, for the most part, journal contents are indexed by services and publications focusing on the discipline addressed by the journal. Among such indexing guides are the following:

- *Science Citation Index* (now a subscription database from Reuters named Science Citation Index Expanded)

- *Social Sciences Citation Index* (now a subscription database from Reuters retaining its original name)
- *Index Medicus* (1879–2004 coverage), which has been replaced by the freely available MEDLINE index of medical journals
- *Essay and General Literature Index* (now a subscription database from EBSCOhost)

Reference staff must be able to select and efficiently use the correct indexing tool to discover journal contents pertinent to fulfilling a need. Although some general indexes, such as Gale's General Onefile, can aid in locating article coverage in popular magazines and a few specialized journals, using the indexing tool that specifically addresses information published in professional serials is a standard search choice.

Annuals

Some serials are published on an annual schedule. Typically, the coverage of these works addresses directory information, as the local telephone book, or a record of the previous year's achievements in a specific discipline, reflected in the *American Reference Books Annual* and any kind of almanac. Because annuals are time-specific and reflective of the immediate past that can be expected to impact the immediate present, their value varies from community to community. For example, a run of old phone books that reflect who was present in the community in the past decade, quarter century, or century can be of great value to ancestry and family tree researchers. Maintaining the current and one five-year-old telephone book, on the other hand, offers no added benefit (unless a particular researcher just happened to need only that five-year-old version). Those annuals deemed to be important to the community for historic purposes should be retained and missing years requested from potential donors. An example of this would be the local high school year book: if your library has a run of most years and is missing the annuals for 1992 and 2000, ask the community if anyone has a copy of one or the other to donate.

Many annuals are now available online. These are typically through paid subscriptions and maintaining backfiles is possible as book producers continue to provide the print analog for the most used or referenced annuals. However, budget constraints in many libraries require making a wise decision between continuing to purchase the annual so that the past record is maintained in future years or responding to needs for the speed of searching for current information from the current online subscription. Rather than deciding that all such annuals will be treated to one format or the other, it is wiser to make a subject-by-subject decision based on the information needs of your community.

Catalogs

Less popular now than before the advent of established and sophisticated e-commerce via the web, paper catalogs of goods—from peanut brittle to electron microscope parts—are another serial publication. An example of a catalog currently still in print is the *Standard Catalog of Vintage Baseball Cards*. Most catalogs have moved online. A few specialty ones that have been standards in print before moving to the web may be useful in your local reference work, such as Sweets (sweets.construction.com/QuickLinks/productcatalogs), which provides access to construction products, or Thomas Scientific (http://www.thomassci.com), which has been in the chemical and science instrument supply business since 1900. Now that such catalogs are online they are no longer serials.

SUBSCRIPTION DATABASES AND PERIODICAL ACCESS

With an understanding of the dynamic aspects of serials publishing and periodical access through indexing, the next step is to understand the formats through which periodicals and some other serials are currently available to consumers. Understanding these contractual and practical constraints of online subscriptions includes awareness of both the indexing and the amount of content that is available in the database once the resource citation is located.

Database access to citation searching through such indexing fields as article subject, author, title, and keyword may also provide at least some of the articles' content, in the form of abstracts. Newspapers themselves, while continuing to be published in traditional format, often provide access to content that may become available once or throughout the day. This may vary from what is made available to different types of subscribers and in different regions of the country. As newspapers continue to expand their online reporting, online report subscriptions (not to be confused with open web news reports) may, in some instances, be more expansive than the paper-based report.

In addition to these already-more complex possibilities for selecting subscriptions and access routes, third parties, such as subscription databases from companies like EBSCO and Gale Cengage, contract with many periodicals to provide unified databases that serve as location tools (indexes), abstracting services, and repositories of full content (minus advertising copy). Unlike the individual publisher's subscription product, such third-party aggregators allow the researcher to locate articles from diverse publications in a single search. In many cases, the backfiles the aggregator database retains may be deeper than those available on the individual title's own site because the content has been enriched with multimedia from other authoritative resources such as reporters' news footage or related interviews with the newsmakers.

Understanding Embargoes

Embargoes create periods of time between the original publication of a periodical issue and the availability of it in a third-party commercial database. Commercial databases, which collect third-party content from periodicals, typically are required by the original publishers to allow that first seller of the periodical time to provide the work in the marketplace and profit from its sale before the database company can assume the right to offer it to the market through the database's services. Contracts with each publication the aggregating database includes that allow the database company to reproduce content vary. The embargo clause in each contract states whether and for how long the database producer must wait before new content from the original publication appears in the database so that the original publisher can maintain rights for selling the information as its sole source for a brief period of time.

A database that reflects the contents of many different journals, newspapers, or other periodicals usually has different contracts with each original publisher, which means that the embargo period on content from one source may differ from the length of the embargo period for another original publishing source. To find out the exact embargo period for each content publisher in a given database, you should regularly check the database contents page where this information is reported. Contracts may change, so an embargo period with one newspaper that may have been 10 days could become 5 or 20 days. When clients show disappointment in being unable to access the very latest issue in a database, you can show them this contents page and explain the embargo period for the title in question.

Commercial Periodical Database Purchase Decisions

Commercial third-party databases can be costly subscriptions in themselves. It is also important to keep in mind that they are only subscriptions: you are not purchasing the database's contents, so if the parameters of access to that database change, you may not retain access to contents previously available to you through it. Determining the most suitable databases for subscription then means a careful analysis of titles in different vendors' databases and reviewing the database company's past performance as a stable provider of content. In areas where databases are shared through state-wide or consortium purchasing, subscriptions tend to be multiyear. That means your library knows what its share of the cost will be for several budget cycles; however, it also means that if the database's coverage becomes less useful, you could be stuck until the subscription term ends and the consortium selects a substitute.

Because third-party commercial periodicals databases have been available for nearly 30 years, database publisher reputations can be evaluated and the stability of coverage can be viewed across substantial time. Among the chief entrants in this publishing market, in terms of fee-for-subscription multi-title full-text access, are the following:

- EBSCOhost (ebscohost.com/title-lists)
- Gale Cengage (solutions.cengage.com/Gale/Database-Title-Lists/)
- ProQuest Newsstand (proquest.com/products-services/newsstand.html)

This is not a comprehensive list, and each of the companies noted earlier provides dozens of different periodical (and other e-resource) database packages. Among the tools the vendors listed earlier provide are some that streamline both discovery and citation to specific periodical articles needed in a wide array of subjects. This includes the capacity to e-mail full-text articles directly from the database to the client requiring the content and the documentation of correct citation style(s) at the article level.

USING ARCHIVAL SERIALS SOURCES

The longest typical backfile reach of most periodical databases is 30 years. Locating information in serials sources that are more than 30 years old requires the use of data stored outside online subscription services. Some of these storage systems reflect mid-20th-century technologies, while others are developing with cutting-edge software and protocols, such as in-house and commercial digitizing, open source sharing of publishers' own digitized archives, and projects mounted by agencies like the Digital Public Library of America, which will be discussed in Chapter 11.

Microforms: Fiche, Film, and the Machines to Read Them

Until the advent of modern computer databases and digitizing technologies, backfiles of periodicals were stored in two basic ways: the paper issues were maintained as such or in bound volumes, or the paper was microphotographed and made available on film (reels) or fiche (sheets). Microphotography preserved many periodicals that would have otherwise disappeared because paper degrades quickly outside regulated environments. Microfilm and microfiche, then, became the preferable method through which to store and retain backfiles of many newspapers and other periodicals. In addition to preserving the content, these formats reduced the storage needed for backfiles.

In order to access these microfilm and microfiche backfiles, special equipment is required. Ongoing maintenance of the equipment has become increasingly difficult in many places. If these formats are your only source of information for back issues of periodicals, you and your staff must be able to use the available equipment and, if it is accessible to the public, be ready to help others make use of it.

Microfiche readers have fewer working parts than do film readers as they don't have reels and the sheet being viewed can be moved efficiently by hand between the glass plates holding it under the magnifier and bulb. Some government offices continue to produce materials in this format, including death record lists and even state statutes, so depending on your community, you may need to be able to access fiche. If that is the case, there are still bulbs to keep replacing and the glass plates also need replacement due to breakage through normal use, so budgeting for these peripherals is necessary. Unlike microfilm, the orientation of documents on the fiche has not even yet been standardized, so each fiche requires a moment's appraisal as to where its content begins and in which direction it moves across the sheet.

Digitized Collections

At the opposite end of the technology continuum supporting archival serials access is the growing abundance of digitized resources, which are discussed both here and later in the book. While such resources go far beyond serials preservation alone, digitized serials archives provide the full view of information appearing in the original source. Unlike databases, the capacity to view advertising and classified copy is restored, as is the ability to understand the relative local importance of news stories based on their page and section arrangements within the digitized newspaper. Researchers can trace the social and fashion changes occurring across time revealed in photos and drawings of consumer products and models. These kinds of information meet a variety of information needs posed by students, genealogists, and other researchers, as well as pique curiosity among browsers because they provide context in which to better understand the world in which the news itself was being reported.

Among digitized newspaper resources of potential value to most libraries are the following:

- Chronicling America: Historic American Newspapers, 1836–1922, from the Library of Congress (chroniclingamerica.loc.gov), which is freely available to all users
- Newspapers.com, affiliated with ancestry.com (newspapers.com/papers/), is part of that company's subscription service
- ProQuest Historical Newspapers includes both U.S. and international papers (proquest.com/products-services/pq-hist-news.htm) and is also a subscription option, costing an amount that the company develops based on population size

In addition to newspapers, another serial that is a popular subject for a digitizing project is the academic yearbook. Yearbooks have value beyond offering a way to recall former classmates' faces or names. They are often used in background checks for writing articles about individuals who have just made the news, whether as astronauts or serial killers. Family members refer to them when planning celebrations of milestone events such as 50th anniversary parties for high school sweethearts or funerals for youth. To locate these, check:

- E-Yearbook (e-yearbook.com) offers subscription access to both high school and university yearbooks from many institutions in the United States.
- Digitalization projects being undertaken at nearby universities, if existing, can save you the expense of accessing a commercial digital or database product to reflect the contents of these yearbooks.
- Video yearbooks have been popular with high schools for over a decade and add the value of preserving voice and action, as well as image, in the yearbook record.

In Chapter 11, you will find information about how the library staff might pursue a local digitizing project to do this type of electronic data preservation.

Be aware that accessing yearbooks through such popular channels as Classmates.com is not advised. Sites like this are collecting data from would-be yearbook viewers as their primary business venture. They are much less interested in providing access to existing data files.

BECAUSE WE CAN'T KNOW SOMETHING ABOUT EVERYTHING

Reference service requires substantiation of anything you or your staff believe you already know through confirming it in independent sources before offering it as a correct answer. It is always easier to start searching for information when you know the topic. However, there are times when someone needs accurate and relevant information about a topic about which you know nothing or very little. In the next chapter, tools are introduced that can help you to start to find out something authoritative about almost every topic. They will not, of course, make you an expert in any subject; instead, you will be an expert in knowing where to begin the search.

NOTE

1. Classified advertisements are brief notices publicizing or requesting immediately available goods and services, such as jobs, housing, or pet location. Unlike the paid advertising that provides and has provided newspaper monies, classifieds are clumped together in one place, each granted a few lines, and paid by the advertising party at a minimum rate for a few days. Much of the classified market has moved online to such sites as Craigslist, which is freely accessible on the web to readers and which charges for the inclusion of such announcements.

CHAPTER 8

Background Information
and Definitions:
Encyclopedias and Dictionaries

In this chapter, the variety of general and specialized resources that provide background information and definitions is discussed. These specific resources are arranged here by the type, encyclopedia or dictionary. The discussion is organized topically, rather than according to format. This approach recognizes the fluid nature of current reference publishing and serves as a reminder that you need to think *first* of what is needed rather than whether to search in an online encyclopedia or a print one for suitable information.

ENCYCLOPEDIAS

As explained in Chapter 5, works called "encyclopedias" provide information contextualizing the topics they address. An encyclopedia's articles are usually written by a variety of authors, often by persons who specialize in the subject or topic discussed within the article.

Encyclopedias in print format are typically organized alphabetically, according to the major articles, with indexing to guide the researcher to content found on that topic in other articles. Those in online or e-book formats include hyperlinks within articles to guide the reader to related information within the encyclopedia. Print encyclopedias may not necessarily be alphabetically arranged. Other popular arrangements of print encyclopedias include the following:

- Thematic, with the themes themselves comprising facets of the major subject of the work—for example, a print encyclopedia of animal life may be arranged according to classification (mammal, bird, etc.) and within each of these major classifications by species (canines, raptors).
- Chronological, with eras of the history pertinent to the subject of the full work appearing in time order—for example, a print encyclopedia of fashion may be organized by sections that move from 1000 CE through 2000 CE.
- Geographic, with articles arranged by country, continent, or sphere. For example, a print encyclopedia of education may group its articles about education systems in each country by arranging the articles for countries in groups by continent.

Print encyclopedias are accessed using the alphabetic arrangement or by the table of contents for thematic or chronologic encyclopedias. It is essential to use the index in almost every search to make certain that all relevant information in the encyclopedia has been discovered. Both *See* and *See also* references, discussed when we examined how indexes are organized, are important to note and follow up when working with print encyclopedia indexes. Online encyclopedias, whether database in structure, e-book, or on the web, don't require these because such references are embedded as hyperlinks.

In contrast, encyclopedias presented online, whether via database, e-book, or the open web, can be accessed through keyword. However, both database and e-book encyclopedias do include indexes, and checking these is helpful because it is the indexing that shows whether the topic is actually treated in this encyclopedia or, although found in the text through a keyword search, is only a passing detail noted in an article about some other topic.

Encyclopedia information included in a database offers the benefit of presenting reliably up-to-date information in contrast with print encyclopedias that need to be replaced with newer editions in order to gain new information. For example, the database encyclopedia that forms part of EBSCO's Explora database, *Funk & Wagnall's New World Encyclopedia*, is maintained within the database with the latest edition. The encyclopedia articles here also are immediately presented with even more up-to-date references drawn from other resources (such as journal articles).

E-book encyclopedias, where pages are presented as they have been in traditional print, carry the added quality of showing you the articles immediately before and after the one you are reading. This can be especially helpful when a particular topic is closely aligned in detail with those topics surrounding it. For example, the e-book edition of *The Oxford Encyclopedia of Food and Drink in America* provides you with the opportunity to realize there is a difference between baking chocolate (a grade of chocolate) and Baker's Chocolate (a brand of chocolate) because the two articles appear on the screen one after the other.

Encyclopedias addressing both specialized and general subjects and in all formats may incorporate visual support, including diagrams, photographs, drawings, or reproductions. In addition to these static images, online encyclopedias may include media clips, both sound and video, to support their information. A few print books, especially for children and including some subject encyclopedias for young audiences, print links to multimedia through QR codes.[1]

General Commercial Encyclopedias for Adults

General encyclopedias may enhance an adult's understanding of history, science, technology, nations, the roles of famous persons, the natural world, inventions, and theories related to all these and more, and thus they should be as up to date as publishing makes possible. Therefore, you must not keep an encyclopedia edition simply because you can't afford to purchase a new one. With one or two exceptions, an out-of-date general encyclopedia has little intrinsic worth as an authoritative information resource. Because subjects treated in general encyclopedia constantly develop and change, general encyclopedias must undergo frequent revision to accurately reflect the who, what, why, where, when, and how presented as factually correct.

One exception to this is the eleventh edition of the *Encyclopaedia Britannica*, which was published in 1910–1911. While no longer a source for discovering information that can support understanding contemporary technology or recent history, this edition is a scholarly, yet highly readable, collection in itself. Each of its main articles was written by a renowned figure in the field it addresses, providing us still with a dynamic snapshot of human intellectual development into the onset of the 20th century. Reference collections serving academic institutions (including community colleges), large public library communities, and independent scholars should retain this edition if it remains present in the collection. It is an inexpensive way to support independent learning about the past.

Chief among the American general encyclopedia publishers who continue to print annual print editions is *The World Book Encyclopedia*. This publisher also provides access to the encyclopedia's contents as an online subscription (at worldbookonline.com), at a relatively small cost to libraries and schools. Articles are authored by writers who place high value on both clarity and balance, and the editing is careful in maintaining authority and suitable bibliographic citation augmentation. The use of well-reproduced color photos and highly detailed indexing (which, in the print edition, fills its own volume) makes locating the desired information relatively quick and reliable. The online version of this encyclopedia has several editions that can be bundled together, including a level appropriate to high school studies, another for very young children, and a platform in Spanish for school-age children.

Another general encyclopedia that is provided online with different interfaces and degrees of depth and scope for different age groups is *Encyclopaedia Britannica*. Although its last print edition appeared in 2010 and continued in presenting contents arrangement designed some two decades earlier that made it difficult for nonspecialists in information retrieval to apprehend, the online encyclopedia is much more thorough and broader in coverage than is the online *World Book Encyclopedia*. Currently, access to the full online *Encyclopaedia Britannica* is a paid subscription, which includes rich multimedia content and straightforward navigation. In addition, a free website offers some of the encyclopedia's content at britannica.com.

English language commercial general encyclopedias, whatever their format, are costly. In their provision of ready access to information that can be helpful when little is known about a topic, their current primary benefit is assurance of editorial quality. However, their role in reference work becomes increasingly less important than it was during the era between their development in 18th-century France[2] and the last decade of the 20th century. Like the card catalog—also developed by those clever French intellectuals as a way of managing information architecture—these print-based publishing constructs are more suited to analog information gathering than digital.

Wikipedia

The most frequently referenced general encyclopedia at the present is not a commercial enterprise. Just as the explosion of printing that developed as the press and increasingly inexpensive paper sources brought a variety of hard copy general encyclopedias for over a century, web-based capacities have brought about an encyclopedia constructed of crowdsourced[3] content. Wikipedia, a product and project of Wikimedia Commons, operates as a repository of articles serving as contextualizing information, or as a general encyclopedia. Wikipedia has an actively contributing community that authors and edits articles that now comprise access to encyclopedic information in over 20 language groups (commons .wikimedia.org/wiki/Wikipedia); the English language Wikipedia (en.wikipedia.org/wiki/ Wikipedia) in fact is the largest of the portals in terms of article number (over five million at this time).

Reference staff working through the period in which Wikipedia rose to popular dominance held legitimate concerns about the authoritative quality of such a publishing project. However, protocols developed by Wikimedia now indicate that early skepticism of the whole should be reconsidered and applied to individual articles instead. Contributors range from government offices to scholars, hobbyists, and experts with an array of legitimate and questionable credentials, so it is at the article level that evaluation becomes useful.

Analogous to this kind of healthy skepticism is the fact that traditional commercial general encyclopedia publishers were, and those still operating continue to be, underscoring a majority power perspective: information in them carries the customary American publishing bias of emanating from a white, male-dominated, middle-class paradigm. As we discussed in Chapter 5, bias is part and parcel of any expression of information. Wikimedia Commons' own protocols call for transparency, and the Wikipedia workforce includes editors with various permission levels. While the belief that "anyone can edit anything" is almost true, editorial changes are constantly fact-checked and anyone who habitually alters articles to reflect a specific bias is denied future access to any Wikipedia editing access.

So, how do you make use of Wikimedia as an appropriately evaluated resource and guide users to assess authority in the information they consider for use? Wikipedia's mission is to provide free web-based access to information that is "neutral and unbiased"[4] and which provides nearly real-time access to information regarding current events. Articles are presented according to a rigorous template structure[5] that eases initial scanning and makes clear why some articles may be tagged as insufficiently elaborated and in need of further editing. In the case of insufficient documentation to demonstrate the reliability of an article, a message at the top of an article clearly states:

This article needs additional citations for verification. Please help improve this article by adding citations to reliable sources. Unsourced material may be challenged and removed. ([Month Year])

As a web-based resource, *See* and *See also* references have been incorporated in concept through article heading notes to help the reader understand the term that may have several meanings rather than be confused by it.[6] These notes are hyperlinked to allow the researcher to go immediately to the article that corresponds to the use of the term in which this user is really interested. For example, the word "phenomenology" applies to a variety of subject-specific theories and activities, so Wikipedia provides a Disambiguation Page, where each of those possibilities is listed and hyperlinked with a single phrase describing the discipline and focus of that specific link:

Phenomenology may refer to:

- Phenomenology (architecture), based on the experience of building materials and their sensory properties
- Phenomenology (archaeology), based upon understanding cultural landscapes from a sensory perspective
- Phenomenology (particle physics), a branch of particle physics that deals with the application of theory to high-energy experiments
- Phenomenology (philosophy), a philosophical method and school of philosophy founded by Edmund Husserl (1859–1938)
- Phenomenology (psychology), subjective experiences or their study
- Phenomenology (science), a body of knowledge that relates empirical observations of phenomena to each other

See also

- Existential phenomenology, in the work of Husserl's student Martin Heidegger (1889–1976) and his followers
- Phenomenology of Perception, a book by Maurice Merleau-Ponty
- Phenomenology of religion, concerning the experiential aspect of religion in terms consistent with the orientation of the worshippers
- The Phenomenology of Spirit, a book by Georg Wilhelm Friedrich Hegel

The structured nature of Wikipedia's articles offers a precise place to begin the authority evaluation process of any specific article. External links provide bibliographic citations to the published work on which article assertions stand. You can click through such links to ensure that they in fact lead to the copy in the linked text. Reviewing the sources used by the article writer provides valuable insight into the writer's level of expertise and bias. The article shows the month and year in which content was most recently edited, which helps you judge the information's timeliness and/or datedness.

Although Wikipedia writers do not sign their articles, it is essential to note many are from reliable agencies and institutions, including the following:

- National Archives and Records Administration (NARA)—This branch of the U.S. federal government has been actively contributing to Wikipedia since 2011. In addition to narrative articles related to its area of expertise, NARA has contributed access to thousands of its digitized images for use in Wikipedia articles by others.[7]
- Other government agencies, including federal, state, and local offices—Throughout the United States and Canada, social media officers, who are charged with sharing their expertise with the public for educational and informational reasons, in a variety of bureaus include Wikipedia contributions in their workflow.
- Research universities—As with government offices, universities also employ "wikipedians-in-residence"[8] in an effort to ensure specialized content coverage is properly discussed and updated.

- Archivists, librarians, professors, and researchers working in libraries, museums, think tanks, and assorted other industries associated with content knowledge in the arts, sciences, technology, social sciences, and other disciplines[9] contribute both articles and editorial oversight on content reflecting their areas of expertise.
- Independent scholars, fans, hobbyists, and others whose credentials as subject experts cannot be attached to an institution also write and edit Wikipedia articles and are, in fact, excellent sources of information about celebrities, travel, and other interests that must be presented, according to Wikipedia standards, with reference to vetted sources for the information they provide.

Because Wikipedia articles are unsigned, evaluation of each article for authority is required. However, some editorial protocols now in place, which were less well developed in Wikipedia's early days, offer assurances in matters related to topics most prone to partisan editing such as descriptions of any political party, most ethnic group histories, and religious belief systems. Among these are "protected pages" that cannot be edited directly; instead, edit requests can be submitted for consideration.[10]

That article-level evaluation is a best practice when using Wikipedia for reference work and serves as an important reminder on two fronts:

- As with any general encyclopedia, Wikipedia is best used for developing broad contextual information in the beginning stages of research, rather than as an expert source to be considered an end point in research; and
- Wikipedia's template-driven presentation of content guides the evaluator through a clear path in assessing authority and offers a schematic that can be imagined when analyzing other resources as well.

In addition, Wikipedia protocols requiring the inclusion of external resources provide any user with reliable resource and bibliographic citations. These external citations include resources available in print as well as in other media.

Students in middle and high schools can be taught the appropriate and valuable use of Wikipedia as a general encyclopedia resource for their homework and personal needs research. Your community's teachers may need guidance in learning about what that means as many teachers either refuse to consider the more developed editorial nature of Wikipedia now, as opposed to some years ago, or, conversely, may not understand the limitations of it (or any general encyclopedia) as a research tool where students are expected to analyze their findings and create original opinions based on comparing different resources.

General Encyclopedias for Younger Teens and Children

Younger teens and children also use general encyclopedias for their school assignments as well as independent research on topics of interest to them. The first research work of most elementary students, traditionally, involves responding to imposed questions such as discovering information about a country, a famous person, or an historic event. General encyclopedias that present multimedia content are attractive to this age group and also help them to fulfill school assignments in which they are required to make visual as well as narrative presentations.

With ending of the paper-bound encyclopedia publishing industry, finding and maintaining quality general encyclopedia options for youth is different from that in searching for such works for adults. How children can and are expected to use general encyclopedias has begun changing. School assignments that once relied on children finding, reading, and regurgitating facts found in encyclopedias such as reports on fourth-grade assignments on various states for the fourth-grade classroom or city helpers for first-grade students have evolved. You need to talk with teachers to determine exactly what the local students are expected to learn through initial research assignments. If students are assigned to find economic information about a state so they can create a flyer that would attract a company to relocate in their state, it will take much more than a look in an encyclopedia. The first-grade class may have a visit from a policeman or fireman from their neighborhood to interview. What they learn from this person makes the encyclopedia only a first look, and it will take more than one book and one encyclopedia article to complete the research for either grade.

Encyclopedias targeting children as browsers with their own questions, rather than as student researchers with needs related to imposed questions, rely on excellent visual components in addition to resource-cited articles. Among these are several works:

- *The New Children's Encyclopedia* (most recently published in 2013)—DK Publishing, in conjunction with the Smithsonian Institute's multivolume general encyclopedia set for children, offers a print general encyclopedia to children as young as kindergarten.
- *The New Book of Knowledge* (last published in paper in 2008)—Now published as Grolier's, receives little attention in the way of publisher upkeep in print and offers a database version that offers the youngest researchers some support.
- *Encyclopaedia Britannica for Kids* (kids.britannica.com) is divided into a product for students aged 11 and up and another for children 8 to 11. This rather fine-grained distinction in audience ages relates as much to selected content as appropriate to the studies of the two age groups as it does to how the information is presented in response to a keyword search. For example, a search in the student 11 and up version for "butterflies" provides, among article sections with direct links, one titled "scientific classification," while the search in the children's 8 to 11 version does not have a link to such a section in the returns list. In both cases, links to articles about swimming strokes as well as fauna are interfiled, and in both cases there are links to additional journal articles and multimedia.

Several websites and even search engines present themselves as "free" general encyclopedias for children. While the information can be suitable, such free resources are generally supported through the presence of advertising among the articles, requiring you to teach children how to differentiate between substantive content and promotional copy. For example, Fact Monster (factmonster.com/encyclopedia.html), from Information Please®, presents an ad-heavy but accessibly designed site of general information likely to address homework details for younger children such as thumbnail descriptions of nations of the world. However, both the advertising and the narrow coverage of topics make this a marginal resource and will certainly need to be supplemented with additional resources.

Alternatively, Simple English Wikipedia (simple.wikipedia.org/wiki/Simple_English_Wikipedia) carries no commercial endorsements on its site, and offers thousands of articles written in short sentences and with vocabulary and phrasing that avoid use of unnecessary complexity. In addition to reading ease, this version of the online work includes helpful images and sidebars, such as traditional print children's encyclopedias would have included to aid in information gathering on a student's part.

Concise general encyclopedias are no longer published in print. If your collection contains any, they should be weeded as their reflection of knowledge makes them unsuitable for reference work.

Subject Encyclopedias

Single-subject encyclopedias such as *The Encyclopedia of Race and Racism*, from Macmillan, and encyclopedias that address general knowledge from a particular and stated perspective such as Catholic University Press's *The New Catholic Encyclopedia* continue to arrive in all formats. They include multivolume works, desk reference–sized books, online subscriptions, and free works available on the web.

The potential uses of such specialized encyclopedias exist in libraries and for users needing brief and focused information to better understand a topic of concern. Authoritative subject encyclopedias, like their general encyclopedia counterparts, present narrative and multimedia information vetted by field experts and arranged for logical access to any desired point of included information. Some, especially those dealing with technologies of any sort, date very quickly and are best maintained online, while others can present useful guidance for information gathering many years after publication, such as those that treat topics such as the Civil War or nursery rhymes.

Selecting and using such works, in whatever format, requires you to have a thorough understanding of the needs of your community. If nutrition and diets are of sufficient interest to high school–age youth, then a subject encyclopedia seems appropriate. *The Gale Encyclopedia of Diets* (2013) provides both a level of information and a structure that befits nonspecialists with a broad interest in the topic. If you are in a location where you are surrounded by hospitals, Elsevier's *Encyclopedia of Human Nutrition* (2009) provides coverage at a level needed by policy makers and health specialists who are trained and work in areas akin to nutrition science without being themselves specialists.

Subject encyclopedias can be valuable resources for representing thematic knowledge areas in a general collection with even-handed coverage. Well-reviewed series, such as those copublished with the Smithsonian Institute or by experienced reference publishers like Oxford University Press, assure reference services staff that there is an authoritative place to begin a search on a topic about which they, or the community members who need to find information, have little knowledge. Such subject encyclopedias include citations to primary sources, clear and well-edited narratives, and indexing that provides guidance when seeking keywords to apply to open web searches.

Because of an interesting confluence of academic priorities and the excellent subject expertise held by professionals in the field, subject encyclopedias that are both free on the web and authoritative are relatively easy to identify in a wide array of knowledge areas. And because sites on the open web need not take up a daily presence in library, they can be "collection ready in the wings" when occasion requires their use.

By identifying fundamentally excellent subject encyclopedias available on the web beforehand, reference staff increase both the speed and accuracy with which specialized knowledge quests can be addressed. The following deserve bookmarking or adding to library guide materials:

- *Stanford Encyclopedia of Philosophy* (plato.stanford.edu)
- *MedlinePlus Medical Encyclopedia* (nlm.nih.gov/medlineplus/encyclopedia.html)
- *Nolo Legal Encyclopedia* (nolo.com/legal-encyclopedia)
- *Encyclopedia of the Nations* (nationsencyclopedia.com)
- *LookLex Encyclopaedia of the Orient* [greater Middle East] (i-cias.com/e.o/index
  .htm)

- *The Canadian Encyclopedia* (English) (thecanadianencyclopedia.com/en/)—also available in French (thecanadianencyclopedia.com/fr/)
- *Encyclopedia Mythica* (pantheon.org/mythica.html)
- *RP Photonics Encyclopedia* [Laser Physics and Technology] (rp-photonics.com/encyclopedia.html)
- *The Encyclopedia of Earth* (eoearth.org)

The selections noted here are examples. Care should be taken to consider the subject and capacity needs of the community served by the library and its reference services.

To identify quality subject encyclopedias in all formats, you can use the following tools, making sure to review them regularly to note if changes have been made in recommendations:

- The reference collections at the Library of Congress (catalog.loc.gov) provide a window on everything that is available and of potential use, nicely organized by subject.
- The encyclopedias listed in Medline Plus (nlm.nih.gov), deemed authoritative by the National Institutes of Health, are online for free.
- University of Buffalo Databases of Subject Encyclopedias (libweb.lib.buffalo.edu/infotree/resourcesbysubjecEncyclopedias.asp) offers good annotations of databases that include subject encyclopedias within their content, making it a good source to check before deciding whether any of these databases might replace older print subject encyclopedias in your collection.
- Free web-based subject encyclopedias included in Best of the Web Encyclopedias by Subject (botw.org/top/Reference/Encyclopedia/By_Subject/) are updated regularly by reference experts.
- *Booklist Magazine*'s online reviews (booklistonline.com) of encyclopedias allow you to perform an advanced search with appropriate keywords and limit the search to reviews of reference titles reviewed to discover new works that might fill a subject encyclopedia need in your community.

Understanding what you need to answer reference questions and a knowledge of the community from which subject area questions emerge are both essential in the selection of appropriate subject encyclopedias. Noting that one or another title has been well reviewed is not enough. Is it a responsible resource for your library? Does it address knowledge for you to use in helping your community find the right level of context support as they begin to explore topics with which they are less familiar? Would acquiring this resource show that the collection needs balancing in other areas of information need as well?

DICTIONARIES AND USAGE GUIDES THAT TREAT ENGLISH AND OTHER LANGUAGES

In contrast to encyclopedias, dictionaries focus on meanings and uses of words and terms themselves, rather than concepts and a discussion of events, places, theories, persons, beliefs, and other systems that give context to the terms they include. Dictionaries afford an explanation of what a word means and how it is used so that users can choose the correct vocabulary word for their intended meaning. Like encyclopedias, dictionaries can now be located and accessed in many formats, with some sources providing better access for some reference needs than others. Pronunciation guidance that includes sound files so that the user isn't relying solely on diacritical interpretation is preferable in most situations where translating diacritical marks into sound can be difficult. Spelling guidance, on the other hand, works well in any print format.

We will consider two types of dictionaries in this section: language dictionaries, which offer general definitions of a wide variety of terms, and subject-area dictionaries, which define the vocabularies of specific disciplines, industries, or other specific topics. Dictionaries of both kinds should be accessed in their most recent iteration; old dictionaries that fail to address new terms (particularly in those disciplines where new discoveries and methods generate new terms), new uses for words, or relevant cultural information about word use should be discarded, except for those that treat linguistics, which we turn to after first broaching tools for understanding language itself.

The thesaurus is a reference tool that provides guidance in locating words that share similar meanings, or synonyms, and words that are the opposite, or antonyms. Thesauri relevant to reference work in various subjects, including language use itself, are noted in each of the following discussions. A thesaurus can be helpful in the search for terms that the reader understands clearly when a less familiar word with similar connotation has been used in either speaking or writing.

The *Oxford English Dictionary (OED)*

The single title that continues to be regarded as the foremost record of the English language, available in a variety of formats,[11] is the *Oxford English Dictionary (OED)*. This icon is out of print in paper copy, so if you don't have one, you probably won't get one unless someone donates it to you.[12] It is considered most useful as the ideal and the scale to judge other dictionaries.

The *OED* supplies word and language use information as follows:

- The *OED* attempts to describe words as they are generally used, rather than making judgmental assessments of the words or their use.
- The contemporary spelling (orthography) of each word is listed first, with any alternate spelling(s) in current use among English speakers noted (e.g., "curb" vs. "kerb").
- Pronunciations, too, are supplied in both primary and alternative variations to reflect common practices in all English-speaking countries.
- Word etymology, or history, notes the first documented use of the word in English, along with subsequent developments of the word to approach its current uses and meanings.
- Definitions are arranged both by part of speech (noun, verb, adjective, etc.), then in the order of most common use, and then with typical support terms ("school of" or "a handle on," for example), figures of speech (idiomatic expressions), and compound terms in which the root word is an essential element ("circus tent" or "cowboy boots," for example).

The previous list serves as a reminder of all the information a dictionary covering any language, discipline, industry, or other range of knowledge can and should be expected to include. Whether you will need full subscription access to the *OED* database or to another version of this English dictionary, you need to be aware of its significance, as well as its authority.[13] It is a reference tool that you might be able to share with your local high school if you can arrange appropriate access from the school to the public library.

Other Authoritative English Language Dictionaries

Although the *OED* is the ultimate unabridged English language dictionary, other dictionaries treating the English language also warrant your consideration. Some focus on the language in general, while others focus on specific elements of language, such as etymology (the history of a particular word) or regional word use.

Evaluating the extent to which English language dictionary coverage is needed locally requires you to be familiar with the community: what kinds of English language needs are expressed? What other ones do you address when helping community members who haven't explicitly asked for dictionary help? Are there school assignments requiring children to access word history information or related dictionary help at the library? While locating definitions, pronunciations, and spellings on the web utilizes a number of different core dictionary texts, there is no free access to a complete unabridged dictionary of our language. Web searching for a spelling or definition, instead, offers much abridged retrievals that may or may not be properly cited so that you can evaluate the resource it quotes. This makes it likely that you need one unabridged dictionary for authoritative English support if you do not have access to the *OED* online. Such online access is preferable, simply because the paper publication of such dictionaries seems to have ceased, with no new ones appearing in a decade. Among print unabridged dictionaries treating standard American English, two remain available:

- *Webster's Third New International Dictionary of the English Language, Unabridged* (Merriam-Webster, 2003)—Now aging, this is the most recent iteration of a general unabridged English language dictionary from the American dictionary publisher.
- *Random House Webster's Unabridged Dictionary* (Random House, 2006)—In spite of "Webster" being in the title, this is the work of another large and trusted publisher, although its age again limits its collection value if it is to be the only unabridged dictionary available.

To address the gap between any lack of access you may have to a print unabridged dictionary along with lacking access to *OED* online, consider acquiring (and maintaining in its most up-to-date iteration) an American English desk dictionary. A desk dictionary is more concise than an unabridged one; however, its coverage is far more thorough than what can be ascertained in an open web search for such sites as dictionary.com. Among up-to-date desk dictionaries are the following:

- *The American Heritage Desk Dictionary* (Houghton Mifflin Harcourt, 2013)—Now in its fifth print edition and having set a publication cycle pattern that suggests it will remain updated, the coverage here is authoritative and specifically treats American English. It is also available as a mobile app at a price (currently about $25), for both iOS and Android.
- *Merriam Webster Online* (merriam-webster.com)—This free source carrying a name that bespeaks word authority is a better alternative than ad-supported sites like Dictionary.com. Definitions are presented in two tiers: simple ones first and then more detailed ones below on the same screen. A big gap in this resource is the lack of presentation of part of speech that traditionally is included with word definitions.

Several subscription database packages, such as Britannica Online and Credo Reference (corp.credoreference.com), include abridged but authoritative dictionaries so that access to the latest edition may be through that database rather than in paper format.

English language dictionaries treating word concerns that you should also know, in order to refer clients to them or to consider for future purchase if your community needs indicate local availability would be more responsive than frequent referrals to other collections, are the following:

- *Dictionary of American Regional English* (Harvard University Press, 2013)—Published in parts across nearly two decades, this comprehensive dictionary includes only terms and/or usages that occur in American regional dialects rather than those that have national and international use.
- *Collins Dictionary* (HarperCollins, 2011)—Published under British auspices, this unabridged dictionary includes regional and dialect English from around the world.
- *The Gallaudet Dictionary of American Sign Language* (Gallaudet University, 2005)—American Sign Language (ASL) has connections to English; however, its visual nature is not a "spelling" of English but rather a language of its own. The dictionary includes a DVD for access to the necessary movements involved for correct replication of vocabulary and nuances of verbal language.
- *Merriam Webster Visual Dictionary Online* (visualdictionaryonline.com)—A free web access dictionary, by its nature defining nouns, is arranged by subjects, including pure and applied sciences, technology, domestic life, the arts, and recreation. The nouns as entries are arranged by written word (and can be located through keyword searching). The dictionary then supplies clear and detailed color schematics showing what the word means in an illustration. The illustration's labeled details are broken out further by spelled words that depict increasing amounts of detail.
- Visual Thesaurus® (visualthesaurus.com)—This subscription database provides dynamic mapping of how words are connected as synonyms and cognates, and also provides voiced pronunciation of the word selected on screen.
- *The Firefly Five Language Visual Dictionary* (2004)—Although aging, this paper visual dictionary provides helpful support where basic communication in English with adult speakers of Spanish, French, German, and Italian warrants.

Dictionaries Documenting Other Languages

In communities where languages other than English are both read and spoken popularly, *unabridged* language coverage of the relevant language(s) is a best practice. Languages develop differently and should not be viewed as a one-size-fits-all proposition. Respecting the community by reflecting their cultural asset of language is a value the library must demonstrate.

Perhaps best known to monolingual English speakers casually considering dictionaries in other languages is what is called a bilingual dictionary. While there are, indeed, thorough and scholarly detailed bilingual and multiple language (polyglot) dictionaries, those most commonly available under this name are actually thesauri or glossaries, translating individual words and occasionally idiomatic phrases from one language covered by the dictionary to the other. For those who need only a discrete term or two, that works. However, any true language dictionary, whether monolingual or encompassing more than one language, contains the elements, or at least most of the elements, described in the section on the *OED*. Definitions, alternative spellings, and subtle idioms should be incorporated descriptively in and for speakers of the language(s) the dictionary claims to present.

Among many fully developed and presented dictionaries of various languages currently available that should be considered as supporting a balanced collection in communities where such languages are primary, these publishers are noteworthy:

- Le Robert (lerobert.com/dictionnaires-generalistes.html)—The French publisher of a host of dictionaries ranging from unabridged to desk, school, and children's to dual language provides works that dynamically explore the language and its words.
- Langenscheidt (langenscheidt.de/unternehmen)—The preeminent German publisher of dictionaries and language reference works, this site offers access to both print and online products.
- Real Academia Española (rae.es/recursos/diccionarios)—This European Spanish publisher offers many editions and depths of dictionaries, both in paper and online. However, most Spanish speakers in North America use one of several forms of Latin American Spanish, so this publisher serves best the needs of those with academic or Continental language needs. The Academia offers free online access to its *Diccitionairio des americanismos* (asale.org/recursos/diccionarios/damer), which addresses the regulated aspects of Latin American Spanish. Barcelona Larousse last published *Diccionario Anaya lengua española* in paper in 2007; this also provides good access to authoritative Latin American Spanish. Access to updated contents in it is available through Vox (vox.es/cgi-bin/index.pl#).
- Chinese dictionaries are available in both Chinese characters and Roman letters, in Mandarin and Cantonese dialects, and with other variables that reference service providers should negotiate with knowledge of local needs. *The Contemporary Chinese Dictionary* (Commercial Press, 2004) has received notice as one Chinese language (as opposed to bilingual) dictionary that can be obtained fairly easily and provides authoritative nontechnical definitions and other basic dictionary guidance.[14]
- Drofa (drofa.ru) is the publisher of dictionaries in Russian, providing content both for Russian language and dual language dictionaries. Access is available in book, online, and app interfaces.
- Sanseido publishes the Japanese dictionary *Shin Meikai Kokugo Jiten* in both paper (most recent edition is 2013) and as a mobile application. The full version provides access both in kanji and phonetically.
- Free Vietnamese Dictionary Project (informatik.uni-leipzig.de/~duc/Dict/) at this time provides the most extensive access to monolingual dictionary treatment of Vietnamese, a language with written roots in both Roman and Chinese. This site's database contains monolingual treatment of 30,000 words; however, its dynamic approach to both access and display permitting search through various character systems makes it a flexible resource for a wide span of users.

While search engines like Google offer word translation as an open and free function, the authority of these, as discussed in an earlier chapter, remains dubious. Where bilingual dictionary coverage is warranted, the following publishers each provide good and affordable resources in multiple formats:

- Collins provides a fully developed and free website (collinsdictionary.com) with quick and complete access to bilingual dictionaries in French, German, Spanish, and Italian. Print dictionaries also provide bilingual authority in Russian, Polish, Greek, Mandarin Chinese, and the previously named languages.
- Penguin Random House's DK imprint publishes visual dictionaries, with detailed and highly reproduced photos, that support bilingual searching in each of Chinese

(Mandarin), Japanese, Polish, Portuguese, and Spanish, in both paper and e-book formats.
- Hippocrene (hippocrenebooks.com/store/c6/Dictionaries.html) provides bilingual dictionaries with English and Cantonese, Vietnamese, Haitian Creole, Romanian, and Indonesian.

Formal English Usage Guidance

Reference staff may be called upon to demonstrate, share, or help to document best English usage practices in both written and oral communications. To support that work, these resources offer authoritative and accessible guidance:

- *A Dictionary of Modern English Usage* (2009 edition)—Traditionally known as "Fowler's," the newest edition is available in both paper and e-book formats. This is the first stop when trying to determine which phrase construction or word/spelling choice is preferable.
- *Practical English Usage* (current paper edition is 2005)—Geared more to those handling English as a student than the previous title, this too offers clear guidance on grammar, idioms, and other linguistic style concerns.
- *The Online Grammar Guide* (world-english.org/grammar.htm)—The work of a Rutgers professor, access here is simple and direct and open on the web.

Reference services that extend to writers and editors, both in academic and nonacademic settings, should provide access to style manuals used for authoritative citation building, pre-publication manuscript preparation, and other writing guidelines. Chief among these are the following:

- *AP Stylebook* (apstylebook.com)—journalism's style authority. This is available as e-resource, app, and in print.
- American Psychological Association (APA) (apastyle.org)—behavioral sciences publication style authority. Available in print and several common points of style are accessible for free at the website.
- *Chicago Manual of Style* (chicagomanualofstyle.org/home.html)—academic and humanities publication style authority. Available in print and as a subscription to its online home.

Contemporary style manuals include such necessary documentation guidance as how to cite tweets, e-mails, and other electronic resources that are published without print-based alternatives. They also guide authors in sourcing and correctly attributing multimedia of all varieties.

Dictionaries for Children

Where children are among the primary focus of reference services, providing appropriate dictionary support, in both language itself and in subject areas of interest to them, is a best practice. The very structure of good children's dictionaries provides practical and concrete experiences: systematic order, browsing possibilities to locate new perspectives, and authoritative explanation of word and term meanings.

While school-age children and young teens should be taught appropriate web searching skills to locate dictionary support on an as-needed basis, print dictionaries address literacy skill building support in their format and capacity for browsing. Among excellent dictionaries for children and reference service support with them are the following:

- *DK Merriam-Webster Children's Dictionary* (latest American edition is 2015)
- *The American Heritage Student Science Dictionary* (latest is 2nd edition, 2014)
- "Eyewitness Visual Dictionary" series (DK Publishing)—While volumes in this subject-specific series are beginning to date, for those topics focusing on historical events (e.g., the Civil War, military uniforms) or popular culture (e.g., Star Wars, LEGO), they provide satisfactory authoritative modeling for young researchers.
- "Let's Learn Picture Dictionary" series (NTC/Contemporary Publishing)—These bilingual dictionaries, offered in Spanish, Portuguese, Japanese, and other languages, are aimed at the youngest audiences of language learners.

As for adults and older teens, children should have access to the most recent editions of dictionaries if they are to rely on them as resources for authoritative information.

SUBJECT DICTIONARIES AND SUBJECT THESAURI

Dictionaries and thesauri that treat the special vocabulary and word uses applicable to specific disciplines and professions are essential to providing reference services that are authoritative. Knowing what a word means in ordinary parlance can misguide both staff and community members when the subject at hand employs that same word in a technical manner that gives it a different or more limited meaning. The subject dictionary is the tool to use when a definition is required to understand meaning as the word or term is used in the specific discipline at hand. It is essential to recognize when a subject dictionary is more appropriate than a general dictionary, as how the subject area employs terms cannot be substituted with general use and a guess on your part about specialized application within a subject. Among the subject areas where authoritative vocabulary must be that of the discipline, in order to qualify as accurate, are the following:

- Law
- Medicine
- Technology by specific type, including computer sciences and applications, architecture, mechanics, design, and engineering
- Education
- Criminal justice
- Philosophy
- Religion, including distinct theological traditions
- Specific sports
- Specific arts, including literary, film, visual, and dramatic

In the cases of law and medicine, the professional ethics of reference providers requires you to quote discipline-specific definitions rather than make use of more popular understandings of words and terms.

Subject-specific thesauri can help bridge gaps of vocabulary awareness both between disciplines and between languages in which the discipline is practiced. An example of the latter case is the resource called a polyglot medical thesaurus that allows medical personnel to be certain of condition, symptom, and treatment terms from language to language, including standard medical English to simplified yet accurate English.[15] Using such a dictionary is not reserved for medical practitioners at all! You may find it your best support when interviewing a client concerned about a diagnosis given to a family member when the physician who named it for the family member, or described aspects of its course and the intended treatment, failed to communicate meaning due to a lack of shared terminology, either between the original patient and physician or between the patient (quoting the physician) and this client, a family member who is not comfortable with casual English, let alone formal and medical terminology.

Standard subject dictionaries to consider for inclusion to aid reference work that is accurate, authoritative, and ethical include the following:

- *Black's Law Dictionary* (latest edition is the 10th edition, 2014), for which free web-based access is available at thelawdictionary.org.
- *MedlinePlus Medical Dictionary* (nlm.nih.gov/medlineplus/mplusdictionary.html) is free on the web from the U.S. government and includes a tutorial on "Understanding Medical Words" (nlm.nih.gov/medlineplus/medicalwords.html).
- *Black's Veterinary Dictionary* (latest edition is the 22nd, 2015), available in both paper and e-book formats.
- *The Dictionary of Criminal Justice* (latest edition is the 7th, 2011), available in both paper and e-book formats.
- *A Dictionary of Art Terms and Techniques* (latest edition is the 2nd, 1991).
- *The Game Developer's Dictionary: A Multidisciplinary Lexicon for Professionals and Students* (2012), available in both paper and e-book formats.
- *The Brill Dictionary of Religion* (revised edition, 2006).

In response to community needs and expectations of locating authoritative guidance in understanding specialized uses of terminology, reference staff may need to consult World-Cat (discussed in Chapter 6) to locate specific dictionaries that respond to these. While looking up words and phrases on the open web may lead to instant response, care must be taken to design the query so as to retrieve definitions that are appropriate to the discipline.

WHERE WE ARE GOING NEXT

In the next chapter, we turn to a wide array of resources useful to respond authoritatively to nonresearch-level fact needs, or ready reference information gaps. Dictionaries discussed throughout this current chapter are among such ready reference resources. As you proceed with the next chapter, you will see some discussion of mobile applications (apps) recommended for some ready reference use. Keep in mind that, as with dictionary apps discussed in this chapter, evaluating both the authority of other ready reference apps and their contribution to local ready reference needs is required.

NOTES

1. Quick Response (QR) Codes are printed within paper-based information—from magazines to billboards and including print books—and can be read by cellphone technology. Each coded image carries any of a vast amount of data that, in the case of print

books, for example, directs the phone's user to a media link affiliated with the text in which the code is printed.

2. The modern encyclopedia grew from Enlightenment scholars active before and through the French Revolution. See, among others, Donald J. Mabry, "Diderot's Encyclopedia," *Historical Text Archive*, 2016, http://historicaltextarchive.com/sections.php? action=read&artid=780.

3. Crowdsourcing has become an element of both commercial and volunteer ventures and refers to the effort to acquire and generate new developments and improve current availability through the solicitation of a peer community.

4. See the discussion at "Wikipedia: Neutral Point of View" (en.wikipedia.org/wiki/ Wikipedia:Neutral_point_of_view), which provides an incisive and detailed presentation on the factors to be considered and the authorial approaches permitted and not permitted to maintain this ideal.

5. Access to the various templates, which vary by content type they are intended to expose as well as topical coverage specificities (e.g., articles addressing topics in technology as opposed to those designed to present information about people), is at simple.wikipedia.org/wiki/Category:Wikipedia_templates.

6. Wikipedia adopted a strategy developed by linguists to explore the problem of how to understand a word that itself carries various meanings within the specific context it is being used.

7. *Citizen Archivist Dashboard: Improving Access to Historical Records through Crowdsourcing* (crowdsourcing-toolkit.sites.usa.gov/files/2015/09/citizen-archivist.pdf) provides an overview of the case study related to this work with Wikipedia.

8. This work is supported for the purposes of quality control and outreach by the Wikipedia Visiting Scholars program (en.wikipedia.org/wiki/Wikipedia:Visiting_Scholars).

9. A list of the current Wikipedian in Residents is listed in LinkedIn (linkedin.com/title/ wikipedian-in-residence) and describes each one's institutional affiliation and area of expertise.

10. A dynamic list of pages that are protected and semi-protected from open editing can be found at en.wikipedia.org/wiki/Wikipedia:List_of_indefinitely_protected_pages#-Main_Page_and_component_templates.

11. The 2010 print edition of the unabridged *Oxford* is, for now, the final paper.

12. For a thorough critical review of the *Oxford English Dictionary*'s claim to definitive, see Pius ten Hacken's "In What Sense Is the OED the Definitive Record of the English Language?" (*Proceedings of the 15th EURALEX International Congress*, 2012, pages 834–845) (euralex.org/elx_proceedings/Euralex2012/pp834–845%20ten%20Hacken .pdf).

13. "The OED in Two Minutes" (public.oed.com/resources/the-oed-in-two-minutes/) provides a slideshow that further explains the creation and development of this resource.

14. Wikipedia provides a good description of the attributes of and controversies surrounding this work at en.wikipedia.org/wiki/Xiandai_Hanyu_Cidian.

15. How to Write Easy-to-Read Health Materials (nlm.nih.gov/medlineplus/etr.html).

CHAPTER 9

Finding Facts Fast: Ready Reference

Among terms common in reference staff jargon, "ready reference" now describes a somewhat different service support area than it did before web access became so ubiquitous. For more than a decade now, veteran reference service providers have struggled with each other, as well as with those outside the profession, to determine how, when, and why to sever their professional service identity from community needs for simple fact delivery.[1] This does not mean that reference staff anywhere are discussing whether to refuse to provide quickly found facts. However, instead of counting such fact-finding mini-missions as demanding high-level staff intervention, many library administrators now recognize that handling ready reference response, whether as a library staff member or for one's own personal information collection, can be done well by someone with just a tiny bit of training and practice in evaluating sources. That training, then, becomes part of the fact-finding service.

Furthermore, the old model of placing a librarian at a desk to await demands for quickly located facts from a nearby book collection has also evolved. Ready reference needs are expressed all over the library building and in every other public venue, while also surfacing for individuals who may not articulate them to anyone else. This new reality removes the expectation that reference staff can perform their job by sitting and waiting to answer clients' self-identified information needs for a phone number, map coordinates, anniversary year gift tradition, or how to boil an egg. Understanding staff's emerging roles, then, requires nuanced analysis. In this chapter, the expertise reference staff must have in locating authoritative facts quickly and in any setting is discussed. Because of the ubiquity of access to many of the resources that provide authoritative ready reference, including mobile apps and free government websites, reference staff can use each ready reference interaction as an opportunity to support and expand information literacy skills among community members. Sharing and encouraging community information literacy does not pose a job threat. Instead, it provides both active clients and the community at large with the opportunity to reach a better understanding of how to make good evaluative decisions in their daily lives.

Reference tools, whether in print or electronic format, that are appropriate and valuable to quick fact-centered searches include both commercial products and truly free resources ("truly" free in that many of these cost-free tools also carry no advertising). Our discussion of ready reference online sets the stage for applying rigorous evaluation methods to more complex web-based resources, discussed in the following chapter. Our focus here is on tools that are authoritative and that present factual information with little to no searching involved. Reference staff should also learn to recognize when the presentation of a simple fact question may actually signal a larger question or a broad information need beyond ready reference.

DATA TRADITIONALLY DELIVERED THROUGH GENERAL ALMANACS

As its name indicates, the general almanac maintains a record of events in time, with the data it provides stripped of any interpretation. General almanacs report such information as anniversary gift traditions, final polling numbers, the number of combatants who took part in the Boer War, the largest recorded earthquakes at a specific Richter scale level, and in which locations, and in which time zone you will find Schenectady. We all need this type of information, from time to time and for a variety of reasons. Sometimes such facts are needed to settle an argument among friends or to bring a frame of reference to a current event. Simple, fact-seeking questions that invite such information in response will always be with us simply because humans, in general, can carry only so many memorized facts in their heads (the order of the alphabet, the dates of our own, and perhaps our loved ones' birthdays).

The moment any question involves any level of analysis or interpretation, the almanac is no longer useful. It is simply a collection of organized facts. This serves as a good illustration of the difference between "ready reference" questions and those questions in which you must invest more analytic effort to determine the subjective aspects of the client's need by assisting in the articulation of a more complex question.[2]

In light of the development of authoritative commercial databases and sophisticated web search engines, the need to acquire print copies of general almanacs for ready reference has diminished. However, where libraries have maintained a series of historical editions, these may provide quick access to year-by-year data that can be uncovered more quickly through their annual arrangement than by consulting a variety of resources to find such basic facts as heads of government in various countries during pre-1980 specific years or historic weather events. Depending on your community's interest in history or use of the collection for such activities as planning class reunions and other historical celebrations, such series can remain in-house if room and use indicate continuing local value.

General almanacs provide concise cultural guidance through relaying such details as changes in traditional wedding anniversary gifts. While the sapphire is the precious stone associated with the fifth anniversary, traditionally, with items made of wood also noted as common, a general almanac also notes that "modern" anniversary gift giving moves items of wood to the sixth anniversary. General almanacs, then, serve as a minimalist cultural history, helpful to party planners and curious historical fiction fans for serving up the briefest of notes documenting what was happening in their period of coverage.

Some excellent contemporary general almanacs include the following:

- Infoplease (infoplease.com/almanacs.html) is available for free on the web, providing an excellent standard with the exception that the site carries paid, and happily clearly marked, advertisements. In addition to a detailed directory page, and a detailed navigation menu that remains available across searches, content can be searched using keywords. Because this free almanac is linked directly to an atlas, dictionary, and encyclopedia, the user can easily move to more data. The user should understand that facts in this resource are grounded in authority, while also recognizing that the advertising content is separate from the authoritative facts in the almanac itself.
- *The World Almanac and Book of Facts* continues to be an annual publication in paper with its usual publication date in early December of the year before the cover date. Because of this publication schedule, this almanac cannot include information that comes from events occurring after late October or early November, and, of course, does not address data accumulating during the cover year. For example, the *World Almanac* for 1996 was released in late 1995 and so does not contain any numbers related to voting in the 1996 presidential election. While this once served as a simple and authoritative ready reference tool, its role in reference work has shifted to one of providing a concise and orderly record of the past—albeit from the viewpoint of its publishers.

DIRECTORIES

Directories cover many different topics, and some of them, including those concerned with financial aid, require more than ready reference checks to be useful. Other areas of interest, however, suit quick and accurate information access. These include telephone directories and those about companies.

Telephone Directories

Telephone directories continue to be available in print format, and you probably receive annually your local one for free. Like other print resources, the paper telephone directory must be organized and printed weeks before it is available for use and, of course, people and companies listed in it can move, change numbers, or be no longer viable. Even for local telephone directory information, then, the web is a better alternative to paper.

The most reliable free online directory for locating people and others with telephone numbers and addresses is AnyWho (anywho.com/whitepages). Entries are updated weekly. In addition to the white pages, there are yellow pages reflecting the same level of information you find in print telephone book yellow pages, and a reverse lookup function that allows you to search a (publicly listed) telephone number to find out whose it is.

Business Directories

Clients may want the address of a corporation to write a letter complaining about a product. They may want the address to see if any jobs are available in the company. They may also want names of corporations with which they can do business. Those needing details of corporations can find these particulars in company directories:

- Where the company is headquartered
- How its offices can be contacted through mail, online, and via telephone
- Names of individuals who: function in specific roles within its structure
- In which industry sector they conduct business, in terms of the North American Industry Classification System (NAICS)[3] (which would allow further exploration of competitors)

To make sure you are able to provide accurate information, you must trust the quality and timeliness of the resource you are searching. Any directory must be corrected and updated when new officers are installed, when new locations are established, or when former locations are abandoned. Quality business directories providing this up-to-date information take the form of online subscriptions. While it is possible to find directory information in free online resources, you would need to do considerable researching to locate all the facets of data contained in an easily searchable way, in a commercial database.

Among the most well-reviewed business directory databases, the following have been designed for ease of use and are produced by publishers with long and authoritative histories in the compilation and updating of business directory information:

- Million Dollar Database (Dun and Bradstreet) provides coverage of both publicly and privately owned businesses operating worldwide, including those in North America. It is updated constantly to reflect fact changes.
- ReferenceUSA (InfoUSA) coverage includes companies in the United States and private individuals' contact listings (although not for anyone with no publicly published phone, e-mail, and/or street address). It is updated constantly, and can be searched using structures familiar from telephone yellow page–style querying.
- Corporate Affiliations (LexisNexis) includes access to subsidiary and other linkages among corporations. It is international in scope and updated constantly to reflect changes in ownership as well as contact information.

Your consortium package of databases may also include the Gale Directory Library (cengage.com), which brings together several directories that have been published for many years, first only in paper and now both in paper and online. Its coverage includes directory access to associations, publications, and nonprofits. Be sure to check to see if this database is available to you locally so that you can use it instead of trying to search the open web for up-to-date authoritative information in these areas.

LOCATING LITERARY QUOTATIONS

Life events can occasion the need to locate specific quotations or to seek a group of quotations for a particular occasion. Wedding toasts, funeral speeches, epigraphs in both professional and student writing, and a not-quite-remembered echo of a line once memorized are among the circumstances when a quick search for a quotation is needed. Tracking the specific quote attributed to a contemporary or even historical politician or philosopher in order to support or debunk an argument can lead to looking for the correct quote. Finding authoritative wording for attribution for a quotation is a good example of how some more complex reference queries may begin with what sounds like a ready reference need for just a simple fact. Finding the desired quote is indeed a ready reference task; analyzing the quotation goes beyond ready reference.

The literature of authoritative quotation resources is rich and deep, so using these resources for ready reference will save you time and frustration over attempting to verify a quote in an open web search:

- *Bartlett's Familiar Quotations*, in formats ranging from paper copy to e-book to web-based open files, has been recognized as an exemplary resource for nearly 100 years. The latest edition is 2012, and the depth of historical coverage reaches back millennia. When considering community need and expectations, this standard may be a welcome resource to have on hand for ready reference, or it may well be that free web access to older editions, available at Bartleby.com and including through the edition published in 2000 as the 5th edition, may be sufficient.
- *Oxford Dictionary of Quotations* (latest is the 8th edition, 2014) is also a serviceable resource for general ready reference. However, unlike Bartlett's this one lacks a North American focus both in terms of sources and in terms of cultural sensibilities.
- *The Columbia Granger's World of Poetry* (Columbia University) is a database providing exemplary access to locating lines as well as other facts associated with poems from every era and heritage, providing poetry in its original language accompanied by an English translation, where applicable.

HANDBOOKS AND MANUALS FOR QUICK FACTS

Handbooks, which explore a discipline or technology, and manuals that offer instruction for undertaking processes are closely related. While handbooks and manuals usually have much more information, some quick facts can readily be found using such tools. Recognizing when such a resource provides both the most authoritative and quickest route to identifying the needed information means being aware of what can be found in the reference as well as how it is arranged. For example, a general-purpose cookbook, like *The Fannie Farmer Cookbook* (Knopf, now in its 13th edition, 2011), which offers such information as the temperature and time needed to adequately roast a turkey, also includes practical shortcuts and alternatives to roasting. It provides quick access to substitutions, such as how to create soured milk if no naturally soured milk is on hand.

Both handbooks and manuals typically include easy access to tables that provide specifications that may be needed to determine a process, a method, or how to perform a calculation that practitioners of the technology or discipline need on a frequent basis, such as converting teaspoons to tablespoons, for measurement, or weights of specific foods, like sugar, to substitute for volume.

Here is where you can provide expert guidance toward independent ongoing research by community members. After conducting a reference interview to identify the exact nature of the fact(s) needed, identify the likely resource for a fast, efficient, and authoritative answer by showing the client the most efficient path into the related handbook or manual. You need not be an expert in the topic covered by the tool, if the client is; your expertise is in showing how to use the resource to the client's best advantage.

Ready reference questions that can rely on manuals and handbooks should be up to date. If an older edition of a manual, such as the one used for automobile repairs of vehicles of a specific vintage, is relevant to your community, be sure to explore replacing historic paper volumes with a database that includes manual information for many generations of models. Your library's consortium database package may include the Chilton database (chilton.cengage.com), a very popular repair manual authority. Be sure to become familiar with it so you are prepared to use it for ready reference purposes.

FACTS ABOUT COUNTRIES AND CULTURES

As human beings, we generally are curious and interested in other human beings, and in commonalities and differences between individuals, classes, cultures, and nations. Members of your community may have questions about the religions of a country or the age when a student may leave school. These are questions that have quick answers. Other questions regarding countries and cultures can be complex and require much more research than ready reference. Recognizing which kind you are addressing is the first step in providing appropriate resources for answering it. Among the ready reference questions that regularly arise are the following:

- Where is . . . a country, a city, a body of water, another natural landform?
- How many . . . seeking population figures for specific places?
- When did . . . a specific place have an official name change, gain independence, become recognized by the UN, enter a war?
- What is . . . the capital, the official language, the government structure?

General almanacs once were used to answer many of these sorts of ready reference quickly. The open web, unless the query is carefully structured, yields too many possibilities that need to be evaluated for authority to provide a quick response to such fact needs. This is an area of reference service design in which a few very specific sites can be learned and bookmarked for quick and ready access to authoritative information.

Excellent resources for quick fact-finding about countries include the following:

- *World Factbook* (cia.gov/library/publications/the-world-factbook/)—The U.S. Central Intelligence Agency provides a free, up-to-date, and easily searched factual information (as well as obvious more interpretive resources) that include national flags, official languages, populations, name changes, major historical events including wars and elections, and other discrete data.
- World Geography and Culture Online (infobasepublishing.com/OnlineProductDetail .aspx?ISBN=0816043795)—A subscription database, this includes considerable research and interpretative information as well as quick access to fast facts about geophysical locations like large lakes and mountain ranges, currency, heads of state names, maps displaying both political and physical elements, and more.

These two sources overlap and provide roughly the same coverage in terms of fast fact discovery. The *World Factbook* is free, and World Geography and Culture Online is independent of government oversight. If the reference collection holds World Geography and Culture Online, you must keep in mind its usefulness for quick fact checking as well as for more in-depth research beyond ready reference. The *World Factbook* has been a trusted and authoritative source of objective facts about specific data for several generations and should not be dismissed due to its connection with a government office focused on intelligence gathering and use. After all, one should expect that such an enterprise requires having plain facts clearly and constantly available. The World Geography and Culture Online subscription database includes coverage of each of the 50 states, which the *World Factbook* site does not.

Children often pose fact-gathering questions related to nations throughout the world. These tools are particularly helpful to teach them how to find facts as well as to answer children's questions with the assurance that references are both accurate and up to date:

- Culturegrams (proquestk12.com/productinfo/culturegrams.shtml)—a subscription database providing quick facts about each nation, each state, and each Canadian province.
- Country Profiles (news.bbc.co.uk/2/hi/country_profiles/default.stm)—a free and easy-to-navigate site that presents clearly stated facts about specific countries, including territories, along with images and news clips. Note that this site carries banner ads that are clearly distinguishable from the site's content.

MAPS AND GIVING DIRECTIONS

Map-related questions that require considerable interpretation are not ready reference opportunities. However, providing directions, whether to local places or the longer distance to the next town, or even within a building, may have fast responses. If you can use a map with a word description, it can be even more helpful to many people. (Keep in mind, however, that reading a map is a skill that not everyone is comfortable doing.) The concierge at the local hotel pointing out a nearby restaurant usually tells the direction while pointing it out on a map, allowing the person who needs the directions to choose whether the words or the image offers more accessible guidance.

A key to providing useful geographic directions when no map is supplied is to limit any oral series of directional changes to three.[4] If more than two turns are required, then the information should be documented in writing or a map should be provided. A third way of handling this more complex series of steps, especially when giving directions inside a building that is laid out in a fashion that requires four or more changes of direction, is to give only the three steps in such a way that the third and final stage brings the client to another staffing point to ask for further direction.

Other information needed when providing directions of any length in response to a reference query is to establish the seeker's:

- Means of transit, including any mobility aids required
- Knowledge with which to recognize the arrival point, such as a building's size or color
- Working knowledge of compass point directions and accurate right and left

You should consider the previous list as a set of precautions to take to ensure that the directions provided are in fact useful. Giving directions, especially locally beyond a building with which you are familiar, should be done with the same attention to authoritative information as any other questions. Staff members should not guess, but should determine if a street is one way. They should be certain of the appropriate bus line even if they seldom use public transit. Such factual details are essential to determine before offering directions.

Wherever reference staff is working, the following resources should be at the ready:

- Paper or mobile app-enabled link to the building and to the immediate local area
- Local transit map and up-to-date schedules for transit service in the vicinity
- Fault line and/or flood plain maps of the area if either of these natural formations is an immediately local feature
- Up-to-date map, in most accessible format(s) of the wider geographical area with locations of government offices, including social services, emergency response stations, houses of worship, and schools noted
- Up-to-date local landmarks list, or gazetteer, such as you can find in the index pages of street atlases

The sources just noted may be available and on hand in a variety of formats, including print, online, and mobile application. Print resources, in this area of information, may include photocopies of building maps and transit routes, as well as more formal publications. Be sure to note the date on any photocopied directional guides, and if the date looks old, contact the source (such as the transit company) to inquire if a newer edition is available.

STATISTICS AND CONVERSION TABLES

Requests for one particular statistical figure are more frequently posed now than in previous decades. Part of the reason for this is that pollsters and other number collecting agencies can work more quickly with modern calculators and thus make announcements that allude to statistics they have derived. Added to that is that many news and editorial journalists report some statistics from research while not reporting the findings in full, piquing curiosity. For example, a politician may announce that more people have jobs and a news source may report both this and the added information that employment rose 2% last month. People may wonder what the unemployment percentage is, however, and want statistics that reflect that facet of the issue. Ready reference questions involving specific statistics may sound like the following:

- What's the dropout rate in this school district?
- What's the current inflation rate?
- How many [television or computer] screens does the average American family of four have at home?

Some statistical information is easy to provide as ready reference information. Government statistics, such as the rate of inflation, are indeed easy to locate (see U.S. Bureau of Labor Statistics at bls.gov/data/inflation_calculator.htm) and the rate itself is needed for a variety of calculations that require it. However, other such seemingly simple queries require both analysis of need and consideration of whether there is a statistically sound figure corresponding to the question.

For example, a query about the effectiveness rate of last year's flu vaccine requires one to note how far the statistic itself may lie outside the demonstrable and possible. Because some demographic groups are more prone to complications from flu and because some demographic populations are culturally distrustful of vaccination, against what population is the "effectiveness" measured? And because this year's vaccine is likely to differ from last year's, and flu strains differ from year to year, is an indicator of past vaccine performance helpful in determining the "real" information wanted? When asked for statistics, it's important to find out the purpose of the question before deciding whether quick ready reference is really suitable.

Reliable free resources of statistics that can satisfy the need for one figure or another, as might be needed to complete government forms, include the following:

- FedStats (fedstats.sites.usa.gov) is the entry point for U.S. government statistics, including those about the economy, agriculture, transportation, crime, census, and more. In addition to serving numbers, it offers visual aids in the form of infographics and maps to show what the numbers look like comparatively. The indexing is superb, and working your way to the right table is a matter of working step by step in the order your choices are presented to dig further.
- Sports Reference (sports-reference.com) gives you a starting point for finding statistics related to team and player statistics for most popular American sports, both at the professional and collegiate levels. If sports statistics are popular in your community, you can bookmark the particular site you want to reference frequently or download the mobile application version.
- National Center for Education Statistics (nces.ed.gov) includes numbers related to influences on education and learning, such as hearing tests, as well as academic performance. Coverage ranges from early childhood (preschool) through postgraduate.

Conversion tables and charts translate one method of measurement expression into another. Such information needs can be satisfied quickly. Among conversion data regularly needed are the following:

- Between currencies, such as the factor by which to calculate the U.S. dollar to the Canadian dollar or the euro to the U.S. dollar.
- Between the temperature measurement systems of Fahrenheit and Celsius
- Between the metric system and the English system, which is the one the United States continues to use

Such conversion needs can find authoritative responses in a wide variety of free sites and mobile applications. Places to know well enough to access quickly include the following:

- XE Currency Converter (xe.com/currencyconverter/) is updated in real time and allows you to find exchange rates for every currency in use.
- Infoplease Online Almanac's Conversions and Equivalents (infoplease.com/ipa/A0873852.html) tables include ordinary measurements like temperature, weight, and length, and also address conversions for applications of these measurements, such as screw or bolt sizes from metric to English.
- Infoplease Almanac's Measurements (infoplease.com/ipa/A0873851.html) also address areas of measurement beyond just systems like metric and English, including standard measurements used in sports.

A variety of free mobile applications offers authoritative data for such needs as well, although more than a single app may be required to collect different conversion sets. Knowing the aforementioned sites reduces the number of different resources to check in a timely manner. It may be further useful to a particular client to share the availability of the app version with them so that they can use it when the need arises again.

AUTHORITATIVE BREAKING NEWS SOURCES

Understanding the difference between authoritative breaking news resources and those that echo rumors and unsubstantiated reports is critical to good reference work.

Whether you work inside a building or on a bookmobile, there is the possibility that your surroundings may be impacted by an event that occasions the need to know immediately what is happening, who knows, and what to expect next, not only for your own peace of mind but also for the community members in your vicinity. For example, a neighborhood fire can lead to increasing calls by firefighters to evacuate the immediate area and seek shelter in public buildings, such as your library. The people who arrive need to know that you can keep them informed correctly about what their prospects may be for the ensuing hours. Other events can demand your information leadership attention as well, presenting you with the need to find correct news quickly before reporting rumors that will need to be amended. Here is a situation where saying "I don't know and I am trying to find out" is more appropriate than repeating uncertain information or simply referring someone elsewhere.

Judging the *medium* in which the breaking news occurs is not an element of determining its authority. From a technology angle, different media can serve authoritative news more or less quickly. Therefore, it is more useful to judge the authority of the source making use of a medium, than deciding what is right based on the technology employed to communicate. That kind of critical judgment should take place well before an emergency situation arises so that when an event breaks out, you already know where to turn for authoritative news regarding it. As we shall discuss in detail in Chapter 12, Twitter should number among the channels reference staff use for this critical ready reference need; using Twitter well and appropriately to that need requires an understanding of how this social medium functions and an awareness of which resources exposed through it are authorities on hard news.

Breaking news, as we discuss it here, affects the public, rather than being personal, and delivers new factual information essential for immediate practical purposes such as planning and decision making affecting the public.

While we are all familiar with broadcast and online journalism sources announcing "breaking news," much of what is presented as such in these venues has not yet been verified and/or has no immediate essential practical influence locally. However, the authentic breaking news data reference service staff should have at the ready include the following:

- Unforeseen immediately local events that place human life in peril or require daily activities to be immediately altered in the vicinity—such events, depending on your environment, might include major earthquake, fire or flood, a hostage-taking situation, or major construction equipment failure.
- Verification of a major national or international event that likely imperils family or homes of local community members—such an event might be the assassination of

a head of state, the verified size of a large natural disaster, or crash of a passenger liner.

- Major national government events that are accomplished by actions at a specific moment—such an event might be a presidential resignation, the death of a sitting justice, or the arrest of a senator. This third set of events is unlikely to require that you take action. However, you may be called upon to quickly locate and share authoritative news details.

While any such events as those just named can be the precursor to ongoing news stories, the moment that the news breaks, or becomes public—and has been verified—it becomes a matter that ready reference providers need to investigate and verify. The best way to ward off speculation, gossip, and unsubstantiated conjecture, any of which wastes time and energy, is to find the facts quickly and make them readily available. For example, your job may include neighborhood work aboard a bookmobile and en route to your assignment you pass a horrific collision being handled one town away from your day's destination. Clients who will be visiting the bookmobile may well have friends and family in that town. Instead of gossiping about what you saw, you would prepare yourself with the facts you collect from emergency workers' public news sharing (often through Twitter). Now you are prepared with factual information, both to share if you are asked and to inform yourself about how the community you are visiting may be responding to an emotional event.

The nature of true breaking news—unexpected, verified, essential for immediate practical purposes—is such that it is brief in both sound bite length and the amount of time it is fresh and needed. To be aware when such breaking news occurs and to be preparing for its fallout within the milieu of reference services in the community, the following resources should be part of your portable toolkit:

- Twitter feeds from local emergency services, including police[5] and fire.
- Where geography indicates the presence of specific events' likelihoods—such as earthquake or hurricanes—Twitter feeds from the appropriate government offices with watchdog responsibilities to note, record, and analyze emerging episodes.
- A trusted and highly evaluated local news outlet should be identified for its authority, credibility, and speed in identifying breaking news as discussed earlier. Following that source on Twitter and keeping its website bookmarked, in a tab, or as a mobile screen icon, aid with making a quick connection when an event occurs.
- Listening skills can be essential to noting when a rumor may in fact indicate essential breaking news. Rather than engage in gossip, when surprising and major events are speculated as having just occurred, investigate and find the facts at once.

Awareness of authentic breaking news is a ready reference need in every type of library or library-sponsored setting. Identifying which sources provide solid information for such purposes requires reference staff to carry out both investigation of options and evaluation of each for its veracity, speed, and most readily accessed output stream. At the local level, this must be undertaken with specific knowledge of the community, climate, culture, and traffic patterns. At the national and international levels, events that can affect the information thirst of residents with distant families require attention, too. The following offer exemplary publication of verified breaking news:

- Reuters (reuters.com/news)—Top news stories can be followed on Twitter, while the news agency's website can be set to specific parts of world, to specific editions, and to a top news feed which is easy to scan and which includes a time stamp to indicate a news item as breaking.

- *The Independent* (independent.co.uk)—Breaking news displays at the top of the opening web page. In addition the All Topics page (independent.co.uk/topics-list) provides an alphabetical list of narrow and specific topics allowing instant searching by event, place, and other attributes. There are minimal ads on the free site that are readily distinguishable from content.
- Associated Press (hosted.ap.org/)—The opening page presents breaking world news headlines in a single box and breaking stories to the left, the latter with about a paragraph of information presented with the headline. Top news stories are refreshed frequently to display current information. Most sections are available in Spanish as well as English. There are ads, clearly identifiable as such.

Note that what does *not* appear on the previous list are specific news business networks. While many valid stories emerge from their work, editorial bias may intrude early in reporting. For the sites listed earlier, the sole portion of the landing pages that is recommended for breaking news appears near the top and news that qualifies as breaking should have minimal interpretive content. This aspect of news is specifically for ready reference, essential fact-checking purposes, not for analysis of news stories.

LOCAL GOVERNMENT INFORMATION

Ready reference questions regarding local government information may include the following:

- Where's my polling place for today's election?
- How do I notify the garbage pickup that I have an oversize item for pickup?
- Is there recycling pickup scheduled next week in spite of the holiday?
- What's the address of the office I need to visit to get a building permit?
- Where can I get a copy of my birth certificate that is good enough for a passport?
- What is the date kids have to turn five to enroll in kindergarten for September?

You should have city and county websites available for quick access and be familiar with how each of these sites is structured. In addition, you should be aware of the frequency and accuracy of site updating. If a client asks about a civic service about which you can't find sufficient and current detail, place a call to the appropriate government office to ask and relay the correct information to your client.

Vital records, like birth, marriage, and death certificates, are maintained at the state level. In some states, county governments also keep records of such events that occurred within the county. Each government district, both state and county, handles requests for these certificates independently, and most charge a small fee for authorized copies. Of course you may be asked for guidance to contacting such a vital records office out of county, out of state, or even in another country since people do move from place to place. The best resources for finding information on obtaining copies of vital records are the following:

- Where to Write for Vital Records (cdc.gov/nchs/w2w.htm)—This page on the Centers for Disease Control and Prevention's website provides links to each state's listing of where to obtain each type of vital record, the cost of each certificate, exceptions to coverage (such as a year span for which alternate sources must be used), and every other detail needed to make a successful request.

- Foreign Birth and Death Certificates (cdc.gov/nchs/w2w/foreign.htm)—This alternate resource from the Centers for Disease Control and Prevention provides similar guidance for requesting these two types of vital records from abroad for U.S. citizens only.
- Web Sites of Foreign Embassies in the United States (state.gov/s/cpr/rls/dpl/32122 .htm)—This is the starting point for locating vital records information from another country when the person or party reflected in the records was not or is not a U.S. citizen.

MOBILE APPS

Many mobile applications (apps) are available for free or at a nominal price to satisfy repeated needs for ready reference data of any specific type. Some have associated website and mobile website configurations. You should be careful in selecting apps for service use, especially when multiple apps would be needed to replace a resource with broader content coverage. For example, acquiring a measurement conversion application, a perpetual calendar application, and a weather application as separate pieces to consult depending on need may not be as efficient as knowing the Infoplease online almanac site (infoplease. com) discussed at several points throughout this chapter.

However, there are mobile apps that can greatly speed up location of certain information sets, such as quotations, local maps, and dictionaries. For reference service provision that is actually on the go, rather than situated in a brick and mortar building with hardwired Internet access and a materials collection, the following mobile apps, under $5 or free, can offer excellent ready reference support. App purchases are one-time, with updates to each one occurring regularly and at no cost.

- Bartlett's Familiar Quotations (bartlettsquotes.com)—Provides access to the latest (18th) edition
- *Merriam-Webster Dictionary HD* (merriam-webster.com/dictionary-apps/android-ipad-iphone-windows.htm)—Far more complete than general search engine returns for word definitions and is functional when cell or Internet access is unavailable
- OffMaps (offmaps.com)—Crowdsourced maps can be downloaded and remain available when no connectivity is available for mobile device

In addition to these general ready reference applications, many other ready reference apps are available that may be appropriate for reference service work in particular communities, both geographic and those of interest.[6] The U.S. federal government develops free applications (usa.gov/mobile-apps) that respond to a variety of information needs, including some that may be ready reference requirements for some librarians. State and local governments may also be appropriate sources in many reference service situations, such as local parking meter maps indicating open spaces or recycling schedules that indicate different dates for green waste than for recycling.

While providing quick and reliable guidance to fast facts, reference work often requires much broader research. In the next chapter, we explore the open web as a medium in which to locate authoritative, timely, and complete information in response to more complex knowledge needs.

NOTES

1. A summary of sorts can be reviewed in the "Room for Debate" series, "Do We Still Need Libraries?" that ran in the *New York Times* in 2012 (nytimes.com/roomforde bate/2012/12/27/do-we-still-need-libraries/).

2. A simple test of where a question departs from a need for a specific fact is whether the question, or stated information quest, involves qualifiers or adjectives.

3. At the time of this writing, the 2012 NAICS is in use and can be consulted at census. gov/cgi-bin/sssd/naics/naicsrch?chart=2012.

4. This is based on the need to confine such directions to being truly ready reference in nature. More than three and there are likely to be alternate routes to be analyzed, landmarks to be identified accurately, and more details that should be discussed and queried. Retaining a series of steps that include two alterations of directions is manageable by most human memories above the age of 10, and for many who are younger.

5. Many local police departments and other government agencies in the United States have joined a service called Nixle (nixle.com/about-us/) that provides notification services via text, phone, e-mail, and social media to civilian subscribers in the immediate community. Explore Nixle as a model of serving breaking news that is needed, concise, and updated in real time.

6. See Nicole Hennig's *Apps for Librarians* (Libraries Unlimited, 2014) for a full discussion of specific apps as well as library service provision using them.

CHAPTER 10

Using the Web to Guide Your Community to Authoritative Information

The largest and most quickly changing information resource available to reference librarians is the World Wide Web. It is a dynamic utility through which information, knowledge, commerce, opinion, and creative expression all flow freely.[1] A website's general identifying attributes were discussed in Chapter 5. In this chapter, how to mine the web for effective and efficient reference help is followed by recommendations of specific resources of high value to your virtual reference collection.

THE WEB AS A REFERENCE TOOL

The best use of any tool requires that we understand the tool's purpose and methods of applying the tool appropriately to the job for which we use it. As we begin an in-depth exploration of best practices utilizing the web as a reference tool, then, we begin with noting some essential aspects of the web as a reference tool. The first is that the availability of the World Wide Web has led to changes in both searching capacities on the parts of many and the amount of free information available. The web can be accessed from most geographic locations, and on any device with connectivity, from desktop computers to mobile phones. The presence of the World Wide Web and the apparent ease with which it can be used have made many to think that it is the ultimate resource and that no research skills are needed to find correct answers. Others think that the lack of verification of some information found on the web makes the whole web unreliable as a source for authoritative fact-finding. The truth, however, lies between the two extremes. Discovering verified and authoritative information on the web can be achieved. However, that requires more conscientious work than the simplistic approach of accepting just any result a casual search presents.

In addition to being widely accessible from almost any location, the web is media-neutral, allowing you to access video and sound recordings as well as written documents presented as lengthy texts, single entries from a database, slide shows, and computations. This advantage addresses various literacy and information gathering (visual vs. auditory) needs and preferences, as well as presents types of information in the medium best suited to communicate a concept: a sound clip of the narrator discussed in an audiobook review, the schooling appearance of sardines moving through their natural environment, and so on.

The web can also connect you to resources suited to different knowledge levels on a specific subject, from novice to expert, and, often, in the language (casual or formal, as well as English or Farsi) that is most useful for the researcher's comprehension, You can also locate instructional support in virtually any discipline, engage in live meetings and discussions with distant peers and subject experts, and share work on group projects that can support local reference service delivery.

All of these possibilities further the rapid growth of the web as a whole, making it constantly richer in content. Taken together, these factors of accessibility, duplication for various skill levels, and an omnipresence that encourages the development and improvement of diverse ways to search make the web an excellent *means* through which to perform reference work. However, it is essential to remember that the web is not itself a resource, or an *end*, for locating authoritative and appropriate information. Confusing the means and the end with the web is rather like confusing a product with the place where you acquired it: the end by which you fed your midmorning hunger was the apple you ate, while your means for acquiring the apple was the fruit stand on the corner. When you research a fact in print books, you specify which particular print book contains the fact, rather than saying "I looked on the shelf and found it there."

FINDING AND USING FREE WEB SOURCES

Both discovery and practical use of authoritative information involving open web searches require knowledge. Before turning to a search engine, the following questions should be considered:

- Is the information best found on the open web, with "best" describing both authority and efficiency?
- Would an open web search enhance discovery in other formats as well?
- Which search engine is the best to use in this particular discovery search?
- Are enough details already in hand to support the creation of a sound and useful search?
- Are more details or clarification needed before a useful web search can be designed?

If any of these questions elicits the answer of "no," pause before digging into the web and find what is needed to get to "yes."

The Web Is a Fluid Collection

Unlike information recorded in any other medium, including books, film, sound files, or databases, the contents of the open web are fluid and always open to changes in availability, location, appearance, and completeness. And this fluidity carries no alert system to inform searchers where and how content at a specific potential destination may have altered since yesterday or this morning. However, there are hundreds of thousands of relatively stable and authoritative sources on the web, so becoming versed in where and how to locate and relocate them is an essential reference service task. Fifteen and even ten years ago, some of this was achieved through professionally crafted website directories that gave reference service providers explicit paths to authoritative, up-to-date, and subject-specific sites. Library staff may have become accustomed to thinking of such directories as the best way to locate authoritative sources, but that era is now over and learning how to search on the open web is a necessary skill for librarians to know and to help others understand. Contemporary use of the web calls for understanding searching, rather than awareness of a few key tools presenting guidance from others who have undertaken direct searches and distilled the focus of these into directory descriptions.

SIDEBAR 1   REFERENCE SERVICES INHIBITED BY FILTERED INTERNET ACCESS

Reference staff working in schools and libraries where full Internet, and thus web, access is partially disabled through the application of filtering software face several issues. Searching techniques employed must be configured to avoid filtered terminology and blocked websites. Teaching and modeling search skills via search engines are compromised.

Filtering software has been problematic for youth-serving libraries for years. Among the problems are the inadequacy of software to be *intent*-sensitive, which means that a search employing a specific word cannot be completed without regard to the intended use of the word or the purpose of the work the employment of the word entails. In addition, blocking sites displaying images, video, and sound removes the prospect of discovering valuable information needed to supply certain access needs (such as video explanation for a student with low literacy skills), information about wholly mainstream topics presented in the format best suited to its exposure (e.g., what something looks or sounds like), and even current news events and other citizenship-supporting concerns.

Reference providers working in such situations need to understand both the intention and the outcome of deploying such inhibitions against open web searching. If library staff cannot supply the necessary training for appropriate use of web searching to the community members, then there is a failure of staff development that should be addressed. If library staff have been shut out of organizational and administrative decision making concerning the application of filters, then attention needs to be called to the fallacy of omitting them from participating in planning that directly affects both their expertise and professional responsibility.

When conducting reference services without access to the open web, service providers must work closely with teaching staff and families to design assignments that can be undertaken without full access to resources, current data, and technology literacy protocols.

The web *as a whole* should be considered a part of the reference collection. It differs from other parts by virtue of both its fluid state and its omnipresence wherever there is connectivity. However, without accessing it, reference service providers eliminate the richest and deepest resource available for their work.

Search Engines

Specific websites are most readily discovered through the use of search engines, which are proprietary computer scripts written to seek identifying terms, images, or sounds within web pages. Different search engines:

- Crawl the web according to unique algorithms that point up different facets of data
- Present results according to engine-specific ranking criteria
- Intentionally offer specific degrees of search privacy to support presumed search efficiency
- Provide different levels and quality of support in the way of advance searching, strategy tutorials, and other web-based applications

Reference service providers should be conversant with all of the search engines in dominant use and learn their individual strengths and weaknesses for deployment in search of specific subjects, for specific audiences, and with regard to associated concerns such as search privacy, the need for relevancy ranking transparency, and more. There are several steps to take to gain this level of familiarity and to maintain it:

- Beginning with the search engines discussed in Chapter 5, review current support pages and subscribe for updates.
- Undertake searches in each search engine on a regular basis to remain flexible and aware of changes in displays, rankings, and on-screen support.
- Check some searches in multiple search engines to note differences in number, kind, and quality of sorting each search engine provides with its use.

The following search engines are the most popular in current use:

- Bing—Microsoft's proprietary search engine
- Duck Duck Go—Targeting privacy of simple searches
- Google—Targeting ubiquity and comprehensive web coverage
- Google Scholar—Focusing discovery on research and expert information
- Ixquick—Presenting metasearch access with stringent privacy settings
- TinEye—Providing reverse image searching

Google's interest in education, in addition to its current domination of the web search engine market, has led the company to produce and freely share large amounts of search training in a variety of formats, including online courses, self-paced tutorials, detailed support pages, and YouTube playlists. While these clearly optimize customer awareness of products, the quality of Google's various training materials is excellent, with some takeaways applicable across search engines as best practices guidance. Check through Google's Search Help Center (support.google.com/websearch/?hl=en#topic=3378866) monthly to note any relevant developments in searching paradigms generally as well as developments in Google's own search engine design.

At the opposite end of the support spectrum, at least now, is the privacy-oriented search engine Duck Duck Go (duckduckgo.com). While its searching capabilities and its attention to privacy for the searcher are okay, search support and search engine education for the user are limited. Microsoft's Bing search engine also provides only a small amount of explicit training in search structuring. Third-party contrasts between Bing and Google discuss pros and cons of each and how these relate to the search returns' appearance and the corporation's power to buy smooth integration with some social media sites. However, Bing's power as a search engine of scope, or one with highly customizable search building capacity, has not yet arrived.

Ixquick differs from the aforementioned four in that it is a *meta*search engine. That means that it crosses search engines to pull results in response to a search, rather than executing the search directly. Like Duck Duck Go, Ixquick is concerned with privacy preservation as a primary value. In some reference service situations, this metasearch engine has a regular role in good search construction and search deployment. In others, including most public library and school settings, Ixquick is helpful occasionally without needing to be the primary search engine used. Its advanced search menu is less detailed than is Google's, so the original search term structuring must be undertaken with more care to employ Boolean operators, discussed next, to limit the collection of website returns to the most pertinent.

Later in this chapter, we will discuss the open knowledge and open resource movement, which is taking hold in Europe and North America at the time of this writing, in academia. Taking advantage of this web growth, search engines such as Google include the ability to search by content licensing (copyright and the various levels of Creative Commons[2] protection).

Google Scholar (scholar.google.com) offers more direct discovery of academic and research published on the open web. Delimiters include searching for patents and case law. (Note that Bing also has a patent delimiter available in its default search, which should be unchecked if patent information is not part of the search at hand.)

TinEye (tineye.com) is an interesting image search engine that works in reverse from searching a verbal term to discover image content. The searcher uploads an image that the search engine analyzes against its crowdsourced collection to identify it for the searcher with narrative terms, such as name and links to where it appears in use on the web. As with most search engines, this one has a mobile alternative, which makes it useful when trying to identify nearby plants, public art, and other environmental objects.

Constructing a Good Search

Building a good search relies on techniques akin to indexing. The search terms should recognize the following:

- The most germane keywords associated with the information need
- Language in which the information is both needed and most likely to be discovered
- Level of understanding needed, beginning, general, or scholarly
- Date of the information's publication, if the facts are subject to frequent change
- Appropriate invocation of delimiters such as last updating of the source, file type (such as web page or video), and domain (such as .gov or .edu) from which the information is desired

For example, the address to which a U.S. citizen living abroad in Ireland should submit his income tax payment to the Internal Revenue Service (IRS) can be located readily by creating a search in which the search terms "living abroad" and "income tax payment" are used, with the added delimiters of the selected domain of ".gov," and the last update range to "past year."

Becoming familiar with basic Boolean operators[3] can be helpful for reference service providers. Combining parameters can serve as a memory aid even when searching through a template that does not require them. Because search engines typically do have advanced search templates, however, there is no need to memorize a full Boolean complement. Think of Boolean as multiplication tables: these once had to be memorized in order to function efficiently, but now understanding the multiplication table's structure and how to find a multiplicand is probably sufficient for many people.

Determining the best search engine and most appropriate search string for locating a specific data set responsive to a question for information should return potentially useful results. To move from all potential qualifiers for searching to those that produce actual and efficient results takes practice in choosing key terms, noting strengths and weaknesses of search engines related to the specific topic under research, and the necessity of evaluating search results for authority.

Evaluating Search Results

Evaluating the results of the search should be dynamic:

- Evaluating the *credibility and authority* of the information retrieved
- Evaluating the *fit* of the source to the person with the information need
- Evaluating the *completeness* of the source—did it cover the entire subject?
- Evaluating the *amount* returned—was it enough information?

The relevancy rankings—or result order—provided by the search engine in a resulting list of items returned from the search may or may not be useful to the evaluation process. Noting the number of search results, however, is a first step. If the results are fewer than three, either the search was almost perfectly constructed or—and more likely—a key term was so badly misspelled that even the search engine's spell-checker didn't recognize it as an error. At the other end of the spectrum, results that form more than five to ten pages of possibilities indicate that the search as constructed was too broad and the results likely to include many that are not helpful in pinpointing the specific information needed.

Once the searcher is satisfied that the list of results of the search includes potentially valuable information, evaluation of the promising site(s) begins. The following criteria become the measures by which reference staff should evaluate open web discoveries to determine their adequacy to fulfilling an information need:

- Authority of the site host and page author as relevant to the specific information it portrays
- The currency of the information
- Completeness of the information
- The purpose with which this information is made available for free here
- The scope and organization of the presentation of the information

We shall now look at each of these criteria to gain a better understanding of what each reflects and what evaluation can be made of each.

Authority

Authority refers to who is providing the information and information source. Evaluating authority requires these questions:

- Whose website is this?
- Is it hosted by an individual, an organization, an educational institution, a government agency, a corporation, or another entity?
- How is that entity's field of expertise related to the information presented here?

The factual answers to these questions allow one to make the judgment as to whether the source has the right grasp on the area of information to suit the gap that needs support.

Currency

Once the site and page's authority have been established, the next aspect to evaluate is how up to date the information posted may be. In some situations, this may be of minimal importance because the need is not for time-sensitive information that changes swiftly, whether from the discovery of new data or the reinterpretation of older data. If it is important, checking for currency is quick and serves to establish whether the page is still being kept up by its host. The questions to ask here include the following:

- When was the site last updated?
- When was the page last updated?
- Do the links on the page still go to live sources, or do they lead predominantly to dead ends?
- Does the age of the information here suit the information need?

There is no perfect and one-size-fits-all way to determine when a site was most recently updated. Sites associated with government, most institutions of higher learning, and many organizations include such notes as "last modified" or "updated" and a specific date. However, the reference may be to the site rather than to a specific page.

There are scripts that can be run against URLs to determine the age of page that is static rather than one that is updated with each access.[4] However, if the information appears to be so suspect as to currency and the last modification date cannot be ascertained, an alternative, and more authoritative and forthcoming, source might be better.

Purpose

Asking critical questions about why this information is provided is essential to determining bias. Evaluating the site requires the potential user of its information to ask the following:

- Why is this information provided? Is the underlying intent to make sales? To sway opinion? To supply informed support or connections with a community of interest? To explain policies of the organization or government supplying the information?
- Who profits from the presence of this site in commercial terms? Is it supported by paid advertising? Does the advertising detract from accessing the free information readily? Does the advertising, even if visually minimal, suggest that the informational content is less than complete?
- Does the site use cookies[5] or require registration even though, post registration, access carries no charge?

As discussed in Chapter 5, all information sources can be disclosed to have a bias. Evaluating the purpose of providing "free" information can expose unacceptable biases. For example, the information may be biased for the benefit of the advertisers as they have invested the cost of providing the information. Such bias may be one of inclusion, of promoting specific products or services, or exclusion, failing to include negative observations related to the advertisers' interests.

Even when advertising isn't involved, bias may be unacceptable due to the hosting site's particular political, social, philosophical, or theological subscription. This is not always the case, and determining whether a political or theological bias, for example, would matter in the specific knowledge search at hand must be considered to draw a conclusion about whether this site's purpose is acceptable.

For example, if the need to find expert information about the tenets of Seventh-day Adventist beliefs about an afterlife took the searcher to a site hosted by a Seventh-day Adventist divinity school, the question of bias due to the host's affiliation would not be problematic. On the other hand, evaluating the purpose of that same site's information about the health factors associated with eating meat should determine that, Seventh-day Adventist beliefs holding with vegetarianism, bias intrudes on the quality of that information.

The use of cookies and other tracking efforts by sites is controversial for web users who value their privacy and don't want to make their search habits known. However, cookies are not malicious software (malware) and their deployment can allow a website host to refine the organization of a site in response to traffic patterns, among other ends to which the collected data can be put. When teaching members of your library's community how to search the web efficiently and use a critical eye to evaluate what is discovered, you should explain "cookies" and other tracking capacities website hosts may use to gather data from them. However, such a warning should be specific and address their situation in conducting this search, rather than present a caveat against any sites using cookies; it relates to their expectations for privacy. To keep up to date on specific sites, reference staff should remain abreast of news, including legal changes that can alter whether and by whom tracking software may be used. One source is Homeland Security's "Cookies: Leaving a Trail on the Web" (onguardonline.gov/articles/0042-cookies-leaving-trail-web). A discussion of privacy and ad blocking can be found at the Electronic Frontier Foundation's Privacy Badger project page (eff.org/privacybadger).

Scope

Evaluating the scope of a resource discovered through a web search focuses on the specific needs and attributes of the specific person needing the information rather than on the information on its own. Evaluating a web resource's scope can be done in a vacuum—that is, without having a specific information void in mind to address—but it's not the best way to start the evaluation process. Here are the critical questions to consider when evaluating the scope of a page or a site found on the web:

- Does it address the subject being researched in a direct and substantive way?
- Is the information it presents offered at a level of expertise that matches the capacity of the person with the information need?
- Is there sufficient content, presented in a mode that can be accessed by the searcher, to make using it worthwhile in terms of efficiency and completeness?

Locating a resource that is authoritative, current, and intended as a sharing of expert insight can still fail as a good resource to use or recommend in this situation. The language it uses may be one the community member cannot read or the content may be presented in narrative form when images are actually necessary for transmitting the information well. A site or page may provide excellent and authoritative data about one small element of the subject—for instance, a comprehensive list of mystery authors active between 1950 and 1968—while the question involves a different scoping criterion—mystery authors active since 1925 and to the present day.

Scope speaks to the organization of the information provided as well. If the resource offers too little navigation to make use of it practical, or evaluation of its scope difficult, then a better resource can and should be found.

SEARCHING FOR WEB-BASED REFERENCE SUPPORT

A development of great import to conducting contemporary reference resource searching is the open data movement.[6] While traditional publishers are exposed to shrinking markets for print-based and proprietary publications, including books and journals in both paper and online formats, there is an equally impressive rise in governments, subject experts, and scholars publishing directly to the web. This information may be found on subject websites, in blogs, and even as e-format documents published with Creative Commons licensing that allows for open sharing.

Experts' Sites

Among the many types of experts who publish directly to the open web, government bodies engaged in health and wellness, business and finance, and support for veterans and other unique populations are essential to explore, just as you would look over new reference books entering your collection. Most important of these government resources for you to understand before you need access to the bounty of information and support for research they contain are the following:

- MedLinePlus (nlm.nih.gov/medlineplus/)—This deep resource from the National Libraries of Medicine provides you with medical dictionaries, encyclopedias, up-to-date prescription and nonprescription drug information, and a wealth of other health and wellness information that is presented without any advertising that can confuse users about which content is authoritative.
- Shopping and Consumer Issues (usa.gov/consumer)—Unbiased and authoritative information contained here addresses both proactive concerns, such as how to build and maintain good credit, and remediating guidance for handling telemarketing scams, recall notices, and related concerns.
- Where to Write for Vital Records (cdc.gov/nchs/w2w/index.htm)—the U.S. Centers for Disease Control and Prevention provides a readily accessible directory guiding you to the specific information needed to obtain birth, death, marriage, and divorce certificates. Because this directory is kept up to date, you can use it knowing that the information is accurate as to addresses, costs, and the many other details included.

- Military Records (archives.gov/research/military/veterans/)—Consulting this site at the National Archives serves genealogists, veterans, and military dependents with both research help and digitized documents.
- American FactFinder (factfinder.census.gov/)—U.S. Census Bureau's data resources that include tools for manipulating downloaded records.
- National Center for Education Statistics (nces.ed.gov)—A wide range of types of data at every level of education derived from government surveys and developed from raw data to include information on bullying, adult literacy programs, and a search directory for U.S. public and private schools and school districts.

The U.S. government is just one type of expert publishing authoritative texts and documents to the web. Other experts with open web publications that can support your reference efforts include the following:

- National associations—Perform an advanced Google search to locate the specific association engaged in furthering the work of understanding a specific topic, such as living with a specific health issue, a prospective career, or grant access for education, business, or other interests. Be sure to evaluate the association's site before using it as a reference source: use the website evaluation criteria of noting authoring body, purpose, scope, and updating.
- Field stations—Agricultural and natural resource information located at field stations and agricultural extensions of research universities supports practical information needs as well as student inquiries for homework. You may need to look beyond your immediate geographic area to locate such an environmental concern that handles the specific topic at hand if it is one that reflects a subject that is beyond local concern. Searching "field station" coupled with the issue—"water" or "wind resources," for examples—will return expert sites.
- Museums—Finding information about natural history, visual arts and artists, exploration, ethnic history, and any area of inquiry that can be addressed through a curated collection can be done easily by searching "museum" and the specific area of concern. Larger museums have significant web presences and share some of their holdings, exhibits, and information documentation on the open web. Smaller ones describe their holdings and usually provide the name(s) of whom to contact for further guidance in exploring a question related to their holdings.

Searching Blogs

One type of open web resource that can be of high value when expert information is needed about a small and specific universe of knowledge is the professional blog. While anyone can publish a blog, just as anyone can present a website, searching for blogs from such experts as libraries, science societies, academicians, and many others who are involved in presenting factual information for users requires you to use just the same evaluation skills you do when vetting a website or even a book.

Beyond discerning the authority of the blogger, here are specific attributes of a well-maintained blog:

- Frequent addition of new posts (articles)—Whether daily, weekly, or biweekly, there should be some frequency maintained in the arrival of new information.
- Tags on each post—These call out significant coverage areas of the individual post and allow a reader to follow a topic, position, or other detail between different posts sharing the same tag.

- Categorization of posts—Broader than tags, categories are established within the blog's architecture so that multiple significant streams of subject areas are defined for the reader.
- Responsible and responsive reader contributions—Blog writers engage their readership in an effort to expand everyone's understanding and awareness of the topic under discussion.

Of course, not all blogs are of high quality and many are authored and maintained by nonexpert individuals or are hosted by agencies or institutions that provide no oversight of the blogger's authority. However, authoritative blogs can provide resources and discussion more quickly and nimbly than can be located through traditional publishing, making these resources on the open web essential to consider when seeking news about facts or recent discussions of events or theories. Most government bodies maintain blogs, as do many researchers, authors, artists, and libraries.

Many websites of all types and domains, including blogs, provide search engines within them that utilize Google to locate points within that site. The following blog sites require well-constructed searches to locate specific data, but they can expand reference service access to open web-based information:

- ScienceBlogs (scienceblogs.com)—Aggregates blogs from 10 disciplines associated with both hard and applied sciences, including scientific work that involves aspects of the humanities and education.
- Pew Research Center (pewresearch.org)—Blog postings by staff experts in technology, health, religion, American attitudes and habits, and more are highly searchable and contain both quantitative data and description of methodology used to obtain them.
- JJ's List (jjslist.com/blog/)—Blog entries on this site that serves as a meeting place between business interests and Americans with disabilities provide access to information on disability law, practical guidelines associated with human resources management, housing, specific kinds of disabilities, transportation, and more.
- U.S. government blogs are maintained by virtually every department, including Occupational Safety and Health Administration, NASA, and U.S. embassies.

In addition to using a search engine to discover blogs of high value in locating specific expert information, WorldCat (worldcat.org/) includes records for thousands of cataloged blogs. While searching for a specific, unknown one in this manner would be time-consuming, WorldCat's own search term building does allow for some helpful refinement. When you find an especially helpful blog using this methodology, you may want to subscribe to it so that updates are delivered to you as they are published. Here are the steps to finding blogs via WorldCat:

1. Enter the term "blogs" in the initial search box.
2. Limit format to "website."
3. Add further delimiters, such as particular language, author, year, and/or topic.
4. The displayed record for a specific blog includes, where available, direct linkage to the blog and to any archives maintained by a WorldCat member library.

As with any resource reference staff plan to use in resolving an information gap, blogs must be evaluated according to the criteria discussed earlier in this chapter. However, unlike Wikipedia, in which each article requires evaluation before vetting it as authoritative, a blog, similar to a journal or other serial, can be evaluated as a whole rather than individual posts. Separating blogs that deal in opinion from those dealing in fact is as necessary as distinguishing between high-caliber news channels from gossip-driven productions. Of course, anything that tweaks your skepticism in a post should be further researched. However, the format of blog itself should not be viewed with skepticism.

Digital Collections from World Libraries

Libraries around the world use the free web and open data concepts through their digital collections. While the digitizing of holdings in material formats has been under way for over a decade, permitting free access to digitized files is becoming increasingly available. Some of the libraries offering these digital collections are listed here. While these collections may offer much more at the physical site of the library, the available digital resources continue to offer access to rich information in a variety of formats, including visual, sound, and documentary.

- Library of Congress Digital Collections (loc.gov/collections/)—More than 250 themed collections of digitized records that originated in print, sound, and visual media can be searched online. Many of the collections require physical presence to view the contents completely. However, the descriptive cataloging of all pieces, and the availability for experiencing many of them via the web from anywhere, makes this an important resource for exploring American, and international, arts, culture, politics, and history.
- Library of Congress State Resource Guides (loc.gov/rr/program/bib/states/)—Each state and territory that supports digitized collections reflecting its history and cultural experiences can be located from this page, leading the researcher to the state's digitized records directory and from there to specific collections held by libraries and institutions in the state. Working through this series of links can bring the researcher directly to galleries of images, recordings, and other primary source materials immediately available for research via the web.
- Smithsonian Libraries Books Online (library.si.edu/books-online)—Books no longer protected by copyright are fully accessible via the web and provide topics and research possibilities difficult to pursue elsewhere. The Smithsonian's focus on history, science, and culture includes information about practical crafts and trades, early photography, and international exhibition catalogs.
- British Library Sounds (sounds.bl.uk)—Digitized sound recordings made all over the world range from accents, the environment, and literature, to various music genres and oral history. Fully accessible via the web, except for some music recordings that can be played only where European Union copyright prevails, this collection can aid researchers needing help with identifying natural sounds, understanding how to pronounce names of people and places, and finding primary source material related to author presentations.
- The New York Public Library Digital Collections (digitalcollections.nypl.org)—Freely accessible visual collections in a range of themes, including historic menus, infographics, nature, gay and lesbian liberation, and works of famous photographers and iconic architects can be discovered and accessed in full readily.

Pursuing a fact-hunting reference question into digital resources such as these may seem an inefficient task; however, relying on such collections to uncover details, complete, and illustrate topics and further inform a community member is an improvement over lengthy waits for interlibrary loans or costly site visits to consult archival holdings in the libraries. Such digital libraries offer even isolated communities with ready access to people, places, events, and ideas that are both remote and difficult for them to visit in person.

THE REFERENCE SECTION OF THE LIBRARY'S WEBSITE

A web presence presented by your library that offers reference resources available 24/7 is an exciting challenge.[7] Building a reference resource hub on the website requires consideration of design protocols that support independent research and use of the resources presented. It requires attention to the overall site design that introduces the reference resources to site visitors who may not know where or how to search to find it.

Discussion in this section is limited to open web links to include in your library's site-based reference collection. While access to subscriptions, including databases, can be expected to be included on the library's site, the discussion here is related to linking to resources that do not require a library card to access. It begins with a request to consider the amount of information you give your viewers. More isn't always better.

Just as in a reference interview, well-chosen, authoritative resources that specifically address information needs are more important than an abundance of resources. Where reference services are detached from the presence of a reference librarian to guide the user, as will be the case when community members access your website from outside the library (and often outside hours they can phone for added guidance), too many options may hinder identifying the best resource needed.

With greater public use of, and self-confidence in using, the web, librarians are more likely to frustrate users rather than attracting them by presenting directories of open websites. Presenting a few carefully chosen, useful, and relatively unique websites that may fill popular needs beyond reference service hours is a better approach. Placement of these selected resources from the open web, with any descriptive matter needed to support effective and efficient use of the site, should serve potential library website users as easy points of access to resources that they may have difficulty locating and evaluating as authorities without your guidance.

Mingling free websites with subscription databases on the library site can confuse and frustrate when a user would need to put in a library card number for one resource and not another. Make sure your website clearly indicates which websites require the library card number and which websites are freely available to users without first entering any identifying information.

To reduce some of the potential for confusion, reference staff are wise to select no more than three to five highly significant external sites and place access to them either on the library's web page or through the catalog. When they are placed on the main web page, the five chosen can be rotated fairly easily. When the cataloging approach is taken, many more sites can be selected for inclusion. However reference staff must then keep frequent and careful oversight of each one in the catalog to ensure that it continues to fit its description as well as present the content for which it was first selected.

One open web link that may be valuable for any library type to include is the link to WorldCat (worldcat.org). That inclusion provides your library's website users with the prospect of pre-searching thousands of collections for the data source needed as well as the opportunity to find specific information immediately regarding bibliographic citations, links to open source publishing, and guidance in terminology that may enrich their online search term choices elsewhere.

Depending on your community's needs, providing access to one of the alternative and content-specific search engines discussed in the first part of this chapter may also be of high value. Including TinEye on the front page of a public library located near a popular nature area can provide just-in-time information without the need for the library's physical collections or staff support.

Seasonal Resources

A helpful approach for the community is to serve direct access to websites that are of immediate urgency to resolving practical matters. Among seasonally significant information sets in high demand and with excellent website support are the following:

- Internal Revenue Service (IRS) (irs.gov)—Relevant for a variety of reasons and needs all year-round, the call for information from the largest group of American residents occurs January through April. The site is comprehensive and well designed, and includes forms and publications, tools, and a full site in Spanish.
- Health Insurance (usa.gov/finding-health-insurance)—Many ramifications, including geographic, employment status, and age, combine to make this issue complex. With annual open enrollment now nationally set for mid-November through December, this site's guidance responds to the nuanced nature of the need for individual understanding of health insurance obligations and opportunities.
- Access to local voting information, including final date for registration, polling locations, and unbiased candidate information, can be placed on the library's opening page about 45 days before a local election. To locate websites that provide factual information regarding local elections, check the local County Registrar and the local League of Women Voters (lwv.org/get-involved/local-leagues).

Care should be taken to remove external links that no longer present enough immediate value to the community to warrant them calling attraction to their presentation on the opening page of the library's own website.

One further and highly valuable website that libraries should include is access to any open web digitized collections for which the local library is responsible. This concern leads nicely into the topic of the following chapter, which is concerned with contemporary models of reference service delivery.

NOTES

1. And this is what the World Wide Web was designed to do. Sir Tim Berners-Lee has been as committed to open data as to computer innovation. See the World Wide Web Foundation's biography (webfoundation.org/about/sir-tim-berners-lee/) for details about him and his current project—the Open Data Institute.
2. See Chapter 3 for a discussion of Creative Commons and copyright as related to professional ethics.
3. An excellent presentation of Boolean operators and web searching can be located in Case Western Reserve University's "Harris Library Boolean Logic Tutorial"

(socialwork.case.edu/wp-content/uploads/2014/12/Boolean-Logic.pdf) created by Sharon Gravius.

4. Read advice from Laurel Storm on "How to Find Out When a Web Page Was Last Updated," posted July 19, 2015, on e-How (ehow.com/how_5097865_out-last-updated.html).

5. In this context, "cookies" refers to the data packet sent from the server to the browser. Subsequent visits to the site are tracked by that site via this script, thereby collecting information about the searching patterns of that Internet access point.

6. The British Open Knowledge Foundation supplies a helpful *Open Data Handbook* online that explains the attributes and purposes of open data (opendatahandbook.org/guide/en/what-is-open-data/).

7. There are too many details concerning best practices in library website design to repeat them here. Refer to the Library Success Best Practices Wiki's page on Website Design (libsuccess.org/Website_Design) for an introduction to issues and models.

CHAPTER 11

Reference Service Delivery Models

Reference services are a means to finding and evaluating authoritative information at the point and time of need. How this service happens today is very different than it was even 20 years ago.

Our understanding of both the place to find information and the speed with which that information can be found has been altered by technology's capacity to allow the transfer of data from the virtual "anywhere" to the person. Making the request is immediate. Should that person be a reference librarian who will help find the answer, a choice of models is available to conduct the search. The models help deliver expert services. In-house training, if needed, will help library staff retool reference services.[1]

Staff have moved from fixed desks near a print collection of basic reference tools to a computer. Patrons no longer need to go to the library during scheduled open hours; they can also telephone during library hours and also at other times for answers. New tools are in place.

NEW TOOLS

In 2015, 76% of all adults in the United States made regular enough use of the Internet to identify themselves "Internet users." During the past decade, Americans' adoption of social networking media has continued to rise across such demographics as gender, age, and ethnicity.[2] Smartphones providing access to cell phone service with full Internet access are currently owned by 68% of the nation,[3] while 15% of the population who are younger, poorer, and more likely to be identified as ethnic minorities are "smartphone-dependent" for Internet access.[4] The translation from this degree of access to expectations of information delivery indicates the following:

- Increased value placed on immediacy
- Increased focus on data points over data sets
- Increased access to sources of high-value information
- Increased need to build capacity in evaluation skills relevant to information collecting

Growing Internet and smartphone usage increases user independence. It is easier to find correct and up-to-the-moment currency exchange rates when and where they are needed. Learning the correct spelling of the poet Percy Shelley's middle name, reviews of books on sale in an airport newsstand, and facts to settle a barroom bet no longer require going to a library.

Librarians will continue to be asked when a client doesn't know where to begin a search. Not all community members are as skilled with social media. At other times the information needed is complex or the resources located seem to be contradictory. Finally, not all the information that could be used is available in an electronic format.

EVALUATING REFERENCE SERVICES

The ease with which quantitative data could be analyzed became increasingly easy with computers developed in the mid-20th century and led to institutional and government trust in counting as a way of expressing value. Anecdotal reports that "the reference room is always busy and the seats are usually full" was no longer accepted as authoritative evidence. Rather, this was replaced with "46 people asked 58 questions between 10 and 11 a.m." Added data included the size of the population from which these 46 were drawn. The ease of collecting and reporting numbers and the faith that quantitative data are objective began to mean that policy and budget decisions were based on measuring service outputs.

Recently, reports of best practices in libraries are moving beyond an under-informing numerical picture of reference use to what the outcomes of the service are. For example, for those 46 people asking questions and getting answers, what change happened after their experience? While significant long-term outcomes cannot be identified without longitudinal studies, some studies with numbers can play a useful role. Here are some possible questions:

- How many of the library's formerly uninsured clients who attended a series of health programs now gained health insurance, whether through employment benefits, private purchase of policies, or Medicare/Medicaid registration?
- How much has the attention span increased for children aged 3–4 who attended story hour regularly?
- How many out-of-work community members secured jobs within six months of using reference services at the public library?
- Have newly formed activist groups presenting cogent documentation gathered at the library been successful in their efforts to gain city council/school board/police department as a working ally?

The outcomes are demonstrably related to reference services practices and show the benefit and value of expert information guidance and evaluation.[5]

SIDEBAR 1   TECHNOLOGY-SUPPORTED SERVICE DELIVERY METHODS THAT HAVE ALREADY MATURED

Reference service delivery methods providers have continued to term "new" long past their maturity date include:

- Telephone clients who are treated with the same deference, and in the same order as in-library service applicants—at least since the passage of the Americans with Disabilities Act (ADA), in 1990, service providers have been and should be assuring equitable service to those making use of telephone access. Environmental diseases, mental health issues, and, of course, a range of mobility disabilities can intrude on a community member's ability to present himself or herself in person to receive services that involve the discussion of a knowledge need and information collecting.

- E-mail communication between community members and reference service providers is only slightly younger, with this mid-20th-century technological advance penetrating library work methods before the 1990s. With the popular growth of e-mail use after the advent of the World Wide Web, service standards for e-mail reference work were being codified as early as 25 years ago.

- Web-based service interactions, including virtual reference services configured through proprietary software, have been in use for nearly 15 years at the time of the writing of this book. Consortia staffing and behavioral protocols for service virtual reference delivery through the web have been developed, and continue to develop, just as evaluation methods continue to develop as professional skillsets mature. However, virtual reference itself is no longer a "new" model of service delivery, and plenty of data and guidance have been published to assist staff who may be new to working within it.

Service delivery development relies on both staff development and community expectations of service. Harmonizing these two capacities continues to require attention and the development of best practices.

IN-HOUSE MODELS

Many public libraries in the United States usually provide the following reference support systems within their buildings:

- Single-point reference stations
- Roving reference staff
- Readers advisory
- Interactive reference support
  - E-mail reference
  - Live virtual reference
  - Texting and tweeting
- Electronic support
  - Computers
  - Checkout to individuals and other agencies

- Internet access—Access to the Internet may be provided through government support. This is especially important for community members who live in homes with no Internet access. Electronic equipment—computers are available for in-house use and laptops, notebooks, e-book readers—may be available for checkout.
- Database subscriptions—Access to commercial databases are available for in-house use for all and often for use away from the library with access through a library card.
- Training for community members

Single-Point Service Desks

Staffing points in libraries where reference guidance can be obtained include a range of staffing configurations. Traditional desk models are placed near reference collections as well as at building entry points. Someone at the entrance to the library will likely be asked directional questions such as, "Where is the children's room?" At the reference desk, the questions are more likely to be ready reference questions or in more depth.

Such models require both staff and library users to recognize their own capacities in finding references. If the reference desk is crowded, the client may decide to conduct the search independently of a librarian's help. When the person at this desk is not helping anyone in the library, the librarian may take some telephone calls or read e-mail for questions submitted that way.

Roving Reference Staff

Staff for reference service are not always assigned to a fixed station within the library. Mobile technologies have expanded this style of meeting the library user at the point of need rather than expecting someone to find the location of the single-point service desk.

Roving reference staff must be well tuned to cues from strangers they encounter in stack areas and at computer stations. Recognizing that guidance is needed before the user asks helps those who may be reluctant to ask. Staff must be especially sensitive to whether asking if help is needed may be felt by the person to be invasive rather than welcome. Certainly staff must appear to be approachable, but they must also honor the client space.

To reveal both their presence and availability to assist, the roving staff member must do only those tasks that can easily be interrupted such as shelf reading or putting up a display. These activities in an area where it is likely that help is needed, such as near the library catalog or by computers designated for public access for database searching or word processing. Having a roving librarian near forms at seasonal times, for example, at income tax time, should help clients get the correct form. Roving librarians should not move too quickly through an area or the library visitor may hesitate to ask for help. The advent of tablets and their deployment with staff in roving reference have begun to popularize this method of providing point-of-need and technology-enhanced reference support in academic libraries as well.[6]

Some libraries are able to install video cameras near the computer area. This helps users who want to contact staff for guidance without leaving the computer station where they are working.

Another point of need location for roving librarians includes helping people who are using their personal electronic equipment in the library. Helping them navigate the Internet is a reference assignment, whether the search is on a library's computer or a client cell phone, tablet, or laptop.

Commercial expert assistance models that are gaining attention as potentially adaptable to in-house reference services include Apple's design of providing "genius" help as well as small class instruction within their retail stores.[7] It should be noted that the popularity of this service, as an enterprise promoting commercial products, differs from the provision of much broader and more diverse information. The need to clarify what kind of information can be obtained from the library for potential service users to turn in the same droves as they do to Apple stores for device support is problematic. However, some of the procedures employed in the store site consultation should inform reference staff:

- Community member ability to set appointments for consultation through the company's website or by telephone
- Appointment and class scheduling that includes time slots much earlier than store opening hours
- Well-trained staff who seem to hold commensurate skill sets among them so that any particular "genius" or small group instructor offers guidance that is complete and courteous
- Clear message delivery about wait times, presence of seating options during waits, and availability of diversionary activities for small children accompanying care providers waiting for service
- Information provision scoped to the specific client need and skill level

Providing this sort of assistance requires some knowledge of technology and might need to be done with the help of someone from another city office to help train when the library doesn't have anyone on staff with this type of technical expertise.

An area of rising interest and activity is the growth of mobile applications to benefit collection access. Apps that display call number locations, provide database access designed for mobile screens, and offer technology and staff appointment booking solutions are among the directions this development is already taking.[8]

Reference staff customization of technology to enhance library resource access can be presented as screencasts: short video prompts through steps needed to perform such functions as online form completion. Screencasting can make use of staff knowledge of typical questions posed by local resource users, local language and literacy needs, and the library's own website arrangement of resources within it to communicate at the point of need quick guidance to optimal access.[9]

As with formal attendance at community events, reference staff presentations to community groups, ranging from service organizations to other library staff, should be a two-way communication path. Tools and resources chosen to highlight in such sessions should be those that can be understood by the general population expected to attend as high value, easy to access, and intuitive to use. Listening to other presentations at such meetings should also inform the attending reference provider(s) about aspects of community information needs and capacities they might not have expected to learn. Time for questions and discussion should be used actively for both listening and making more detailed presentations.

In addition to one-off opportunities for sharing reference service tools, there may be good reason to allocate library reference resource tools to kindred agencies and organizations serving similar populations. For example, providing one-step access to databases created by library reference staff to provide comprehensive access to social and educational supports within the community so that staff at schools, social services, and kindred agencies can make good field use of their contents with clients serves the information needs of the community, through reference expertise, via collaborative outreach.

Interactive Reference Services Online

Interactive reference services, as discussed in Chapter 2, may include voice, visual, or shared resource components. Reference staff need to develop their technology skills to be able to offer interactive reference services online. Familiarity with the platforms used by the library for interactive communications must be familiar to reference staff.

E-Mail Reference

E-mail reference allows a thoughtful analysis of the question. If questions arise, the reference librarian can send a message asking for clarification. The need to clarify what exactly is needed reduces the chance of drowning the information recipient in too many links, options for web exploration, and other resources. Otherwise the librarian may swamp a user who is expecting specificity and simplicity in a response. Reference e-mail exchanges should occur using a generic institutional address rather than the work e-mail of a specific staff member. Generic names are suggested for the librarian just as in some libraries, staff wear name badges with only a first name. E-mails should be acknowledged upon receipt, and an honest estimate of time needed to begin the search should be transmitted to the senders immediately. The capacity of e-mail to carry links to websites and database records, screencasts, and other digitized information improves this method as an answer to a reference question.

Live Online Chat

Virtual reference occurs when the person needing information requests help from the library through an electronic means such as a live chat or an interactive session through a management system such as Blackboard. Live chat software assigned specifically for reference typically includes a platform robust enough to support screensharing in addition to voice and/ or text instant messaging exchanges. Live chats may also occur on Skype. Reference can occur with various options for supporting an ongoing virtual presence. These are the following:

- Live chat from remote staffing spaces within the library during hours the library is open.
- Live chat with a reference librarian responding for a narrowly defined community, usually during limited hours
- Consortium-supported access to full-time reference experts who respond to chat appointments 24×7.

Guidance for planning such service developments is available from the Reference and User Services Association. "Guidelines for Implementing and Maintaining Virtual Reference Services" (ala.org/rusa/resources/guidelines/virtrefguidelines) address both best practices and administrative concerns.

Texting and Twitter Reference

While virtual reference services support fully developed sessions that include interviewing and data delivery providing a wide variety of resources, providing reference support through texting and Twitter can only augment a researcher's need for quick and limited guidance. The limits are set by the technology itself and not by the librarian or the library. While users who text regularly are very fast in creating messages, these are on small screens and the people sending and receiving messages do not anticipate long responses. Twitter feeds can be automated as well as real-time messages to those to share out specific updated messages daily, such as the library's readers', advisory blog in as well as real-time messages to those pursuing information through authoritative virtual resources and contact with experts on staff.[10]

Formal Readers Advisory

Contemporary advisory services reach community groups interested in casual reading as well as exposure to other media format appreciation. Reference staff may create playlists to enhance popular books, host film screenings accompanied by public discussion, and provide blogs and other social media publication discussing the literary and artistic treatments of subjects, themes, and individual authors and other creative artists.

In some libraries, face-to-face consultation with the community has the librarian involved in an analysis of reading preferences. Prescriptive suggestions are then offered to clients. Subject specialist reference staff can provide guidance to those beginning to explore areas of reading and viewing interest through formal discussion groups. Libraries are developing form-based advisory services for remote community members, collecting information to suggest fitting suggestions from the collection.[11]

Considerable guidance is available for reference staff pursuing readers' advisory initiatives with all age groups. Professional books, subscription databases for community and staff use, and abundant free websites, many with high-quality content, can support this service direction. Advisory work supports community capacity building for independent learning, participation in culture events, and building literacy. Where the advisory service provides guidance in multimedia, the community gains from the availability of guidance in multimodal literacy as well.

COMMUNITY-BASED DELIVERY MODELS

Confining reference services to the library buildings makes little sense in the wired culture of the 21st century. Often the services provided by library staff are used by those who are well equipped with independent connectivity options.

In addition to providing remote access to both virtual collections and staff communication, staff members themselves are working physically beyond library buildings in the support of community reference service access. In keeping with the shift from library practices being centered on library and library staff perspectives to methods looking to community attributes, needs, and capacities, reference staffing may function more effectively beyond the physical library.

One of the most important attributes of accessible services moving beyond the library building embodies is that service can become reality even for community members who have not self-diagnosed a need for reference assistance. The model is akin to delivering public health value by working within the community to resolve issues community members recognize instead of requiring community members to determine when and if they should seek emergency room attention that goes only so far as amending an obvious health problem.

Deploying Reference Staff Outside the Library Building

Placing embedded reference librarians in such capacities as service in non-library government agencies is not new. However, moving beyond siting an information expert at city hall to expecting library reference staff to be available in community venues is developing more fully in both public and academic library service planning. Skill sets for reference staff working in field settings that range from classrooms to cafes to social services offices require such staff members to:

* Become familiar and comfortable with work surroundings developed for needs and expectations perhaps unlike the traditional library setting
* Value and undertake collaboration across both agency and job qualification classes
* Build relationships readily and easily without relying on the librarian identity as one according automatic recognition as an expert
* Demonstrate facility with such technology as mobile devices and virtual resources

Delivering reference services support in the field has a high likelihood of placing staff in information gathering situations where an interaction requires immediate resource support while the fuller project to which the need adheres goes unrevealed. In communities where trust is gained in such embedded library support, reference staff should develop insights about community information needs and capacities that they lacked previously. Instead of working with library users who elect to turn to the established library for guidance, embedded reference services make access to expert support more visible to a community's non-library users.

Encounters in the field by embedded reference providers should be focused on understanding, clarifying, and responding to expressed information needs, rather than as opportunities to market visiting the library itself. Embedded library staff can expect that those who make use of their presence are busy and in need of guidance and support rather than diversion to another place for services.

Reference Staff Presence at Community Events

Often the public library director is asked to provide an exhibit or a booth or a table at a community event. Whenever possible someone from the reference department should volunteer to join others on the library staff. Attending community events to share information allows the reference librarian an opportunity to explain the reference services. Such events may include job fairs, where reference staff can both promote library and information science as a career and also explain library resources available for persons looking for a job, looking for a different job, or looking for a way to change careers. Reference librarians can share information about the help they can give to support school homework or to parents homeschooling their children.

Such opportunities also allow the reference staff to listen and collect information about the information needs of the community. Asking those stopping to talk about their information needs can assist all present in developing a more accurate picture of the library in the lives of the members of the community.

Training, too, in such areas as desktop publishing, mobile application evaluation, and digitalization projects sited at non-library organizations can become an appropriate reference service to offer. The broader sharing of reference service expertise creates library value, even when the immediate goal satisfied lies beyond the library's own resource curation.

TAKING REFERENCE SUPPORT INTO THE COMMUNITY

Earlier in this chapter we discussed embedded librarian delivery of traditional reference information articulation. However, reference service providers are also now called upon to develop and support services that go beyond intellectual research or episodic practical problem troubleshooting. A number of library service models that depend on reference staff capacity as information developers and communicators provide support to casual readers, content creators, and those exploring ideas in the arts and sciences, current events education, and cultural connections all provide content for reference service providers to disseminate and support.

Such information access support can take the form of passive services such as recommendations and research guidance publications in popular topics. They can also be treated through active and interactive programming both within the library and in other community venues.

Publishing and Other Production Support

While a few reference libraries specialize specifically in patent research, many more are going directly in the area of supporting production in the community. Book publishing, makerspace labs supporting participation in craft and fabrication, and other initiatives tap into the creative efforts of community members and supply guidance and institutional support for their efforts at exercising literary and artistic output.

The roles of reference staff members in such efforts include community analyses of interests and access points to self-expression, service planning to allow staff oversight of any space or equipment with which community members may require guidance, and engaging community connections to further assist in the establishment and running of any such ongoing program. Turning reference services curation of such community connections back into a collaboration that aids further community development through creative expression can be highly valued in some communities and can demonstrate the high value of well-evaluated choices of means and collaborators to support their efforts.

Publishing, in particular, has a fairly long history within reference services offerings. This may range from support of individual authors—professionals, students, and others—through supplying both information for content and information about content formation. In the past decade, libraries have been experimenting with adding equipment for community use that makes in-library book printing possible.[12]

Some public libraries, especially where reference services concerning music are supported by specialized staff, also offer practice rooms for community musicians. Furthering this support, Denver Public Library staff vet local musicians' recordings and select from them for inclusion in Volume: A Local Music Project (volumedenver.org), which is curated by the library. This program makes use of digitizing equipment, an area of reference expansion in some libraries that we will discuss in more detail next.

Supporting Civic Engagement through Reference Programming

Exploring current events and cultural concerns sometimes can better be achieved through group programs that bring together subject experts and the general community than through published resources on hand. Reference service providers who maintain close contact with agencies and experts who also serve the library community, and who attend to news stories and events that impact civic life, such as government or institutional initiatives, can heighten community understanding both of these matters and the roles that they, as community members, can take in meeting them.

Literacy and lifelong education are means toward the ends of both developing individuals to their fuller capacities and engaging the community as a whole in supporting culture. Speakers, performers, and discussion leaders provide contextualized opportunities in which the community can explore:

- Multicultural misapprehensions and needs
- Changes in law and custom
- Opportunity to appreciate new forms of artistic expression
- Background information necessary to more fully and accurately understand current events

In addition to collaborating with appropriate guides to lead such programming, reference service providers can further support community exposure and consideration of issues by supplying appropriate reading, listening, and viewing lists, along with identifying sources of authoritative information on the web or in the physical community. Rather than considering attendees at such programs as audience, reference staff can encourage participation, activating the community to engage with the subject matter and contribute perspectives that may be unique to their own experiences.

Among such programming topics as may be relevant in both academic and public libraries are those related to current domestic and international events ranging from the unexpected to the planned. For example, presentations on student political movements, the practical local aspects of new federal laws, and the opportunity to engage with a cultural segment of the population with whom the larger community has had little personal experience can all support the growth of civic and institutional capacity as well as enhance the awareness and confidence of its members.

Building Community Archives through Crowdsourcing

An area in which technology, the library community, and the library collection can all be brought into a unified initiative involves the preservation and curation of the community's own archives. Libraries are more frequently undertaking digitization projects of archival collections by making use of the community itself to crowdsource tagging newly available digital files.[13] Such a reference staff–led service provides the community with the value of preserving its past, while also supporting the valuable opportunity for participating in that preservation.[14]

Among such crowdsourced projects inspiration can be gained from New York Public Library's invitation to online volunteers who have helped to make both the Map Warper (maps.nypl.org/warper/) and What's on the Menu? (menus.nypl.org) digitized collections available on the web. Perhaps the best-known reference resource that is achieved through crowdsourcing is Wikipedia. Universities and other institutions explored topics for entry in this source.

In order to sustain an accurate up-to-date and active role in community access to and evaluation of information, reference staff development is an ongoing need. The final chapter describes continuing education opportunities currently available, and some predictions of new methods of professional development that will continue to emerge in the future.

NOTES

1. See Julia K. Nims, Paula Storm, and Robert Stevens, *Implementing an Inclusive Staffing Model for Today's Reference Services: A Practical Guide for Librarians* (Rowman & Littlefield, 2014).
2. Andrew Perrin for the Pew Research Center, "Social Media Usage: 2005–2015," October 8, 2015 (pewinternet.org/2015/10/08/social-networking-usage-2005–2015/).
3. Monica Anderson for Pew Research Center, "Technology Device Ownership: 2015," October 29, 2015 (pewinternet.org/2015/10/29/technology-device-ownership-2015/).
4. Aaron Smith for Pew Research Center, "U.S. Smartphone Use in 2015," April 1, 2015 (pewinternet.org/2015/04/01/us-smartphone-use-in-2015/).
5. Martha Kyrillidou, "From Input and Output Measures to Quality and Outcome Measures, or, from the User in the Life of the Library to the Library in the Life of the User." *The Journal of Academic Librarianship* 28: 42–46 (2002).
6. James R. W. MacDonald and Kealin McCabe, "iRoam: Leveraging Mobile Technology to Provide Innovative Point of Need Reference Services." *Code4Lib Journal* Issue 13 (April 2011).
7. Brian Matthews writing at *The Ubiquitous Librarian* blog (chronicle.com/blognetwork/theubiquitouslibrarian/2011/07/11/a-future-space-for-reference-services-an-inspiration-from-gale/), July 11, 2011.
8. Nicole Hennig's blog post "50 Ideas for Creative Uses of Mobile Apps in Library Services" (nicolehennig.com/ideas-for-creative-uses-of-mobile-apps-in-library-services/) March 28, 2015, includes many associated with reference services provision within library walls.
9. An overview of screencasting can be reviewed at Kelly Turner's post to the TechSmith Blog February 9, 2015, "Screencasting from Script to Screen" (blogs.techsmith.com/tips-how-tos/screencasting-from-script-to-screen/).
10. Besiki Svilia and Leila Gibradze, in "What Do Academic Libraries Tweet about, and What Makes a Library Tweet Useful?" *Library & Information Science Research* (2014) preprint explores both large academic library use of Twitter and determining usefulness of tweets from the academic library to its community.
11. Williamsburg (VA) Regional Library developed an early version of such form-based customized advisory service. See their current online intake form at wrl.org/books-and-reading/adults/find-good-book/looking-good-book-reader-profile-forms.
12. See Sacramento (CA) Public Library's community publishing program at saclibrary.org/services/i-street-press/.
13. The Digital Public Library (dp.la) provides extensive guidance for both the technical and curatorial aspects of such projects. In addition, the Library of Congress offers a host of tips and tutorials for digitizing projects to be undertaken by individuals as well as institutions (digitalpreservation.gov).
14. Rose Holley, "Crowdsourcing: How and Why Should Libraries Do It?" *D-Lib Magazine* 16: March/April 2010 (dlib.org/dlib/march10/holley/03holley.html).

CHAPTER 12

Networking and Professional Development

As discussed in Chapter 3, reference staff have the ethical obligation to pursue professional development and to encourage it in their peers. In this final chapter, both formal and informal routes are described to maintaining and building reference service skills and knowledge into the future.

One certainty a career in libraries provides is that technologies will change. Another is that community expectations and information needs will change because events will generate new information needs. Reference work is an art as well as a science and, as such, altering how reference work is carried out responds to changes in technology and your clientele and their needs. Making these changes is essential to quality reference performance. Keeping up with these changes can be accomplished with professional development in many formats from formal to less structured experiences.

PROFESSIONAL DEVELOPMENT TECHNOLOGIES

An array of easy-to-learn technologies is available for staff development. Making use of the various means of access to development opportunities should improve every reference staff member's performance. Learning how to use a specific medium is, itself, professional development.

Webinars

Professional development webinars are presented by many groups, agencies, organizations, and individuals for different lengths of time, at various fee levels from free to any amount up to and even over what you might spend on registration for a library conference. Many sponsored by professional associations are free to members. Others, which may carry no registration fee, are supported through advertising.

A webinar allows an individual up to a large group to hear and see a remote presentation on their own local computer screens, often with the ability to engage with the presenter(s) through either text chatting or even voice. Learning to participate in a webinar requires one to read or listen to the specifications provided by the host. These should come with the acknowledgment of your registration for the webinar. Such details include where to look on the screen for what content, where to click to download handouts, whether the webinar includes text chatting or voice capabilities, and so on.

At this time, most webinar presentations can be accessed either as a voice presentation over an Internet protocol (VoIP) or by dial-in from a telephone for the audio portion. Each webinar provider relates the capacity for either or both access means at the time of registering for the webinar. If a sponsor of a webinar does not provide this in the publicity, you should try to get it because trying to access it on the day of the webinar may become stressful.

Web-Based Course Participation

Asynchronous online learning opportunities have been available for over a decade. While webinars may be free, courses usually have a fee attached unless an agency such as a state library is sponsoring the training. Software on which they are distributed may require downloading a management program such as Blackboard to your computer. Many of the popular programs[1] can be accessed on mobile (smartphone or tablet) devices as well as computers.

Participation in an online learning course does require participants to have access to an up-to-date browser and web access. Expect to spend an hour or two each week of a multiweek course to complete the actual session and to complete reading assignments and coursework that may include written work, online discussions, or reporting on fieldwork.

E-Mail Lists

Organizations ranging from state libraries and library associations to government interest groups provide access to e-mail lists among their members; these are often called "listservs." Some of these are moderated, while others rely on subscribing members to notify the list provider if inappropriate postings are made. Most listservs are free and can be accessed in a regularly delivered digest form allowing recipients to scan daily or weekly messages in a single mailing.

Such e-mail subscriptions are participant-driven. They give you access to your peer group, and you can ask for information and contribute information or advice to others' questions. Discussions on these lists allow the group to discuss a topic potentially of interest to the group. You can choose to participate or delete the discussion.

Some e-mail lists such as those for professional associations may add you to the group when you send in your membership fees. If you must join yourself, the e-mail list will include protocols for subscription, content coverage, subscription cancelation, and expectations of user behavior on the list. Managing one's subscription is placed on the subscriber.

Using Professional Blogs

"Blog" is the term for journalism created to live online, including the discussions that can ensue through replies to any post. A blog may be editorial, instructive, descriptive, evaluative, or personal. They were discussed in Chapter 10 as a resource for reference information and, when used as a reference source, librarians stay in touch with blogs that provide up-to-date content from authoritative sources related to subjects, technologies, government initiatives, and other areas of information. When a blog is accessed for professional development you should find bloggers who are on the cutting edge and can introduce you to trends and issues in the profession, new technologies, and a great deal about what is going on in the world of libraries and information science.

Blogging software is simple to use and can be obtained for free from several sources. The most popular free blogging tools come from WordPress (codex.wordpress .org/New_To_WordPress_-_Where_to_Start) and Google (blogger.com/). Both sites offer salient information about blogging and paying attention to blogged content in a larger scheme of things than those using their particular software.[2]

Access to blogs for reading and participating in discussion through comments on posts is free. Learning the protocol for respectful discussion participation is simple. Different blogs are updated more or less frequently. Access as a reader can be gained through site visits to the blog, e-mail alerts when new posts are published, and through syndication to which a reader subscribes.[3]

Most blogs can be viewed on mobile devices as well as computers. Their previous contents usually reside as archives on the blog, and both categorization and tagging of individual posts allow in-site searching. Blog postings can take the form of written narrative, images, and/or recordings.

Twitter

This social networking medium is a decade-old in 2016. As discussed in the previous chapter, its timely, highly interactive, and focused content delivery makes it a suitable candidate for use for reference. For the same reasons, Twitter can be an excellent way to discover, follow, and participate in professional development opportunities.

Twitter's support pages and Help Center (support.twitter.com/categories/281) are well written and provide the documentation needed to use this network for professional development guidance. Because anyone can maintain multiple Twitter accounts, just as one can maintain multiple blogs and subscribe to multiple listservs for different purposes and from different e-mail addresses (work and home), you should consider whether to make use of Twitter only for professional purposes rather than only for your private life.

Librarians active on Twitter for professional use must pay attention to their "feed" daily. Following subject-specific hashtags[4] back through time can be helpful in many situations when you are trying to catch up with events and highlights of a conference you couldn't attend. If you attended the conference, you might be interested in hearing the viewpoints of others who attended the same sessions you attended.

As with any other social communication, civility cannot be underrated. It is wiser to hesitate than to react with an emotional response. You need not express your opinion of a statement. If something someone else says takes you aback, take a moment to collect yourself and then respond with the voice of reason; there is no communication in the library, beyond a call for summoning emergency responders, to which you must react instantly.

Twitter, and any social networking medium, takes time, and often balancing your capacity to attend effectively to incoming information becomes overwhelming. Making informed choices about whom and how many accounts to follow is best done through experience and analysis of the degree of appreciation of content and comfort with keeping abreast of the flow. Then cancel any that you no longer appreciate.

NETWORKING WITH THE LOCAL COMMUNITY

Access to segments of the library's community, beyond its active users, should be pursued in order to ensure that all community sectors find reference services accessible. Addressing information needs, in turn, gives the library and its reference services community value.

Reference Staff's Role in the Local Community

As we discussed, especially in the previous chapter, reference services staff must be proactive in the 21st century. Service design must be pursued with the community served, rather than as a commodity competing for possible selection by consumers of what happens to be available.

The community the public library serves is the general population of a geographic area, and that area may have a boundary line around it that limits cardholders to those who pay taxes within that boundary. Your community includes individuals and groups affiliated with the library such as foster care families, retirement communities, schools and colleges in the area. Networking with affiliated groups can enhance your understanding of information needs in the larger community served and the community's understanding of how, when, and why to seek information from the library and what can actually be provided.

Among the face-to-face networking opportunities reference staff should consider are the following:

- Physical visible presence outside the library or reference department, engaging in such activities as chatting with non-reference staff members of the larger community and using public transit (where community members do) with sufficient frequency to build an awareness of how local commuting patterns might affect information needs and vice versa
- Services on a cross-departmental initiative affecting community health, welfare, or continuing education
- Attendance ceremonies recognizing achievements by staff members in other departments and using the social time these include to meet and listen to the others in attendance
- Participation in community-based initiatives when there is a call for volunteers to help support activities it may involve

- Active membership in such service groups as the Chamber of Commerce, Rotary Club, or the League of Women Voters

What does this look like in practical terms? Each face-to-face encounter of this nature requires that you learn about the community that goes beyond reference service. What you may learn could require workplace support. Equity for both the community and the reference staff member group, then, requires that such encounters be spread among staff and/or staff members so that these activities balance their workplace duties rather than burden coworkers. These caveats all fall within the ethical principles, discussed in Chapter 3, of "enhancing our own knowledge and skills, by encouraging the professional development of co-workers" (Principle VIII).

Where staffing is too small to engage in face-to-face networking in the community on a regular basis, you have other opportunities to enhance you connections virtually. Among these relevant to all library types are the following:

- Participating in listservs of such community groups as schools, local organizations supporting education (such as the Parent–Teacher Association, Head Start), and those providing social support (such as community policing, homeless service providers beyond government agencies, independent living and other disabilities service providers)
- Identifying and following Twitter feeds of the authoritative spokespersons for any group suggested earlier
- Responding to requests for information from community groups via social media networking, as a reference services provider, with timely and evaluated information

As we discussed, particularly in Chapter 2, participation in any communication, including networking efforts, requires a balance of writing messages to "advertise" reference services and listening to and responding to messages sent to you for information. Maintaining this balance means "lurking" on social media and that can be time-consuming. To be effective, you must ask questions, answer with suggestions, and point out the information available to answer the question. It is more than simply bragging about potential services or information; it is offering information services to an audience who can use them immediately.

NETWORKING WITH OTHER LIBRARIES AND LIBRARY STAFF

Networking within the profession is essential. Like networking with the local community, it requires good communication and the willingness to both give and receive information, observations, and questions.

State Libraries, Regional Consortia, and Local Systems

Government and quasi-governmental agencies with library services oversight and support responsibilities usually have listservs intended to provide local and just-in-time assistance to subscribers. Reference staff should subscribe to any that apply to their work and follow the protocols it supplies for participation. In most areas, the state library can be the best source of reference help.

State library web addresses can be found at lib-web.org/united-states/state-libraries/.[5] From these, the researcher can locate such resources as social media networking channels each one uses and publications of interest to all staff in libraries. It is very important to the reference staff because they will offer information about potential access to professional resources within the state. When a state subscribes to a statewide database service, it is most often managed through the state library.

Regional library systems and neighboring libraries may include intranet access to work policies and procedures, which can help you understand whom to contact to update practices, the promotion of locally available training opportunities with details about applying to attend, proposed joint purchase of library supplies or subscriptions, or joining in a funded research proposal and other joint projects. Where intranets are underdeveloped or underutilized for locating quality networking and training guidance, reference services providers are among those staff best able to address concerns with information quality and facilitate improvements.

Library consortia and neighboring libraries frequently use social networking channels to promote attendance at and interest in both professional and social events targeting reference librarians. Such opportunities can lead to face-to-face meetings with others who have interests in common practices and should not be judged as lacking any but social hour value.

Professional Association Membership

Professional library associations offer many opportunities for you to network, meeting valuable colleagues and participating in opportunities to explore trends and issues in reference service. You can both learn and improve your leadership skills by participating on formal committees, reading listservs, blogs, and Twitter feeds with other experienced practitioners. You can contribute by answering another's questions and offer guidance. This will help you build your credibility as a knowledgeable reference librarian. Among the associations most relevant to reference staff are the following:

- Reference and User Services Association (RUSA) (ala.org/rusa/about)—This division of the American Library Association (ALA) offers guidelines on the website (ala.org/rusa/resources/guidelines) that is accessible without membership. However, to join, one must first join ALA and then add RUSA membership. Members can participate in a variety of networking channels and on committees, and some RUSA sections (ala.org/rusa/rusa-sections) are focused on specific areas of reference service. RUSA's Reference Services Section (RSS) (ala.org/rusa/sections/rss) has committees established to address more specialized reference areas such as health and medical reference, job and career reference, and virtual reference situations. Other committees in this section are dedicated to exploring reference work with special populations: Spanish speakers, older adults, and teens.
- Public Library Association (PLA) (ala.org/pla/)—This division of ALA is made up of public librarians and also provides opportunity for members to participate as applicable to reference. Professional tools accessible on PLA's site (ala.org/pla/tools) without membership include those addressing digital literacy support, e-government initiatives for library, and planning related to accessing e-resources as information tools.
- Association for Rural and Small Libraries (ARSL) (arsl.info)—An ALA affiliate with a focus on librarians working in smaller libraries where staff share responsibility for

multiple services and often with isolated populations. This association develops policy templates, free webinars, and job boards.

Reference librarians will be more competent in their jobs when they belong to and participate in one or more of these professional association. They offer one of the best professional development possibilities.

REFERENCE STAFF TRAINING

While national, regional, and state library associations and agencies organize and offer training opportunities for reference librarians, other organizations and agencies do as well. Among these are the following:

- Language training, including American Sign Language—Contact local community colleges for affordable language courses in Spanish, Russian, Mandarin, Cantonese, and American Sign Language (ASL); where Mango Languages (mangolanguages.com) database is maintained as a subscription in a local public library system, use it to build recognition and beginner fluency in community languages.
- Accessibility awareness training—The Accessible Technology Coalition (ATC) (atcoalition.org) is a clearinghouse for technical training; professional development; product reviews; and free professional development webinars. Zero Divide (zerodivide.org/our-services/) offers resources and consultation to help you learn how to network and build connections with your community.
- Government initiatives—At the federal level, opportunities include websites such as Plain Language (plainlanguage.gov/resources/index.cfm) for web writing support. At the time of writing this book, the Affordable Care Act and the regulations for small business compliance (sba.gov/content/affordable-care-act-training-materials) training was a hot topic. State governments also offer training programs in areas such as disaster response and adult literacy.
- Vendors—Publishers and software developers sponsor training opportunities through webinar series. Their training typically includes professional experts who present generic training rather than a session on the sponsor's product. They will, because they are being funded by a vendor or publisher, feature some vendor promotion.
- Allied professions—The Knight Center (knightcenter.utexas.edu), a professional journalism organization, offers some distance learning opportunities (knightcenter.utexas.edu/distancelearning) that address reference staff member needs to understand data sources, mobile devices, and other information-carrying venues, as well as a digital library (knightcenter.utexas.edu/digitallibrary) with texts on such topics as social media guidance and writing for the web. These are all free to download.

Among important resources for reference provider development, the following agencies and programs should be pursued:

- Digitization—The Digital Public Library of America (DPLA) currently supports a Public Library Partnerships Project (dp.la/info/about/projects/public-library-partnerships/) that provides a self-guided course in planning and executing library-based digitalizing projects.
- Library of Congress–sponsored business research training (loc.gov/rr/business/Tutorials/tutorial_home.html) is one of several of the Library of Congress's free development

programs from which reference staff can benefit. Others target training for those interested in the Federal Library & Information Network (FEDLINK) (loc.gov/flicc/education/index_education.html), and its American Memory Project's Primary Source Use series (loc.gov/teachers/professionaldevelopment/selfdirected/).

- WebJunction (webjunction.org/explore-topics/reference.html) offers high-quality webinars and self-paced courses addressing innovative reference delivery, high interest topical modules designed for easy understanding, and tools for reference staff who need help in financial areas.
- Some state libraries provide free training and professional development courses to in-state staff. The continuing education divisions of state libraries in other states may offer courses nationwide free or for a fee.
- Other courses have been developed by professionals working as consultants for a variety of continuing education organizations, including Amigos Library Services (amigos.org), Library Juice Academy (libraryjuiceacademy.com), Lyrasis (lyrasis.org/Pages/Main.aspx). Many of these courses and training events can also be entered on a tuition basis and fees for them tend to be low.

BEYOND FORMAL INSTRUCTION

In addition to formal curriculum, professional organizations, library vendors, and professional journals share information through social media that can lead to valuable staff development finds. For example, OverDrive (overdrive.com), which serves e-content to subscribing libraries, hosts a Library Blog (blogs.overdrive.com/library/), which includes many librarian-contributed posts related to reference service innovation with such populations as prisoners and youth, and staff training posts that detail ways to increase skill and comfort with emerging technologies. RUSA (rusa.ala.org/blog/category/call-for-contributions-or-nominations/) and other professional organizations regularly call for contributions from the field and certainly planning and presenting posters, workshops, chapters, research papers, and other content to peers serve to develop the skillset of the author/presenter as well as the audience.

Certainly the list of professional development areas and resources is not intended to be comprehensive. It is intended to spark creative thought in searching for ways to remain up to date. One of the hallmarks of a professional is dedication to continuing to grow and expand understanding in the field. For reference staff, this includes learning *about* how to improve searching and evaluation skills to information available and how to use available information in new ways. Emerging technologies increase access to information, and these must be learned. Reference librarians join their colleagues working in the library in all efforts to reach larger segments of the community in meaningful ways.

NOTES

1. Moodle and Blackboard are two of the most often used in North America at the time of this writing. Learner experimentation is, as of November 15, 2015, possible, for Moodle, at school.demo.moodle.net/mod/page/view.php?id=46, and for Blackboard an overview can be visited at blackboard.com/new-learning-experience/index.aspx.

2. "What Is a blog?" (codex.wordpress.org/Introduction_to_Blogging) is an excellent introduction to best practices both for reading and for contributing to blogs.

3. RSS means "rich site summary" and is simply a way for online publishers to distribute newly published work automatically to subscribers.

4. Hashtagging is a social networking protocol used in Twitter and elsewhere to allow discussants to identify the subject of their message as it may relate to an event, cause, or other unique matters.

5. While this directory seems to be well maintained, a dead link can be addressed simply by searching "[nameofstate]state library" with a search engine. Once the site is located, compare the URL with that which failed from the directory. The problem is likely to be a change in URL made by the state library that has yet to be recorded in the directory.

BIBLIOGRAPHY

American Library Association. 1996. *Library Bill of Rights*. Available at http://www.ala.org/advocacy/intfreedom/librarybill

American Library Association. 2008. *Code of Ethics of the American Library Association*. Available at http://www.ala.org/advocacy/sites/ala.org.advocacy/files/content/proethics/codeofethics/Code%20of%20Ethics%20of%20the%20American%20Library%20Association.pdf

American Library Association. 2015. *Interpretations of the Library Bill of Rights*. Available at http://www.ala.org/advocacy/intfreedom/librarybill/interpretations/

Bivens-Tatum, Wayne. 2010. "Imagination, Sympathy, and the User Experience." *Library Journal* 135: 8. Available at http://lj.libraryjournal.com/2010/11/ljarchives/imagination-sympathy-and-the-user-experience/#.

Calhoun, Cate. 2014. "Using Wikipedia in Information Literacy Instruction." *College & Research Libraries News* 75 (1): 32–33. Available at http://crln.acrl.org/content/75/1/32.full.pdf+html

Cowgill, Allison A., Louise Feldman, and A. Robin Bowles. 2008. "Virtual Reference Interviewing and Neutral Questioning." In *Technology in Libraries: Essays in Honor of Anne Grodzins Lipow*, ed. Roy Tennant, 37–47. London: Lulul.com. Available at http://techinlibraries.com/cowgill.pdf

Federal Crowdsourcing and Citizen Science Toolkit. Available at https://crowdsourcing-toolkit.sites.usa.gov

Gladwell, Malcolm. 2007. *Blink: The Power of Thinking without Thinking*. New York: Back Bay Books.

Goldsmith, Francisca. 2015. *Crash Course in Weeding Library Collections*. Santa Barbara, CA: Libraries Unlimited.

Google. 2015. "How Search Works." *Inside Search*. Available at https://www.google.com/insidesearch/howsearchworks/

Google. 2015. *Search Quality Rater's Handbook*. Available at http://static.googleusercontent.com/media/www.google.com/en//insidesearch/howsearchworks/assets/searchqualityevaluatorguidelines.pdf

Halfaker, Aaron and Dario Taraborelli. 2015. "Artificial Intelligence Service Gives Wikipedians 'X-ray Specs' to See through Bad Edits." *Wikimedia Blog*, November 30, 2015. Available at https://blog.wikimedia.org/2015/11/30/artificial-intelligence-x-ray-specs/

Hennig, Nicole. 2014. *Apps for Librarians*. Santa Barbara, CA: Libraries Unlimited.

Holley, Rose. 2010. "Crowdsourcing: How and Why Should Libraries Do It?" *D-Lib Magazine* 16 (3/4). Available at http://www.dlib.org/dlib/march10/holley/03holley.html

ICANN (Internet Corporations for Assigned Names and Numbers). 2011. *Beginner's Guide to Internet Protocol (IP) Addresses*. Available at https://www.icann.org/en/system/files/files/ip-addresses-beginners-guide-04mar11-en.pdf

Kyrillidou, Martha. 2002. "From Input and Output Measures to Quality and Outcome Measures, or, from the User in the Life of the Library to the Library in the Life of the User." *The Journal of Academic Librarianship* 28: 42–46.

Maarno, Rauha. 2012. "Information 'Lost and Found': New Models for Library Reference Services." International Federation of Library Associations 78th Conference Proceedings. Available at http://conference.ifla.org/ifla78

MacDonald, James R. W. and Kealin McCabe. 2011. "iRoam: Leveraging Mobile Technology to Provide Innovative Point of Need Reference Services." *Code4Lib Journal* Issue 13. Available at http://journal.code4lib.org/articles/5038

Markey, Morris. 1868. "The Encyclopedists." *Atlantic Monthly* 17 (100). Available at http://www
.theatlantic.com/magazine/archive/1868/02/the-encyclopedists/305188/

Mathews, Brian. 2011. "A Future Space for Reference Services? An Inspiration from GALE." *The Ubiquitous Librarian.* Available at http://chronicle.com/blognetwork/theubiquitouslibrarian/2011/07/11/a-future-space-for-reference-services-an-inspiration-from-gale/

Monea, Alexander. 2015. *A Primer on BigDIVA and the Future of Search?* Available at https://www
.hastac.org/blogs/alexandermonea/2015/10/23/primer-bigdiva-and-future-search

Morse, Grant W. 1980. *Guide to the Incomparable New York Times Index.* New York: Fleet Academic Editions.

National Archives and Records Administration. 2015. *Citizen Archivist Dashboard: Improving Access to Historical Records through Crowdsourcing.* Available at http://crowdsourcing-toolkit.sites.usa
.gov/files/2015/09/citizen-archivist.pdf

Nims, Julia K., Paula Storm, and Robert Stevens. 2014. *Implementing an Inclusive Staffing Model for Today's Reference Services: A Practical Guide for Librarians.* Lanham, MD: Rowman & Littlefield.

OCLC. 2012. *U.S. Academic Libraries: A Snapshot of Priorities & Perspectives.* Available at http://
www.oclc.org/content/dam/oclc/reports/us-libraries/214758usb-a-A-Snapshot-of-Priorities-and-
Perspectives.pdf

OCLC. 2012. *U.S. Community College Libraries: A Snapshot of Priorities & Perspectives.* Available at http://www.oclc.org/content/dam/oclc/reports/us-libraries/214758usb-c-A-Snapshot-of-Priorities-
and-Perspectives.pdf

OCLC. 2012. *U.S. Public Libraries: A Snapshot of Priorities & Perspectives.* Available at http://
www.oclc.org/content/dam/oclc/reports/us-libraries/214758usb-A-Snapshot-of-Priorities-and-
Perspectives.pdf

Open Knowledge Foundation. [2010?] *Open Data Handbook.* Cambridge: Open Knowledge Foundation. Available at http://opendatahandbook.org/guide/en/

Perrin, Andrew and Maeve Duggan. 2015. *Americans' Internet Access: 2000–2015.* Pew Research Center. 26 June 2015. Available at http://www.pewinternet.org/files/2015/06/2015–06–26_internet-usage-
across-demographics-discover_FINAL.pdf

Reference and User Services Association. 2010. *Guidelines for Implementing and Maintaining Virtual Reference Services.* Available at http://www.ala.org/rusa/sites/ala.org.rusa/files/content/resources/
guidelines/virtual-reference-se.pdf

Sullivan, Danny. 2003. "Where Are They Now? Search Engines We've Known and Loved." *Search Engine Watch*, March 3. Available at http://searchenginewatch.com/sew/study/2064954/where-
are-they-now-search-engines-weve-known-loved#

Svilia, Besiki and Leila Gibradze. 2014. "What Do Academic Libraries Tweet about, and What Makes a Library Tweet Useful?" *Library & Information Science Research* 36 (3–4): 136–141.

ten Hacken, Pius. 2012. "In What Sense Is the OED the Definitive Record of the English Language?" *Proceedings of the 15th EURALEX International Congress*, 834–845. Available at http://www
.euralex.org/elx_proceedings/Euralex2012/pp834–845%20ten%20Hacken.pdf

Wikipedia. 2015. *Wikipedia: Principles.* Available at https://en.wikipedia.org/wiki/Wikipedia:Principles

Williamson, Timothy. 2002. *Knowledge and Its Limits.* New York: Oxford University Press.

INDEX

ABOUT THE AUTHOR

Francisca Goldsmith, MLIS, designs and presents curricula in a number of library and information service areas, including contemporary reference methods, following a career that has included public and academic professional positions in reference services and teen services, as well as management positions related to collections and to branch services. Goldsmith is the author of six professional books and has contributed to many others. She earned her master's degree in library and information science at Simmons College and has worked in California, Massachusetts, Nova Scotia, and Maine. Goldsmith blogs at nowportlanding.wordpress.com.